DotNetNuke 5.4 Cookbook

Over 100 recipes for installing, configuring, and customizing your own website with the DotNetNuke CMS

John K. Murphy

BIRMINGHAM - MUMBAI

DotNetNuke 5.4 Cookbook

First published: September 2010

Production Reference: 1300810

Published by Packt Publishing Ltd.
32 Lincoln Road
Olton
Birmingham, B27 6PA, UK.

ISBN 978-1-849511-68-1

www.packtpub.com

Cover Image by Vinayak Chittar (vinayak.chittar@gmail.com)

Credits

Author

John K. Murphy

Reviewers

Jeff Cochran

Sebastian Leupold

Acquisition Editor

Darshana Shinde

Development Editor

Rakesh Shejwal

Technical Editors

Kavita Iyer

Conrad Sardinha

Indexer

Hemangini Bari

Editorial Team Leader

Mithun Sehgal

Project Team Leader

Lata Basantani

Project Coordinator

Vincila Colaco

Proofreader

Lynda Sliwoski

Graphics

Geetanjali Sawant

Production Coordinator

Melwyn D'sa

Cover Work

Melwyn D'sa

About the Author

John K. Murphy is a software industry veteran with more than 25 years experience as a programmer and database administrator. A graduate of the University of West Virginia, he began writing computer games in the 1980s before pursuing a career as a computer consultant. Over the years, John has enjoyed developing software in most major programming languages while striving to keep current with new technologies.

In his spare time, John enjoys scuba diving, skydiving, and piloting small planes. He lives with his wife and two children in Pittsburgh, Pennsylvania.

I would like to thank the many people who made this book possible especially my wife Marianne for all her support, my sons Zachary and Simon, and my editor for her insightful comments and patience. I would also like to thank the technical reviewers for all their efforts and attention to detail.

About the Reviewers

Jeff Cochran is a Senior Network Specialist for the City of Naples, Florida. A large part of his job includes web design and coding, as well as web server management. Jeff has nearly two decades of experience with the Internet, having started one of the first Internet service providers in Southwest Florida, and has worked with Windows and Unix-based web servers. Now primarily concentrating on Windows technologies, Jeff has been a Microsoft MVP for Microsoft's Internet Information Server for nearly a decade and is active in the ASP Classic and ASP.NET communities as well. Jeff co-authored Packt's *"Building an ASP.NET Content Management System"* and has worked on several books by other publishers.

Sebastian Leupold after studying Economics and Business Engineering at Karlsruhe University has acquired professional experience in software applications for about 20 years now. He is the CEO of Gamma Concept, a solutions company specialized in developing database-driven software for PC and the Web, which is part of dnnWerk, the compound of leading DotNetNuke experts in Germany, providing all services around DotNetNuke, including hosting, training, advisory, skinning, and module development.

As a member of the DotNetNuke Core Team, Sebastian added a couple of enhancements to the DotNetNuke Core Framework and is mainly responsible for module release testing. While also being a member of the User Experience Team, he focuses on improvements for DNN usability. In the past, he has been a project lead for UserDefinedTable module. Sebastian creates and maintains hundreds of German language packs for the DotNetNuke framework and modules.

Sebastian is co-founder and co-lead of the German DotNetNuke User Group. He was also an initiator of DNN-Europe, the Network of DotNetNuke Professionals, for which he organized the first European Day of DotNetNuke 2010 in Paris. Sebastian has held a number of sessions in OpenForce DotNetNuke conferences in Europe and the U.S. as well as a number of user group meetings. Microsoft awarded his activities by the "Most Valuable Professional" (MVP) title.

Table of Contents

Preface

DotNetNuke 5.4 is a powerful and flexible content management system for building websites. It comes with many features for publishing content, including tools to create Blogs, Banner Advertising, News Feeds, and much more. The chapters in this book provide example recipes that will show how to download, install, configure, and customize DotNetNuke with your own plugin modules.

What this book covers

Chapter 1, Installation and Setup, explains downloading and installing the tools you need to create your own DotNetNuke website.

Chapter 2, Managing Users and Site Setup, explains creating users, assigning security, and configuring your site.

Chapter 3, Easy Tricks with Existing Modules, discusses installing and configuring the most popular modules.

Chapter 4, Creating your Own Modules, explains installing the development tool and creating your first custom module.

Chapter 5, Building, Debugging, and Deploying Modules, has in-depth examples of module development and debugging.

Chapter 6, Data Entry Tricks, takes a look at common data entry controls for DotNetNuke.

Chapter 7, Cool Web Controls, shows examples of web controls such as TreeView, TabStrip, and CAPTCHA validation.

Chapter 8, Basic Skinning, explains how to style your site by creating custom skins.

Chapter 9, Working with Foreign Languages, explains how to use localization to create a bilingual site.

Chapter 10, Advanced Tricks with Existing Modules, shows examples of more complicated modules demonstrating Flash, jQuery, XML feeds, URL rewriting, and more.

Chapter 11, Challenging Custom Modules, shows examples of searching, importing, and exporting from custom modules.

Chapter 12, Advanced Modules and Security, explains advanced module examples and security techniques.

Chapter 13, Advanced Skinning, takes a look at skinning in more detail with animated menus, CSS, and Widgets.

What you need for this book

DotNetNuke is a web-based content management system that uses Windows Internet Information Server (IIS) and the .NET Framework. To follow along with the recipes in this book, you will need the following:

- ▶ ISS 5 or later found in Windows Server 2003, 2008, or 2008R2. For development you may use Windows XP Professional, Windows Vista, or Windows 7 (Home Premium and above).
- ▶ Microsoft .NET Framework 2.5 or higher.

Who this book is for

If you are a .NET developer with beginner to intermediate knowledge of Visual Basic or C# and want to develop a website/CMS using DotNetNuke, this book is for you.

Familiarity with DNN operation, CSS, and basic web development (ASP.NET) skills is required.

Conventions

In this book, you will find a number of styles of text that distinguish between different kinds of information. Here are some examples of these styles, and an explanation of their meaning.

Code words in text are shown as follows: "We can include other contexts through the use of the `include` directive."

A block of code is set as follows:

```
<asp:TextBox ID="txtSalary" runat="server"></asp:TextBox>
<asp:RequiredFieldValidator ID="valSalary"
                            resourcekey="valSalary.ErrorMessage"
                            ControlToValidate="txtSalary"
CssClass="NormalRed" Display="Dynamic" ErrorMessage=
                            "<br>Salary is required" Runat="server" />
```

When we wish to draw your attention to a particular part of a code block, the relevant lines or items are set in bold:

```
<tr valign="top">
<td class="SubHead" width="125">
<dnn:label id="lblSalary" runat="server" controlname="lblSalary"
                                                 suffix=":">
</dnn:label>
</td>
```

New terms and **important words** are shown in bold. Words that you see on the screen, in menus or dialog boxes for example, appear in the text like this: "If you like how it looks, click on **Apply** to apply the container to your site.".

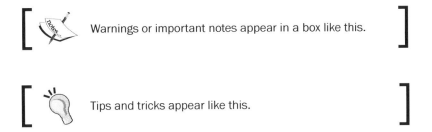

Warnings or important notes appear in a box like this.

Tips and tricks appear like this.

Reader feedback

Feedback from our readers is always welcome. Let us know what you think about this book—what you liked or may have disliked. Reader feedback is important for us to develop titles that you really get the most out of.

To send us general feedback, simply send an e-mail to feedback@packtpub.com, and mention the book title via the subject of your message.

If there is a book that you need and would like to see us publish, please send us a note in the **SUGGEST A TITLE** form on www.packtpub.com or e-mail suggest@packtpub.com.

If there is a topic that you have expertise in and you are interested in either writing or contributing to a book, see our author guide on www.packtpub.com/authors.

Customer support

Now that you are the proud owner of a Packt book, we have a number of things to help you to get the most from your purchase.

Downloading the example code for this book:

You can download the example code files for all Packt books you have purchased from your account at http://www.PacktPub.com. If you purchased this book elsewhere, you can visit http://www.packtpub.com/support and register to have the files e-mailed directly to you.

Errata

Although we have taken every care to ensure the accuracy of our content, mistakes do happen. If you find a mistake in one of our books—maybe a mistake in the text or the code—we would be grateful if you would report this to us. By doing so, you can save other readers from frustration and help us improve subsequent versions of this book. If you find any errata, please report them by visiting http://www.packtpub.com/support, selecting your book, clicking on the **errata submission form** link, and entering the details of your errata. Once your errata are verified, your submission will be accepted and the errata will be uploaded on our website, or added to any list of existing errata, under the Errata section of that title. Any existing errata can be viewed by selecting your title from http://www.packtpub.com/support.

Piracy

Piracy of copyrighted material on the Internet is an ongoing problem across all media. At Packt, we take the protection of our copyright and licenses very seriously. If you come across any illegal copies of our works, in any form, on the Internet, please provide us with the location address or website name immediately so that we can pursue a remedy.

Please contact us at copyright@packtpub.com with a link to the suspected pirated material.

We appreciate your help in protecting our authors, and our ability to bring you valuable content.

Questions

You can contact us at questions@packtpub.com if you are having a problem with any aspect of the book, and we will do our best to address it.

1
Installation and Setup

In this chapter we will cover the following topics:

- ▶ Downloading the Microsoft Web Platform Installer
- ▶ Installing SQLServer Express
- ▶ Downloading and installing DotNetNuke package
- ▶ Running the DotNetNuke installation
- ▶ Setting the site name and information
- ▶ Choosing a skin for the site
- ▶ Choosing a container for the site
- ▶ Adding a module to a page
- ▶ Installing Standard DNN Modules
- ▶ Downloading an extension (skin or module)
- ▶ Installing a new extension

Introduction

DotNetNuke (which for brevity's sake we'll call "DNN" going forward) is a powerful and flexible content management system for building websites. It comes with many features for publishing content including tools to create Blogs, Banner Advertising, News Feeds, and much more. All of this comes right out of the box and if you use the Community Edition, all of it is free.

But setting up a website from scratch can be challenging. There are multiple pieces involved and each piece must be correct for the whole to work. Fortunately, the recipes in this chapter will safely navigate you around the obstacles and have your own website up and running in no time. It is important that you read the instructions of the recipes with care making sure each step is done as described. Following these recipes is very much like following a cooking recipe — if you leave out an ingredient or set the oven to the wrong temperature the result could be a mess.

In the recipes of this chapter you will see the phrases web server and database server. If you are building a website for a company chances are the web server and database server are two different machines located on the network. To install and run DNN you need login access to each machine with privileges to install software.

On the other hand, if you are developing a small test website everything will be installed on your desktop or laptop and the terms web server and database server refer to your machine to which of course, you already have full access.

Internet access is necessary to download the DNN code and installation files but if you have made it this far we'll assume you are properly equipped.

Let's get started.

Downloading the Microsoft Web Platform Installer

In this recipe we will show how to prepare a machine for a DNN installation by installing **Microsoft Web Platform Installer** (**Web PI**). The Microsoft Web Platform Installer is a free tool for downloading applications from the Internet including the DotNetNuke installation, Internet Information Services (IIS), SQL Server Express, .NET Framework, and Visual Web Developer. To make installing DNN as simple as possible, it is best to install Web PI first.

How to do it...

1. Open your favorite web browser and go to the site `http://www.microsoft.com/web/Downloads/platform.aspx`.

2. Click on the **Download It Now** button on the right side of the page.

3. Web PI will now start to download. When the Run/Save dialog appears, click on **Run**.

4. If prompted by the Security Warning, click on **Run**.

5. If you are prompted by the browser, click on the security bar at the top of the browser and allow the file to download.

6. Lastly, if you are prompted to allow access to run the program, click on **Allow**.

7. Web PI will now launch and show the products available for download.

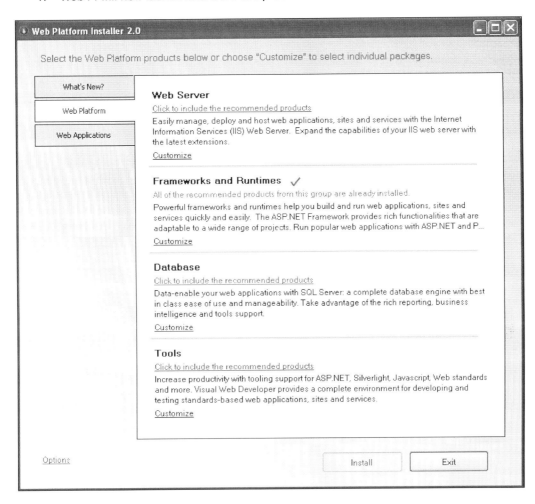

8. From this dialog you can choose the software to download. Click on **Exit** when you are done downloading products.

See also

With Web PI installed you can easily download the tools needed for the rest of this chapter. See the individual recipes for instructions.

Installing SQLServer Express

This recipe will show you how to download and install Microsoft's free version of SQLServer called Microsoft SQL Server 2008 Express. DNN currently supports SQL Server 2005 and 2008, but SQL Server Express is also a good solution for a website developer looking to run DNN from a single machine.

Getting ready

For this recipe you should have Windows Server 2003, 2008, or 2008R2. For development you may use Windows XP Professional, Windows Vista, Windows 7 (Home Premium and above).

In addition, you should complete the following recipe:

> ▸ *Downloading the Microsoft Web Platform Installer*

How to do it...

1. Start by launching the Microsoft Web Platform Installer.
2. When the list of available products is displayed, click on the **Web Platform** tab.
3. Under the **Database** section, click on the **Customize** link.

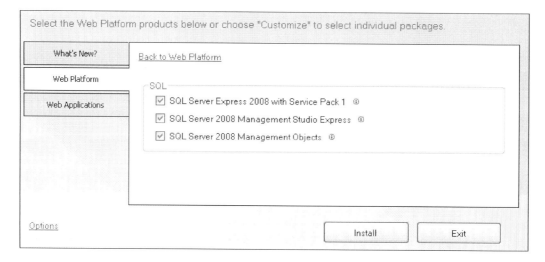

4. Make sure the following products are selected:

   ❑ SQL Server Express 2008

   ❑ SQL Server 2008 Management Studio Express

   ❑ SQL Server 2008 Management Objects

5. Click on the **Install** button to begin the installation.

6. The next dialog will list the file you are downloading and prompt **I Decline** or **I Accept.** Click on **I Accept**.

7. Lastly, you must choose how you want to authenticate users in the database. As this installation is probably just for your local use, you can choose **Mixed Mode Authentication**.

8. Pick a password for the SQL Server administrator (SA). It must be a strong password, so try to include numbers, special characters, and mixed case. Supply a good password and click on **Continue**.

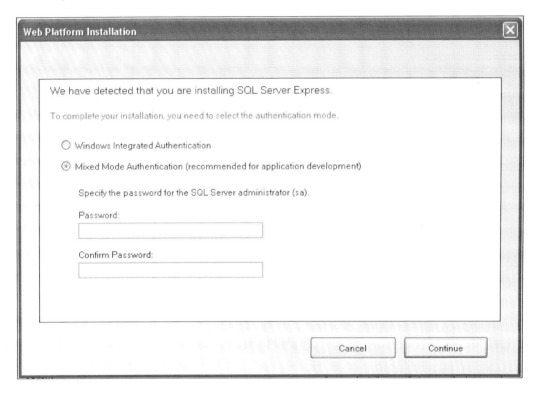

9. Now the file will download and install by double-clicking it. It will take several minutes, even with a fast connection. Halfway through the installation it may prompt if you want to reboot, click on **No** so that the installation will continue.

10. After the installation finishes you will see a congratulations message. If you are prompted to reboot, click on **Yes**.

How it works...

Microsoft's Web Platform Installer handles the details of the file download and installation. Once it is completed, you will have SQL Server Express running on your machine.

Downloading and installing the DotNetNuke package

In this recipe we will walkthrough downloading and installing the DotNetNuke package using the Web PI tool.

Some of the other ways to install DNN are:

Pre-installed by a hosting provider	This is certainly the easiest way. There are many hosting providers offering DNN as part of a hosting package.
Manually uploading and installing	If you are familiar with SQL Server databases and IIS you can download the DNN installation files and manually install the package. This is a good way to see how the individual pieces fit together.
Use DNN Starter Kit for Visual Studio 2008	You can also run DNN from your development tool. For more information, see *Chapter 5*, Building, Debugging, and Deploying Modules

Getting ready

For this recipe you should have Windows Server 2003, 2008, or 2008R2. For development you may use Windows XP Professional, Windows Vista, Windows 7 (Home Premium and above).

In addition, you should complete the following recipe:

▶ *Downloading the Microsoft Web Platform Installer*

How to do it...

1. Start by launching the Microsoft Web Platform Installer.

2. When the list of available products is displayed, click on the **Web Applications** tab.

3. Scroll down until you see DotNetNuke and make sure it is selected.

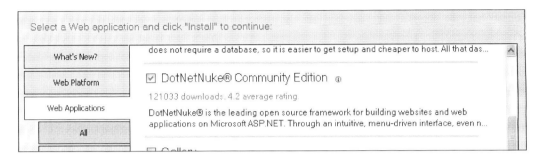

4. Click on the **Install** button to begin the installation.

5. The next dialog will list the file you are downloading and prompt **I Decline** or **I Accept**. Click on **I Accept**.

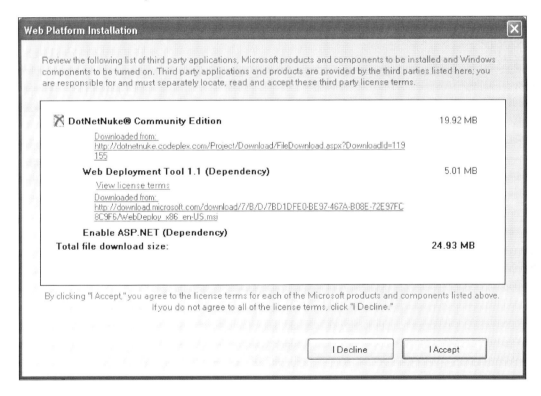

6. Now DotNetNuke will download. Install by double-clicking on it. It will take several minutes, even with a fast connection. Halfway through the installation it may prompt if you want to reboot, click on **No** so that the installation will continue.

7. Once DotNetNuke package has been downloaded, Web PI will immediately launch the installation. It starts by prompting for the details of your new DNN site:

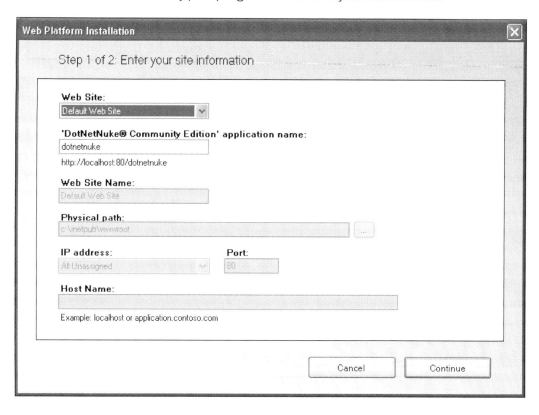

8. Leave the defaults and click on **Continue**.
9. Next is the prompt for the application information:

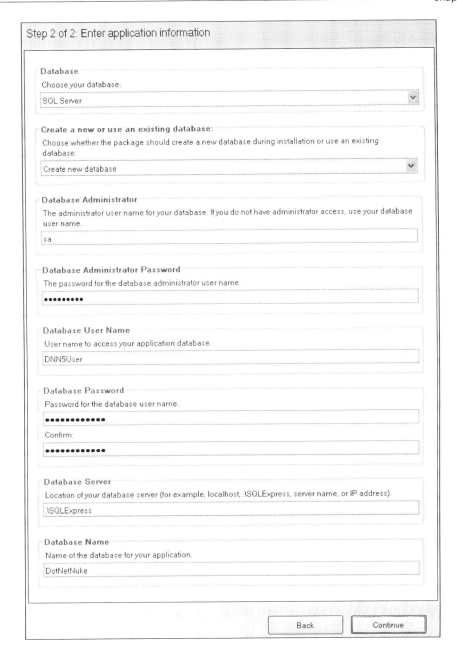

Step 2 of 2: Enter application information

Database
Choose your database:

SQL Server

Create a new or use an existing database:
Choose whether the package should create a new database during installation or use an existing database:

Create new database

Database Administrator
The administrator user name for your database. If you do not have administrator access, use your database user name.

sa

Database Administrator Password
The password for the database administrator user name.

••••••••••

Database User Name
User name to access your application database.

DNN5User

Database Password
Password for the database user name.

•••••••••••••
Confirm:

•••••••••••••

Database Server
Location of your database server (for example, localhost, .\SQLExpress, server name, or IP address).

.\SQLExpress

Database Name
Name of the database for your application.

DotNetNuke

Back   Continue

10. Enter the application information:

- **Database**: SQL Server

- **Create new or use an existing database**: Create New database

- **Database Administrator**: sa

      ❑   **Database Administrator Password**: use the password you choose when the database was installed

      ❑   **Database User Name**: Choose a user name (such as `DNN5User`)

      ❑   **Database Password**: Choose a password (such as `DNN5User2010`)

      ❑   **Database Server**: `.\SQLExpress`

      ❑   **Database Name**: `DotNetNuke`

11. Click on **Continue**.

12. Next, the status screen will be displayed as the installation runs. If you see a login failure instead, check that your database is up and running and you gave the correct password for the user `sa`.

13. You should now see the congratulations screen. Click on **Finish**.

14. Click on **Exit** to close the Web Platform Installer.

How it works...

In this recipe we used the Web PI Installer to download and install the DNN site. To complete the installation, see the next recipe *Running the DotNetNuke installation*.

Running the DotNetNuke installation

Once all the pieces are in place the final step is to access the DNN web and run the final installation code.

Getting ready

At this point you must have successfully completed the following recipes:

▸ *Downloading the Microsoft Web Platform Installer*

▸ *Installing SQLServer Express*

▸ *Downloading and installing DotNetNuke package*

How to do it...

1. Open your favorite web browser and go to the new site (for example, `http://localhost/DotNetNuke`).

2. There will be a pause while the installation begins, then you will see the installation wizard screen.

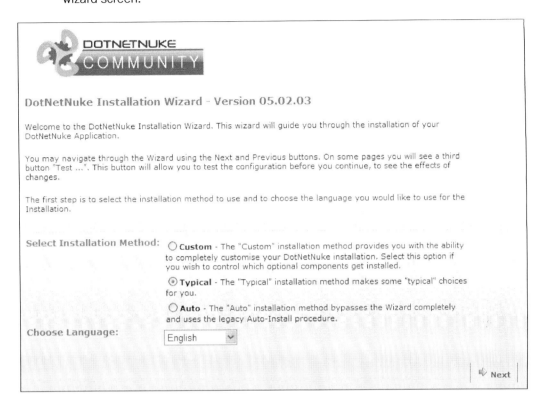

3. Select **Typical** for the installation method.
4. Choose **English** for the language.
5. Click on **Next**.
6. The next page will test the file permissions. The wizard will automatically check the file permission. You should see the message: **Your site passed the permissions check**. Click on **Next**.

7. Now we must point our DNN installation to the database. Make sure **SQL Server 2005/2008 Database** is selected at the top of the page (select this option even if you are using SQL Express. We're not really defining the database here; we're just saying how we want to connect to it).

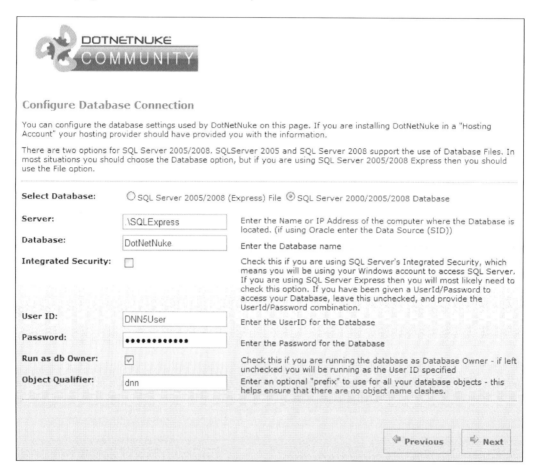

8. For **Server**, go with the default `.\SQLExpress`.

9. For the **Database**, type the name of the database created when SQLServer Express was installed: `DotNetNuke`.

10. Leave **Integrated Security** unchecked.

11. **User ID** should be the user name you selected (such as `DNN5User`).

12. **Password** should be the password you selected (such as `DNN5User2010`).

13. Check **Run as db Owner**.

14. Type `dnn` for the **Object Qualifier**. This is optional, but it helps to separate out database objects that belong to DNN from those that don't.

15. Click on **Next**. You will now see status messages as the database tables and stored procedures are created. At the end should be the message **Installation of Database Complete**. If the installation was successful, pat yourself on the back and click on **Next**.

16. Now the wizard will create two users to start with: the **SuperUser** who controls the entire DNN installation and the Administrator user who administers the portals and has more limited privileges.

Configure Host Account

In this page you should provide the information for the Host or SuperUser User Account. This user has access to all portals created on the site, and care should be taken to provide a UserName/Password combination that is difficult to "hack" by malicious users.

First Name:	SuperUser
Last Name:	Account
User Name:	syshost
Password:	•••••••••
Confirm Password:	•••••••••
Email Address:	yourname@yourcompany.com

SMTP Server Settings

You can configure and test your SMTP Server settings.

Server:

Authentication: ⊙ Anonymous ○ Basic ○ NTLM

Enable SSL: ☐

◊ Next

---

17. For the **First Name**, keep the default `SuperUser`.

18. For the **Last Name**, type `Account`.

19. Select a **User Name** (avoid the standard host for the username. It is too well known).

20. Choose a good password and confirm it. Then write it down as you will need it later.

21. Provide your **Email Address** to get system messages.

22. Click on **Next** and provide the details for the Administrator user.

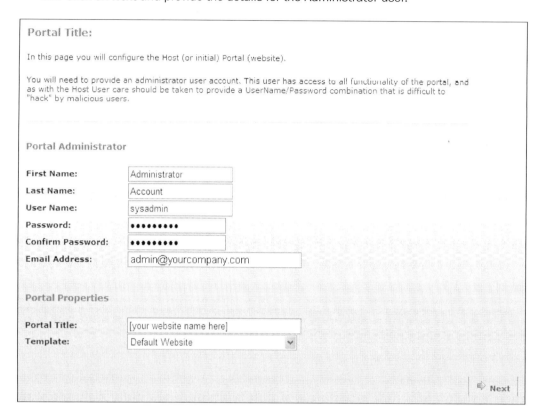

Portal Title:

In this page you will configure the Host (or initial) Portal (website).

You will need to provide an administrator user account. This user has access to all functionality of the portal, and as with the Host User care should be taken to provide a UserName/Password combination that is difficult to "hack" by malicious users.

Portal Administrator

First Name:	Administrator
Last Name:	Account
User Name:	sysadmin
Password:	•••••••••
Confirm Password:	•••••••••
Email Address:	admin@yourcompany.com

Portal Properties

| Portal Title: | [your website name here] |
| Template: | Default Website |

➡ Next

23. For the **First Name**, keep the default `Administrator`.

24. For the **Last Name**, type `Account`.

25. Select a **User Name** (avoid the standard admin for the username. It is too well known).

26. Choose a good password and confirm it. Then write it down as you will need it later.

27. Provide your **Email Address** to get system messages.

28. Lastly, the wizard will prompt for the basic information for your site. Choose a title for your site and type it into **Portal Title**.

29. Select `Default Website` for the **Template**.

30. Click on **Next**.

31. When you see the Congratulations screen, click on **Finished (Goto Site)** to complete the installation.

32. After a pause you should see the Welcome screen to your new website. Congratulations! You have successfully installed and set up a DNN website.

How it works...

When you navigate to a brand-new DNN website, it checks whether the necessary tables and stored procedures exist or not. If they are not there the script will create the tables, views, and stored procedures that DNN needs to run.

There's more...

As this recipe is the final step in the DNN installation it will show an error if any of the previous recipes were not done correctly. This means you may not realize until this moment that a step has been missed in any of the previous recipes. If you do encounter an error the best course of action is to cancel the installation by closing the browser; then review all the previous recipes to confirm every step was done correctly. If the installation continues to fail, it is recommended that you delete all files and the database and retry this recipe from the beginning.

Setting the site name and information

With the installation complete you can now setup your site. DNN is a powerful and flexible content management system so there is much to customize. This recipe will take you through the basics and show you how to quickly set up your site name and copyright message, as well as demonstrate how to upload your own logo for the site.

Getting ready

In this recipe we will demonstrate setting up the basic information for your site. To accomplish this task you must have successfully installed DNN as described in the first four recipes. You will also need to know the host and admin logins, and their passwords as chosen when DNN was installed.

How to do it...

1. Open your favorite web browser and go to the site you set up. If you are developing on your own machine then the web address would be `http://localhost/DotNetNuke/default.aspx`.

2. At the welcome screen click on the **Login** link in the upper right corner of the page (just below the search magnifying glass).

3. Type the username and password you set up for the admin account (`sysadmin` in our examples). Remember: the password is case sensitive.

4. The first thing you'll notice is the Control Panel across the top of the page. It contains useful tools to maintain the site divided into four categories: Common Tasks, Current Page, Admin, and Host. Some of these tools are also available under the host or admin menus, but they're easier to find here in the Control Panel.

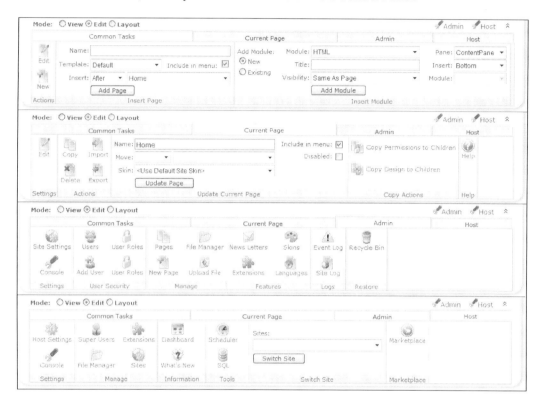

5. Click on **Admin** to display the Admin tasks and click on the **Site Settings** icon in the upper-left corner.

6. This presents the Site Settings form. This is a typical data entry form in DNN. You have fields with labels, but also titles such as **Basic Settings** with little minus signs next to them. These are collapsible panels. You can hide parts of the form by clicking on the minus sign. You'll also see small **Help** icons next to all the fields. Clicking on these might provide more information about the field.

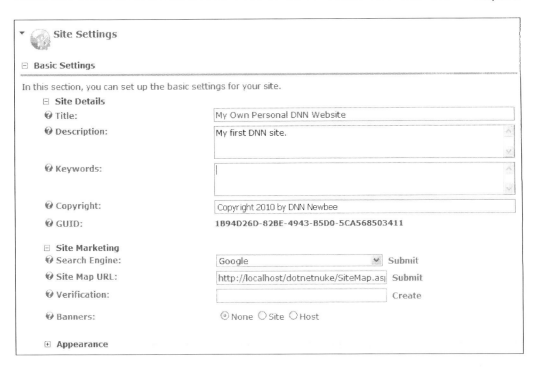

7. Start filling out this form with the following information:

    - **Title**: My Own Personal DNN Website

    - **Description**: My first DNN site

    - **Copyright**: Copyright 2010 by DNN Newbee

8. Click on the small plus sign next to **Appearance** to expand the panel and display fields dealing with the appearance of the site.

9. You can upload your own logo to the site by clicking on the **Upload File** link next to the **Logo:** prompt.

10. This will make a **Browse** button and two new links appear. Click on the **Browse** button.

11. When the **Choose File** dialog appears, navigate through your files and pick an image file to upload. In general, logo images look best if they are wide, but not too tall. Approximately 300 by 100 pixels.

12. Click on **OK** to close the File dialog.

13. Then click on the **Save File** link to actually bring your file up to the web server for DNN to display. The name of the file will now appear in the form.

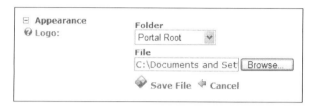

14. Click on **Update** at the very bottom of the page to save your changes.

How it works...

The **Site Settings** page has a variety of options you can set, many of which will be explored in later chapters. Feel free to try different options. If it doesn't look right you can come back to this screen and change it back.

Choosing a skin for the site

This is a quick and easy recipe for changing the color scheme (called the "Skin") of your DNN site. When you download DNN it comes with a basic skin. However, you can download different skins selecting the one which you want your visitors to see. You may even opt for a different skin for the site administrator.

Getting ready

The typical installation of DNN has only one skin. In order to follow this recipe you will need to download at least one other skin to switch. If your site has only one skin you can still follow along to see how to change it. Or try the recipe *Downloading an extension (skin or module)* to download more skins for your site then come back and see how to change them.

How to do it...

1. Log in as Portal Administrator (`sysadmin` in our example).

2. From the **Admin** menu, select **Skins**.

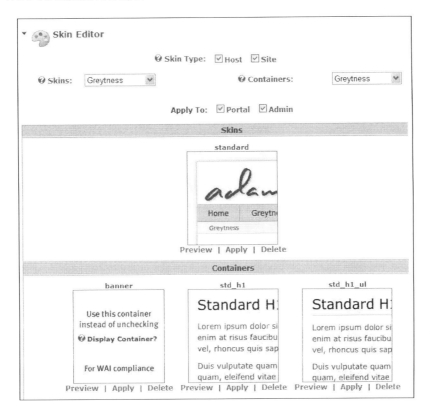

3. Look for the drop-down list showing the available skins that have been installed on your site. If you don't see the skin you want, refer to the recipe *Downloading an extension (skin or module)* to install more skins.

4. Select the skin you want from the drop-down list. Samples of the skin will then be displayed.

5. Click on **Preview** to see what your site would look like with the selected skin.

6. If you like how it looks, click on **Apply** to apply the skin to your site.

7. If you want to have a different skin just for the Administrator user, then find the two checkboxes labeled **Portal** and **Admin**. Uncheck **Portal** and leave **Admin** checked, then apply the skin as described.

How it works...

A skin in DNN is a kind of layout. Visual elements in DNN like the login link, the copyright phrase, and the site logo appear to the skin as simple tokens that are easily repositioned in the layout. The purpose of a skin is to separate the functionality of your site from the visual layout. It allows the artists to design the site without having to worry about how the code works; in turn the programmers can code the site without having to worry about how the graphics work. It provides a consistent look all over the pages of your website.

See also

See the next recipe for more ways to change the visual appearance of your site.

Choosing a container for the site

The skin controls the layout and color scheme of your site but the actual content of your DNN site (the blogs, news articles, and so on) are contained inside visual blocks called Containers. Containers help you lay out your site but you can also choose a visual style for these containers in the same way you pick a visual style for the page itself.

How to do it...

1. Log in as Portal Administrator (`sysadmin` in our example).
2. From the Admin menu, select **Skins**.
3. Look for the drop-down list showing the available skins that have been installed on your site.
4. Select a skin from the drop-down list. Samples of the skin will then display along with the containers within the skin.

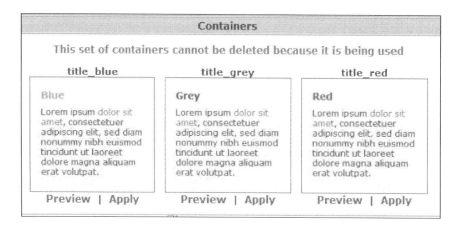

5. Look over the available containers and click on **Preview** to see what your site would look like with the selected container.

6. If you like how it looks, click on **Apply** to apply the container to your site.

7. If you want to have a different container just for the Administrator user, then find the two checkboxes labeled **Portal** and **Admin**. Uncheck **Portal** and leave **Admin** checked, then apply the container as above.

How it works...

Containers are usually found within skins so the styles available for the containers are determined by the skin you have chosen. That is why you have to pick a skin before you can see the available containers. However, DNN is very flexible, allowing you to assign one skin to the pages of your site but also allowing the use of containers from a totally different skin. You are free to mix and match containers and skins to achieve the best appearance for your site.

See also

For more information on how to change the appearance of your site pages, see the recipe *Choosing a skin for the site*.

Adding a module to a page

A module in DNN is a way to organize content into easy-to-use (and easy to reuse) plugins. You create a forum or a blog once, but you can "plug it in" to any page in your site as many times as you like. That is how you build your site by creating pages and plugging in whatever modules you have.

Getting ready

The only thing you need for this recipe is a page in your site. You can add modules to your home page or create a new page to hold your module. In this example we'll add a Banner Ads module to a new page called **Our Sponsors**.

How to do it...

1. Log in as Portal Administrator (sysadmin in our examples).

2. Make sure the Control Panel is displayed across the top of the page (the Control Panel is the set of icons you see when you are logged in as administrator).

3. Click on the **New icon** on the left side. This will create a new page.

4. For the **Page Name**, use Our Sponsors.

5. For the **Page Title**, use Our Sponsors.

6. Leave the rest as default and click on **Update** to create the page.

7. Next, look at the top center of the Control Panel and make sure **Add Module: New** is selected.

8. Locate the drop-down list that appears next to the **Module:** prompt. Select **Banners**.

9. Find the drop-down list next to the **Pane:** prompt and make sure **ContentPane** is selected.

10. In the **Title** box, type A Word from Our Sponsors.

11. In the drop-down list labeled **Insert:** make sure **Bottom** is displayed.

12 Click on the **Add Module** button to insert the Banners module into the page you're looking at.

13. That's all there is to it. Once a module is added to a page you must set the options for the module before you use it. For more details on setting up specific modules, see *Chapter 3, Easy tricks with existing modules*.

How it works...

Adding a module to a page is a simple task and one you will do often. Building a website in DNN is merely adding modules to pages to create the features you need.

The Control Panel offers other options for positioning the module on the page. The example used ContentPane (which is the center pane) but you can also position modules in the left, right, top, and bottom panes.

When you already have modules on the page, the **Insert** drop-down list controls whether the new module should appear above or below the existing modules. Again these are just options to help position the module on the page you've selected. Feel free to experiment with module positioning to get a better feel for what looks good on your site.

Installing standard DNN modules

DNN comes out of the box with many modules, but only the most popular are installed at first. This was a conscious decision by the makers of DNN so that new DNN websites would not be bogged down running a lot of modules that were not needed. This makes for an efficient install, but it also means you'll want to install several standard modules once your site is created.

How to do it...

1. Log in as a SuperUser (`syshost` in our examples).

2. Look at the Control Panel and make sure you're in Edit mode.

3. Look under the **Host** menu and select **Extensions.**

4. Scroll to the bottom and click on the link **Install Available Extensions** or hover the mouse over the module action menu and select it.

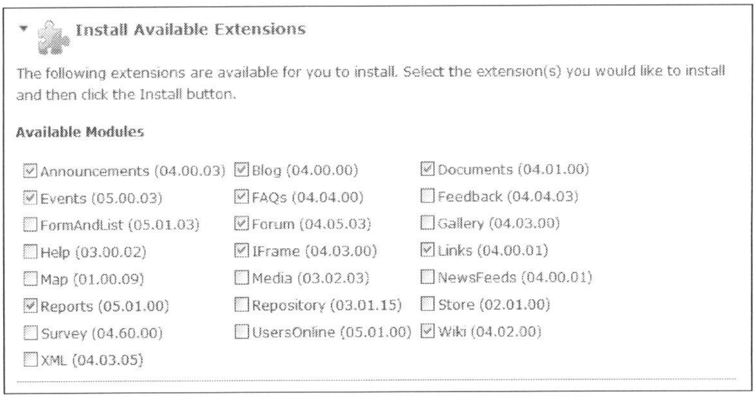

5. Check the modules you want to install. For the recipes in this book, select the following modules:

    ❑ **Announcements**

    ❑ **Blog**

    ❑ **Documents**

    ❑ **Events**

    ❑ **FAQs**

- ❑ **Forum**
- ❑ **IFrame**
- ❑ **Links**
- ❑ **Reports**
- ❑ **Wiki**

6. Scroll to the bottom of the page and click on **Install Selected Extensions**.

7. Now each of these modules will appear in the Control Panel.

How it works...

By installing these additional modules you have many more features you can place on your pages.

Downloading an extension (skin or module)

Extensions in DNN consist of a set of files put together in a compressed folder (also called a ZIP file). To install a new extension you just provide the ZIP file and the DNN extension wizard will do the rest. Only the SuperUser can install new skins and modules.

A good way to get new extensions for your DNN site is to download them from the Internet. Sometimes they are free or cost only a nominal amount. In later chapters you will see how to make your own extensions. No matter how you get your extensions it will consist of a single ZIP file that you need to upload to the DNN server and install before it will appear in the Control Panel drop-down lists as we saw in *Adding a module to a page*.

Popular sites for downloading DNN extensions are `www.codeplex.com` (free open source modules), DotNetNuke Forge (`www.dotnetnuke.com`), and `www.snowcovered.com` (mainly commercial modules). You may need to register for an account with the site, but the registration is free.

This recipe will show how to download an extension (a free skin in this example) but the process is basically the same for all different extension types (such as modules and foreign language packs).

How to do it...

1. Open your favorite browser and go to `www.snowcovered.com`.

2. Find the **Register** link at the top of the screen (next to the **Help** icon) and click on it. If you already have an ID on this site, you can click on **Login**, provide your username and password, and skip to step 4.

3. Fill in your name and pick a Username and Password to use with this site. Fill in any other required fields and click on **Register**.

4. After a successful login or registration, you will see the Welcome page, showing the most recent modules and skins. In the upper left corner, click on **DotNetNuke 5** in the list of **Browse** links.

5. This will show a list of all the modules and skins for DNN 5. We're looking to get a free skin, so find and click on the **Skins** link in the **Browse** list to the upper left.

6. Next, locate the drop-down list that says **Release Date** and select **Price: Low to High**. Then click on the **Sort** link. This will show the free skins first.

7. Look over the free skins and pick one you think will look nice on your site. In this example we'll pick one called **Greytness**, but you can pick whichever one you like. Click on it to go to the skin detail screen.

8. Examine the details of the skin (especially the price which will be $0 if it is a free skin). Then click on the **Add to Cart** link on the right side of the page.

9   A message will confirm the skin is added to your cart. Now click on the link called **View Cart** to complete the transaction.

10. The next screen shows the skin you are downloading. Click on the **Proceed to Checkout** button.

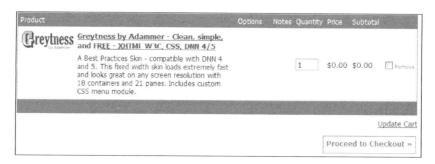

11. At the Payment page, type your e-mail address. Click on the **Continue** button.

12. If you haven't logged into the SnowCovered site yet, you will be asked for your username and password. Otherwise you'll go right to the Payment page.

13. The Payment page will show your account information. Make sure all the required fields are filled in and click on **Continue**.

14. The next screen will show the Sales Agreement and Terms. Click on the **Agree to terms** checkbox and click on **Confirm Order**.

15. The last page will present a link called **My Downloads**. Click on this link.

16. At the list of pending downloads, click on **Downloads** shown next to the skin you purchased.

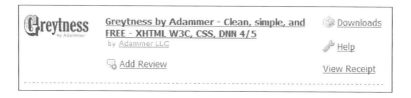

17. On the next page, click on the **Download** link.

18. The File download dialog will ask if you want to Open or Save. Click on **Save** and select a temporary folder to hold the ZIP file.

19. That's all we need from the SnowCovered site so close the browser.

20. There is one more thing we need to do. Often when we download an extension, the ZIP file we really need is inside the ZIP file we downloaded. We'll need to look inside the ZIP file we just got and extract the ZIP file we need. Go to the temporary folder where you saved the download file.

21. Right-click on the file you downloaded and choose **Open With | Compressed (zipped) Folders**.

22. In the file we downloaded, there are several folders inside, one for DNN4 and one for DNN5. Look inside the DNN5 folder and you'll see the ZIP file we really need called `Greytness_01.00.00_Install.zip`. Choose **File | Extract All** from the menu and save all files that were inside the original ZIP to their own folder.

23. Remember the name of the folder holding the `Greytness_01.00.00_Install.zip` file. This is the ZIP we will send up to our DNN site. We will not send up the ZIP file we got from SnowCovered site but the ZIP we found inside that file.

How it works...

A DNN extension is an installable add-on for DotNetNuke that extends the visual experience (Skin, Container), Functions (Skin Objects, Modules), Services (Providers), Localization, or even modules. Modules, skins, and foreign language packs were treated separately in older versions of DNN, but in version 5 they are grouped together under the category of Extension with a single wizard to install them.

See also

Now that you have downloaded the extension in a ZIP file, the next recipe will show how to upload the ZIP file to your DNN site and install it.

Installing a new extension

Once an extension has been downloaded and saved in a temporary folder the last step is to connect to your DNN site and upload the module or skin. This recipe will show you how to install a module you have downloaded from a site like SnowCovered.

Getting ready

To perform this recipe you need to have downloaded an extension file as described in the recipe *Downloading an extension (skin or module)*. In this example we will assume you have a file called `Greytness_01.00.00_Install.zip` ready to upload. Note: some extension packages are zipped with additional material (documentation, install instructions) together and need to be unzipped to be installed. For example, a DNN 5 install ZIP must have a manifest file inside.

How to do it...

1. Point your browser to your DNN site.

2. Log in as SuperUser (`syshost` in our examples). We must use the SuperUser account (not the admin account) because we are adding a new extension to the site.

3. Look at the Control Panel and make sure you are in Edit mode (not View mode).

4. Go to the menu **Admin | Extensions**.

5. Scroll to the bottom of the page and click on the link called **Install Extension Wizard**. You can also select this from the module action menu.

6. Click on the **Browse** button and select the ZIP file (`Greytness_01.00.00_Install.zip` in our example).

7. Click on **Next**.

8. If you see a screen with a warning about a missing manifest, don't panic! It probably means that you skipped the steps from the download recipe and are trying to load the ZIP file that you got directly from SnowCovered. Click on **Cancel** and repeat the steps from the recipe *Downloading an extension (skin or module)* to extract the ZIP file for DNN5. w

9. If all is well, you will see the **Install Extension** page. This shows the details of the skin file. Click on **Next** to install it.

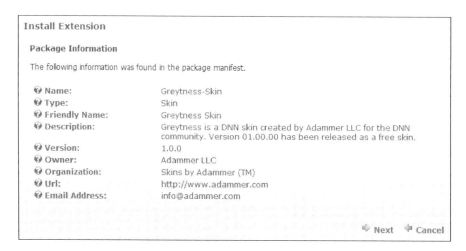

10. At the Release Notes page, click on **Next**.

11. If you see a **Review License** page, check **Accept License** and click on **Next**.

12. The last screen is the **Package Installation Report** which should list all the items loaded for the skin with a final message at the bottom saying **Installation Successful**. If you see an error message instead, there could be a problem with the skin file. Try loading a different skin.

13. Click on **Return** to complete the skin installation.

14. The skin is now available to use on your site. If go to the menu **Admin | Extensions** you will now see that the new skin appears in the drop-down list of skins.

How it works...

The ZIP file holding the extension is uploaded to the DNN site and parsed for a special file called a manifest. The manifest tells DNN whether this is a skin, module, or foreign language extension you are trying to load. From there DNN knows what to do and it will make sure your extension is put in the right place.

There's more...

Installing a module extension is exactly the same as above except that when a module successfully installs it will appear in the Control Panel under the list of available modules.

2
Managing Users and Site Setup

In this chapter we will cover the following topics:

- ► Enabling user registration for your site
- ► Creating users and granting access
- ► Creating and assigning security roles
- ► Granting access to modules
- ► Banning and deleting users
- ► Managing profile properties
- ► Creating and organizing pages
- ► Using the Recycle Bin
- ► Setting up a SMTP server with Gmail

Introduction

Once the DNN site has been successfully installed the next step is to set up the security roles, create your users, and make sure they can only see and edit content they have access to. This chapter covers security, maintaining users, and the tools for configuring the site.

Enabling user registration for your site

Once you have installed your DNN website, the first thing you're going to think about is how to create the users for it. In DNN users are created through the process of User Registration. You control how users can join the site by choosing one of the four membership options:

- ▸ None: Users cannot register themselves. Instead the Portal Administrator must create each user as needed.

- ▸ Private: Users create their own registration but the Portal Administrator approves the user registration before the user can access the site.

- ▸ Public: Users create their own registration and gain immediate access.

- ▸ Verified: Users create their own registration and gain access by clicking on a link in the confirmation e-mail.

In this recipe we will show how to set the user registration for the site and demonstrate how the Verified membership works.

Getting ready

When using the Private, Public, or Verified memberships, both the Portal Administrator and the new user will receive an e-mail alert as part of the registration process. To see this entire process demonstrated in this recipe you need a valid e-mail address and the site must be set up to send e-mails. To set up your site this way, see the recipe *Setting up a SMTP server with Gmail* at the end of this chapter.

How to do it...

1. Begin by logging in as the Portal Administrator (`sysadmin` in our examples).
2. Look at the Control Panel and make sure you are in Edit mode.
3. Look under the **Admin** menu and select **Site Settings**.
4. Look under **Advanced Settings** and expand **Security Settings**.

5. Select **Verified** for the registration type.
6. Click on **Update** at the bottom of the page to save your changes.

7. To test the new setting, log out of the site by clicking on the **Logout** link.

8. By selecting a membership type that is not None, you will now see a **Register** link next to the **Login** link:

9. The register link will now also appear on the Login page:

10. Clicking on the **Register** link will display the **User Registration** form where users can provide their information:

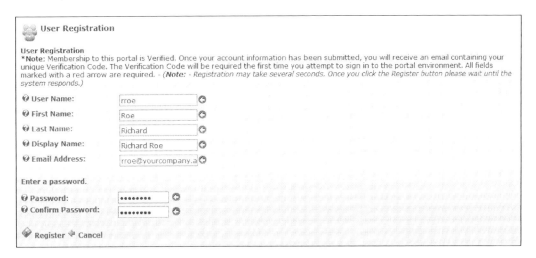

11. Click on the **Register** link to create the user.

12. As the membership is Verified, the new user will receive a special e-mail containing a link that will complete the registration and add the user to the site. The e-mail looks something like this:

```
From: admin@mycompany.abc [mailto:admin@mycompany.abc]
Sent: Friday, September 17, 2010 12:59 PM
To: Richard Roe
Subject: MyCompany Intranet New User Registration

Dear Richard Roe,

We are pleased to advise that you have been added as a Registered
User to MyCompany Intranet. Please read the following information
carefully and be sure to save this message in a safe location for
future reference.

Portal Website Address: www.mycompany.abc
Username: sjones
Password: dnnuser
Verification Code: 0-7

You can use the following link to complete your verified registration:

http://www.mycompany.abc/default.aspx?ctl=Login&username=rroe
&verificationcode=0-7

Thank you, we appreciate your support...

MyCompany Intranet
```

13. When the new user clicks on the link in the e-mail they are taken to the Log in page where an additional Verification Code field now appears. Providing the password and verification code will now give access to the user:

How it works...

Allowing users to register themselves with your site takes the burden of user creation off of the administrator. With the options of Private, Public, and Verified you can control the user registration process as much or as little as needed.

There's more...

When a user has attempted to register with the site, the Portal Administrator will receive an e-mail alert so that the administrator can take the appropriate steps to complete the registration. Here is an example:

```
From: admin@mycompany.abc [mailto:admin@mycompany.abc]
Sent: Friday, September 17, 2010 12:59 PM
To: System Administrator
Subject: MyCompany Intranet New User Registration

Date: Friday, September 17, 2010
First Name: Richard
Last Name: Roe
Unit:
Street:
City:
Region:
Country: N/A
Postal Code:
Telephone:
Email: rroe@mycompany.abc
```

See also

The fields that appear on the user registration form (first name, last name, and so on) are part of the user's profile. To see how you can add your own fields and make them required for registration, see the recipe *Managing profile properties* later in this chapter.

Creating users and granting access

In the previous recipe we saw how to allow users to create themselves in your portal through the user registration process. As administrator you also have the option to create users directly (indeed if you turn off the user registration you must create the users directly). This recipe will show you how to create your own users, assign them a password, and grant them access to the different pages of your portal.

Getting ready

To create users all you need is the Portal Administrator login. But there are some decisions to make. Should the new user get an e-mail to notify them when their account has been created? Should you automatically authorize them so they can immediately log in? Should you give them a random password and force them to change it when they first log in? This recipe shows how to set these options.

How to do it...

1. Begin by logging in as the Portal Administrator (sysadmin in our examples).

2. Look at the Control Panel and make sure you are in Edit mode.

3. Look under the **Admin** menu and select **User Accounts**. You can also select the Users icon in the Admin tab of the Control Panel.

4. The page shows a list of users.

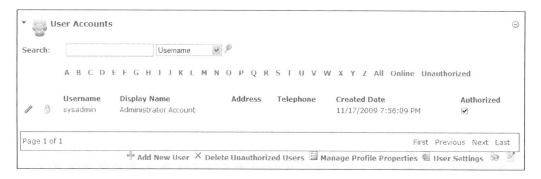

5. To create a new user look at the bottom of the page and click on the **Add New User** link (or select it from the action menu).

6. This displays the **Add New User** form. Fill in the form with the following information:

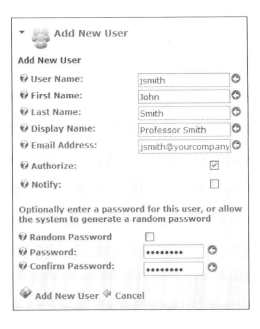

- ❑ **User Name:** jsmith
- ❑ **First Name:** John
- ❑ **Last Name:** Smith
- ❑ **Display Name:** Professor Smith
- ❑ **Email Address:** jsmith@yourcompany.com
- ❑ **Authorize:** Checked
- ❑ **Notify:** Unchecked
- ❑ **Random Password:** Unchecked
- ❑ **Password/Confirm Password:** rfid2010

7. Click on **Add New User** to save your changes and create the user.

8. Next we need to assign the security role. New users automatically get the Registered User role and the Subscribers role. We can also grant our own security roles to jsmith.

9. Find `jsmith` in the list of user accounts. Click on the lock icon next to the name to display the **Manager Roles** page.

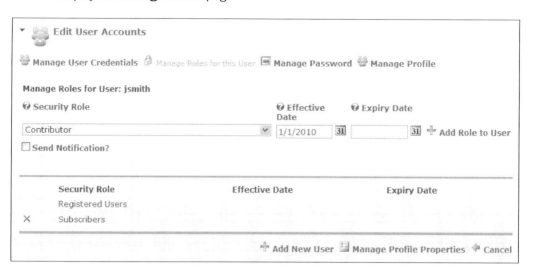

10. On the left side you'll see the label **Security Role** and under that is a drop-down list of all the roles in the portal. Find the **Contributor** role in the list and select it.

11. Pick an **Effective Date** of today and leave the **Expiry Date** blank.

12. Uncheck **Send Notification?**

13. Click on the **Add Role to User** link to save your changes.

14. The Contributor role should now appear in the list of roles in the bottom-left of the page.

15. Click on **Cancel** to close the page as our change is done.

How it works...

As this is a test user we left Notify unchecked so no e-mail is sent. With Notify the user gets an e-mail when the account is created. If we select Random password then a random password appears in the e-mail. A notification e-mail with a random password looks like this:

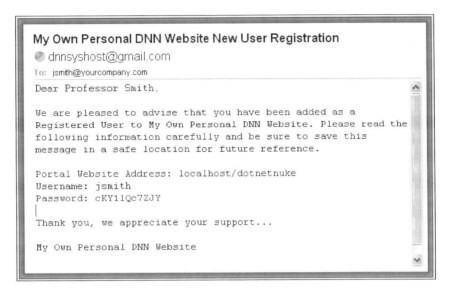

The text that appears in the alert e-mails is completely customizable. You can find it by selecting **Languages** from the **Admin** menu (or from the Control Panel) and clicking on the pencil icon next to the language of your portal. To learn more about localizing text like this see the recipe in *Chapter 9, Editing the language resource file.*

There's more...

After creating a user and defining security access the last thing remaining is defining which security roles can see the portal modules.

See also

To learn how to assign security access to different modules see the recipe *Granting access to modules* later in this chapter.

Creating and assigning security roles

One of the first things you must do as a Portal Administrator is to define the security for the portal. Security roles grant access to all users assigned to the role and when combined with permissions permit some pages to be public and some to be private.

Getting ready

To create a security role you need either the host or Portal Administrator login. To decide what security roles you need think about the different types of users accessing the site. For example, if you have a news site you may create a group called Contributors. By creating a security role for this group you can give them access to edit content that a normal user would not have.

How to do it...

1. Begin by logging in as the Portal Administrator (`sysadmin` in our examples).
2. Look at the Control Panel and make sure you are in Edit mode.
3. Look under the **Admin** menu and select **Security Roles**.
4. This page will display all the security roles you currently have.

5. Click on the link labeled **Add New Role** (or select it from the action menu).

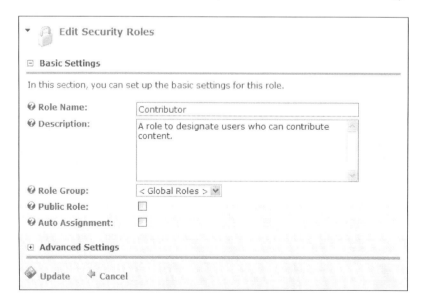

6. When the Edit Security Roles page is displayed, enter the following information:

- ❑ **Role Name**: Contributor
- ❑ **Description**: A role to designate users who can contribute content
- ❑ **Role Group**: <Global Roles>
- ❑ **Public Role**: Unchecked
- ❑ **Auto Assignment**: Unchecked

7. Click on the **Update** button to create the role.

How it works...

Once a security role is created you can assign it to a user then take advantage of DNN's flexible security and assign it to either the pages or the modules in your portal. This will control access to your portal's content.

There's more...

When your DNN was installed, five security roles were created for you:

- ▸ **Administrator:** This role grants full access to the selected portal.
- ▸ **Registered User:** This is any user who has been given a username and password for the website.
- ▸ **Subscribers:** This is a sample for a public role, intended to be used in Newsletter modules. Users can register and unregister for role membership by themselves.
- ▸ **Unregistered users:** These are public users who are visiting your site but have not logged in.
- ▸ **All Users:** This special role is used when you want to give access to all users, regardless of whether they are logged in or not.

These security roles can provide most of the security control your portal needs, but sometimes you need to create roles that make more sense to your business.

See also

For examples of how to use the role you've created see the next two recipes:

- ▸ *Granting access to modules*
- ▸ *Banning and deleting users*

Granting access to modules

Once security roles are defined and assigned to users the last step is to decide which users can access the modules in the portal. You specify access to modules in two ways: a module can inherit access from the page where it is placed or you can turn off inheritance and specify directly on the module what security roles can access it. Some modules are available to all users while others are private. If you don't have the security role required by the module you will not see the module when the portal page is displayed.

Getting ready

For this recipe you need a module. The default DNN portal includes a small HTML module called **Sponsors** that displays some of the companies that support DNN. We will take the normally private module and make it public so everyone can see it. Keep in mind that the recipe below will work with any module in DNN, not just with Sponsors.

How to do it...

1. Begin by logging in as the Portal Administrator (`sysadmin` in our examples).

2. Look at the front page of the portal and scroll down to the bottom of the page. Look for the **Sponsors** or just use any module you see on the page.

3. Locate the module action menu. It's the small triangle next to the module name. Hover your mouse over the small triangle and the action menu will display.

4. Select **Settings** from the action menu. This displays the **Module Settings** form.

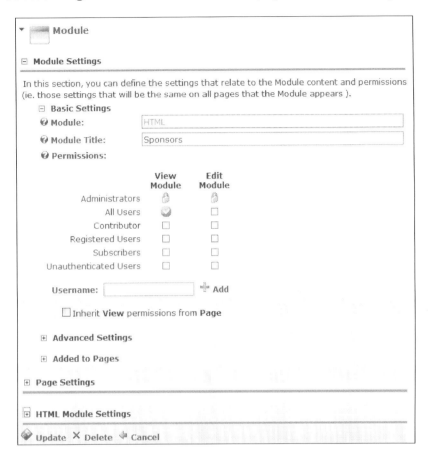

5. Make sure **Inherit View permissions from Page** is unchecked. This will allow you to set the security at the module level.

6. Listed under the Permissions prompt will be the five security roles that came with DNN plus any security roles you created. To give view access to unregistered users (that is the general public) make sure that:

   ❑ **All Users** is checked

   ❑ **Registered Users** is unchecked

   ❑ **Unauthenticated Users** is unchecked

7. Click on **Update** at the bottom of the page to save your changes.

8. To test the security, click on the **Logout** link to become an unauthenticated user.

9. Look at the home page and scroll to the bottom. The **Sponsors** module should now appear even when you're not logged in. It is now a public module.

There's more...

In this recipe we saw a simple example of controlling user access at the module level, but security in DNN is determined at several different levels. You can control access at the page level and the let modules on the page inherit the same access or you override at the module level for additional control. But there may be additional factors to consider when choosing security for your site. Users can have multiple security roles and some modules (such as the Blog module) have additional layers of security built into them as well. It is best to think carefully about your security decisions and test them before deploying them on a production site.

See also

For more examples of user account security see the next recipe, *Banning and deleting users*.

Banning and deleting users

Once you have created users and given them access to your portal you have two different ways to remove that access. You can ban them by stripping them of their privileges or you can delete and remove them all together.

Getting Ready

For this recipe you will need some test users to ban and delete. See the recipe *Creating users and granting access* for more information.

How to do it...

1. Begin by logging in as the Portal Administrator (sysadmin in our examples).

2. Look at the Control Panel and make sure you are in Edit mode.

3. Look under the **Admin** menu and select **User Accounts** or click on the **Users** icon in the Control Panel.

4. The **User Accounts** page will display all the users in the portal. Look for an existing user or create a test user. Do not pick the administrator user! The administrator user cannot be banned or deleted.

5. To ban a user without deleting you need to unauthorize him. Find the user you want to ban in the list and click on the small pencil icon next to their name. This will display the **Edit User Accounts** page.

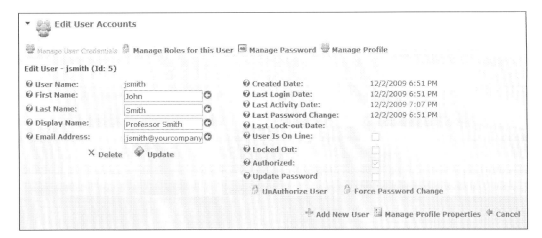

6. Click on the **Unauthorize User** link at the bottom of the page. You will see a message saying **User successfully Un-Authorized**.

7. Click on **Cancel** to return to the list of users.

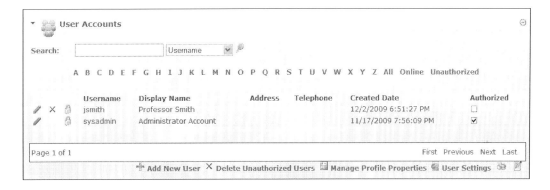

8. The test user is still listed but the **Authorized** checkbox is now unchecked. This user is now banned and can no longer log into the portal.

9. To completely remove the user and their profile you can delete the user by clicking on the small red **X** that appears next to their name. If you have several unauthorized users to delete you can click on the **Delete Unauthorized Users** link.

10. When asked to confirm your decisions, click on **OK**.

11. After a pause a message will display confirming the users are deleted.

How it works...

A user can only log into your portal if they exist and are authorized. By removing these you effectively block access.

Managing profile properties

Before we leave managing users and move on to site setup there is one more thing to demonstrate. The user accounts page has fields such as First Name, Last Name, and many others. These are called Profile Properties. But as Portal Administrator you can control the fields that appear on the user profile. You can streamline user registration by removing properties you don't want. You can also create your own profile properties if there is special user information you want to collect.

Getting ready

For this recipe you will need some test users to modify their profile. See the recipe *Creating users and granting access* to create a test user.

How to do it...

1. Begin by logging in as the Portal Administrator (sysadmin in our examples).
2. Look at the Control Panel and make sure you are in Edit mode.
3. Look under the **Admin** menu and select **User Accounts** or click on the **Users** icon in the Control Panel.

4. Click on **Manage Profile Properties** (or select it from the action menu).

Manage Profile Properties

You can change the order of the profile fields, and whether they are Required or Visible on this screen. Click on the "Apply Changes" button to save any changes you make. To edit other properties of each Profile Property click the pencil icon in the first column of the grid.

Edit	Del	Dn	Up	Name	Category	DataType	Length	Default Value	Validation Expression	Required	Visible
										☐	☑
✎	✕	⬇	⬆	Prefix	Name	Text	50			☐	☑
✎		⬇	⬆	FirstName	Name	Text	50			☐	☑
✎	✕	⬇	⬆	MiddleName	Name	Text	50			☐	☑
✎		⬇	⬆	LastName	Name	Text	50			☐	☑
✎	✕	⬇	⬆	Suffix	Name	Text	50			☐	☑
✎	✕	⬇	⬆	Unit	Address	Text	50			☐	☑
✎	✕	⬇	⬆	Street	Address	Text	50			☐	☑
✎	✕	⬇	⬆	City	Address	Text	50			☐	☑
✎	✕	⬇	⬆	Region	Address	Region	0			☐	☑
✎	✕	⬇	⬆	Country	Address	Country	0			☐	☑
✎	✕	⬇	⬆	PostalCode	Address	Text	50			☐	☑
✎	✕	⬇	⬆	Telephone	Contact Info	Text	50			☐	☑
✎	✕	⬇	⬆	Cell	Contact Info	Text	50			☐	☑
✎	✕	⬇	⬆	Fax	Contact Info	Text	50			☐	☑
✎	✕	⬇	⬆	Website	Contact Info	Text	50			☐	☑
✎	✕	⬇	⬆	IM	Contact Info	Text	50			☐	☑
✎	✕	⬇	⬆	Biography	Preferences	RichText	0			☐	☐
✎		⬇	⬆	TimeZone	Preferences	TimeZone	0			☐	☐
✎		⬇	⬆	PreferredLocale	Preferences	Locale	0			☐	☐

◆ Apply Changes 🖹 Refresh Grid

➕ Add New Profile Property ◀ Cancel

5. You'll see a list of all the current profile properties. To hide some of these look under **Visible** column and uncheck the following:

   ❑ **Biography:** Unchecked

   ❑ **TimeZone:** Unchecked

   ❑ **PreferredLocale:** Unchecked

6. Click on **Apply Changes**.

7. To add a new property click on **Add New Profile Property** (or select it from the action menu).

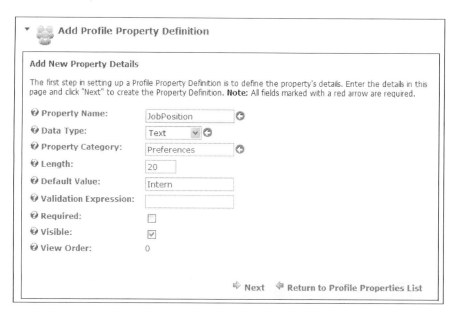

8. Fill in the following information:

   - **Property Name:** JobPosition (no space)
   - **Data Type: Text**
   - **Property Category:** Preferences
   - **Length:** 20
   - **Default Value:** Intern
   - **Validation Expression:** Leave blank
   - **Required:** Unchecked
   - **Visible:** Checked

9. Click on **Next**.

10. On this page we provide the Help, Validation, and Error messages for the new profile property. Fill in the following information:

    ❑ **Property Name:** JobPosition (no space)

    ❑ **Property Help:** Your position in the company

    ❑ **Category Name:** Preferences

11. Click on **Save Localized Text**.

12. Click on **Return to Profiles Properties List**.

13. The new property will appear in the list of properties. Click on **Cancel** to return to User Accounts.

14. To check your results, click on the pencil icon to edit a user.

15. Click on **Manage Profile**.

16. Confirm that JobPosition now appears as a property for the user.

17. You can also use profile properties as part of the user registration process. If we want to add the example JobPosition to the user registration we start by going to **User Accounts** under the **Admin** menu.

18. Select **User Settings** from the action menu or by clicking on the link at the bottom of the page.

19. Scroll down to the bottom of the page until you see **Require a Valid Profile for Registration**.

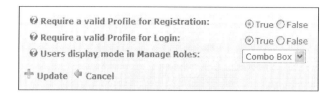

20. Set **Require a Valid Profile for Registration** to **True**.
21. Click on **Update** to save your changes.
22. To see how the user registration form looks, click on the **Logout** link.
23. Then click on the **Register** link.
24. The new `JobPosition` property now displays along with the other properties:

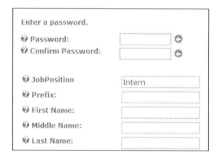

Creating and organizing pages

In this example we will create a few blank pages to show how to create new content and organize it in a menu. We will create one page that will be the parent of several smaller pages.

So what is a page? A page in DNN is really a place holder. When you create a new page it appears in the menu of your site and acts as a blank layout to hold your modules.

In this recipe we will create a few blank pages, organize them into a hierarchy and then delete some of them to see how it is done.

How to do it...

1. Begin by logging in as the Portal Administrator (sysadmin in our examples).

2. Look at the Control Panel and make sure you are in Edit mode.

3. Look under the **Admin** menu and select **Pages** (or select **Pages** from the **Admin** tab of the Control Panel).

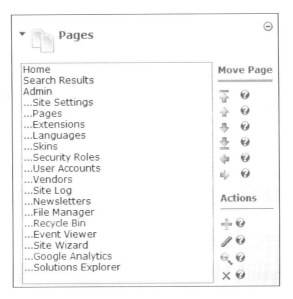

4. On the left side you can see the list of all the pages in your portal arranged in a hierarchy just as they will appear in the menu. The indented pages represent submenus.

5. Click on the **Add New Page** icon under **Actions** on the left side.

6. Provide the following information:

- **Page Name**: My Links

- **Parent Page**: <None Specified>

- **Insert Page**: Click on **After** and select **Home** from the drop-down list

      ❑ **Template Folder**: <None Specified>

      ❑ **Include in Menu?** Checked

      ❑ **Permissions**: Check **View Page** for **Registered Users**

7. Click on **Update** to save your information.

8. Now we have a new menu item that appears on every page of the site (like the Home or Admin menu). Let's create another page, but put it under this new menu item.

9. Click on the **Add New Page** again.

10. Provide the following information:

      ❑ **Page Name**: Announcements

      ❑ **Page Title**: Announcements

      ❑ **Parent Page**: My Links

      ❑ **Template Folder**: <None Specified>

      ❑ **Include in Menu?** Checked

      ❑ **Permissions:** Check **View Page** for **Registered Users**

11. Click on **Update** to save your information.

12. See how our second page appears underneath our first page. This is because we choose the first page as our Parent Page.

13. Add another page called **My Blog** and put it under **MY LINKS**.

14. Add another page called **My Forum** under **MY LINKS**.

15. Add another page called **Useful Documents** under **MY LINKS**.

16. Add another page called **Delete Me** under **MY LINKS**.

17. We now have five pages under our original parent page but they are in the wrong order. We can move the **Delete Me** page to the bottom of the menu.

18. Find **Delete Me** in the list of pages on the left side and select it.

19. Press the down arrow button to move the page downwards until it is the last page listed under **MY LINKS**.

20. Now that we know how to move a page in the menu, let's see how to delete a page.

21. Select **Delete Me** in the list of pages on the left side.

22. Click on the small red **X** under **Actions** on the right side of the page.

23. You will be prompted **Are you Sure You Wish To Delete This Item?** Click on **OK**.

24. The page is sent to the Recycle Bin and disappears from the menu and the list of pages. If you delete a page and change your mind later, see the next recipe *Using the Recycle Bin* to learn how to get it back.

How it works...

Creating pages, organizing them in the menu and adding modules to them is a big part of building a website using DNN. We'll see many more examples of adding pages and creating content in the next chapter.

See also

Now that you have blank pages in your site you can start adding modules using the remaining recipes in this chapter and *Chapter 3*.

Using the Recycle Bin

When you delete pages and modules in DNN, they are not actually deleted. Instead they are held in a Recycle Bin just like files on your computer. This recipe will show you how to "undelete" pages and modules.

Getting ready

To follow along with this recipe you'll need a deleted page. See the recipe *Creating and organizing pages* to learn how to delete a page.

How to do it...

1. Begin by logging in as the Portal Administrator (`sysadmin` in our examples).

2. Look at the Control Panel and make sure you are in Edit mode.

3. Look under the **Admin** menu and select **Recycle Bin**.

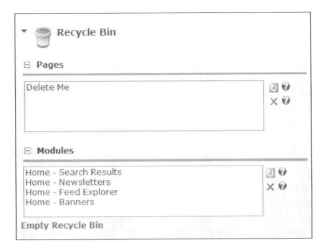

4. The Recycle Bin maintains pages and modules you have deleted. To bring back a page click on the page to select it.
5. Click on the small green recycle icon.
6. After a pause the page will become active again and reappear in the menu.
7. To restore a module, select the module in the list.
8. Click on the recycle icon.
9. After a pause the module will reappear on the page it was deleted from.

How it works...

The Recycle Bin lets you undelete pages and modules but it also offers a link to empty the Recycle Bin. If you click on this link then all the pages and modules in the Recycle Bin will be deleted forever. Use this link with caution.

Setting up a SMTP server with Gmail

DNN uses e-mail in many ways: when a new user is created, when you set up vendors, or when someone responds to a blog post.

You can configure your site to send e-mails using the **Simple Mail Transfer Protocol (SMTP)** but this requires a SMTP Server.

In this recipe, we'll demonstrate how to use a free Gmail account (from Google) as your SMTP server and how to configure DNN to send e-mails via this account.

Getting ready

To follow along with this recipe you must have the following:

▸ A Gmail account (you can get a free one by going to `http://mail.google.com` and clicking on the **Create an Account** button)

▸ The username and password to your Gmail account

How to do it...

1. Begin by logging in as the host (`syshost` in our examples).

2. Look under the **Host** menu and select **Host Settings**.

3. Under **Basic Settings**, provide the following information:

   ❑ **Host Email**: (put your Gmail address here, like `dnnsyshost@gmail.com`)

4. Scroll down and expand **Advanced Settings**.

5. Find **SMTP Server Settings** and expand it.

6. Fill in the following information:

    ❑   **SMTP Server and port:** `smtp.gmail.com`

    ❑   **SMTP Authentication: Basic**

    ❑   **SMTP Enabled SSL:** Checked

    ❑   **SMTP Username:** (your Gmail email address `dnnsyshost@gmail.com`)

    ❑   **SMTP Password:** (your Gmail password)

7. Click on the **Update** button to save your changes.

8. Click on the **Test** link to test your configuration.

9. You should see a message **Email Successfully Sent**. If you see an error instead, check whether you typed everything as shown above and provided the correct Gmail address and password.

How it works...

The information you provide allows DNN to connect to your Gmail account and send e-mail through it.

3
Easy Tricks with Existing Modules

In this chapter we will cover the following topics:

- Using the HTML module
- Creating an Announcement
- Distributing documents online
- Publishing a Newsletter
- Creating a calendar of events
- Creating a Wiki
- Publishing sets of popular links
- Displaying RSS news feeds
- Configuring RSS news feeds
- Publishing a simple report
- Publishing a survey questionnaire

Introduction

In this chapter, we will look at the most popular modules that are included in the DotNetNuke community edition. We will explore everything from announcements to publishing content to displaying reports from the database. These recipes will give you everything you need to build a popular and useful portal.

Most of the modules described in this chapter are included in the current version of DNN but are uninstalled. Limiting the number of installed modules keeps a new DNN site as simple and efficient as possible. Review the recipe from *Chapter 1, Installing standard DNN modules* to install these additional modules before following these recipes.

Using the HTML module

The HTML module is a very simple module but it offers a lot of possibilities. Think of it as an HTML file you can put inside a container on your DNN page. Whatever code you put in the module will be interpreted just like an HTML file placed on the web server.

On the positive side, this means your HTML module can contain the same kind of code you would find in any HTML file: HTML, JavaScript, VBScript, even JQuery. On the negative side, as the HTML module sits inside the DNN page, it means there are some important limitations to what the HTML module can do. The principal consideration is that whatever code you place in the HTML module must play nice with the all the other code running on the page outside of your module. It also means that you are responsible for the correct syntax of your HTML code. There is no error checking done on the code in the HTML module.

In this recipe we will demonstrate simple HTML with CSS code. For more examples of the HTML module, you can look ahead to *Chapter 10*.

Getting ready

To follow along with this recipe, it is handy to be familiar with HTML and CSS.

How to do it...

1. Log in as Portal Administrator (`sysadmin` in our examples).
2. Add the HTML module to a new or existing page.
3. Select **Edit Content** from the module menu (or click on the **Edit Content** icon).
4. On the **Edit Content** page, you will see the editor which has different modes. You can choose **Basic Text Box** for simple text entry. You can also choose **Rich Text Editor** if you prefer to use the automatic HTML formatting features. If you are working directly in HTML you can click on the **HTML** tab at the bottom to avoid any automatic formatting.

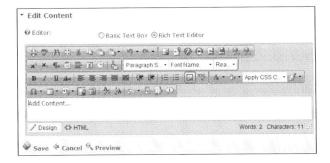

5. As we are working in HTML, click on the **HTML** tab at the bottom.

6. Type the following HTML in the editor to create a list of sample images of DNN vendors:

```
<div class="imagebar">
<ul class="image">
    <li><img alt="" src="/dotnetnuke/Portals/0/aspnet.gif" /></li>
    <li><img alt="" src="/dotnetnuke/Portals/0/redgate.gif" />
        </li>
    <li><img alt="" src="/dotnetnuke/Portals/0/WH4L.gif" /></li>
    <li><img alt="" src="/dotnetnuke/Portals/0/
                                        exacttarget.gif" />
    </li>
    <li><img alt="" src="/dotnetnuke/Portals/0/
                                        maximumasp.gif" />
    </li>
    <li><img alt="" src="/dotnetnuke/Portals/0/telerik.gif" />
    </li>
</ul>
</div>
```

7. Click on **Save** to save your changes.

8. A simple list will display the images as a vertical bar.

9. This demonstrates how the module renders simple HTML, but to format the display we need to add some style information. Select **Edit Content** from the module menu (or click on the **Edit Content** icon) and click on the **HTML** button.

10. Add the following style information at the top of the editor, just before the HTML code:

```
<p><style type="text/css">
.imagebar {
   height: 70px;
   width: 780px;
   border: 1px solid #ddd;
}
ul.image {
   float: left;
   list-style: none;
   margin: 0; padding: 0;
}
ul.image li {
   margin: 0; padding: 5px;
   float: left;
   position: relative;
   width: 120px;
   height: 60px;
}
</style></p>
<div class="imagebar">
<ul class="image">
    <li><img alt="" src="/dotnetnuke/Portals/0/
                                        crystaltech.jpg" />
    </li>
    <li><img alt="" src="/dotnetnuke/Portals/0/
                                        datasprings.gif" />
    </li>
    <li><img alt="" src="/dotnetnuke/Portals/0/easycgi.gif" /></
li>
    <li><img alt="" src="/dotnetnuke/Portals/0/
                                        exacttarget.gif" />
    </li>
    <li><img alt="" src="/dotnetnuke/Portals/0/
                                        maximumasp.gif" />
    </li>
    <li><img alt="" src="/dotnetnuke/Portals/0/telerik.gif" />
    </li>
</ul>
</div>
```

11. Click on **Save** and see the results:

12. The styling has created a border and arranged the images in a horizontal line.

There's more...

This is a simple example of how HTML and CSS are displayed in the HTML module. For other possibilities, see the recipe from *Chapter 10, Using the HTML module with JQuery*.

Creating an announcement

The Announcements module is an easy way to publish regular bits of news or small pieces of content. An announcement consists of a title and a body, optionally an illustrating image and link to continue. In this recipe we will take one of the blank pages created earlier, add the Announcements module to it and create our first announcement.

Getting ready

We'll need some text and a picture to put in the announcement. For this example, we'll imagine we have a technology news site and we want to add some news concerning a new product called "Mir:ror" used for reading RFID tags on a home computer.

How to do it...

1. Begin by logging in as the Portal Administrator (`sysadmin` in our examples).

2. Look at the Control Panel and make sure you are in Edit mode.

3. Navigate to a blank page (like **Announcements** created in the recipe *Creating and organizing pages*).

4. From the Control Panel, pick the **Common Tasks** tab and select the Announcements module from the drop-down list (if you don't see the Announcements module listed, see *Chapter 1, Installing standard DNN modules* for more information).

5. Click on the **Add Module** button.

6. Now that we have placed the module on the page we can use it to create an announcement. Click on the **Add New Announcement** link.

7. Fill in the following information:

   ❑ **Title**: `Get a Mir:ror for Your Computer !`

   ❑ **Image:** Select **URL (A Link To An External Resource)**

   ❑ **Location:** `http://www.thinkgeek.com/images/products/ front/ba0d_violet_rfid_mirror.jpg`

8. In the editor, type the following text:

`Violet, a maker of RFID devices, is offering a user friendly RFID reader called Mir:ror. It plugs into your USB port and will read the tag of an object placed upon it.`

9. Then complete the remaining information:

Link: None

Track Number Of Times This Link Is Clicked? Checked

Log The User, Date, And Time For Every Link Click? Unchecked

Open Link In New Browser Window? Unchecked

Publish Date: Use today's date (as the announcement is hidden until this date)

View Order: 1

10. Click on the **Update** button to see your changes.

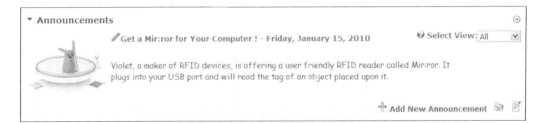

11. You will see your new announcement displayed. If you don't, look for the **Select View** drop-down list on the right side and select **All**.

How it works...

Announcements are a very simple way to publish information on your portal. This works well with a simple text announcement and an image. If you have more complicated content or need options for user feedback try using the Blog module instead.

Distributing documents online

It is possible to publish a variety of documents on a DNN portal such as Word documents, PDF files, internal documentation, and images. This is useful for a company intranet that wants to distribute documents to employees without the task of e-mailing everybody.

Getting ready

To follow this recipe you must have the Documents module installed on your DNN site. See the recipe in *Chapter 1, Installing standard DNN* modules for instructions.

Document distribution in DNN has four steps:

1. The host user decides what document types will be allowed.
2. The host user creates a list of file categories to keep the files organized.
3. A user (like the Portal Administrator) uploads a document.
4. Another user downloads the document.

How to do it...

1. Log in as the host user (`syshost` in our examples).
2. Look under the **Host** menu and select **Host Settings**.
3. Scroll all the way down and look for the section called **Other Settings** and expand it.

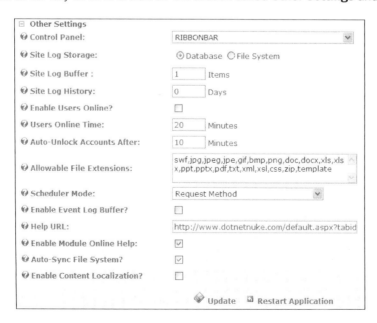

4. Find **Allowable File Extensions**. This list affects both the files available to download and the files allowed for upload. For example, if you want to upload a JPG for the HTML module the extension has to be listed here. Review the list and remove any extensions you will not support on your site.

5. Click on **Update** to save your changes.

6. Log out as host and log in as the Portal Administrator (sysadmin in our examples).

7. Navigate to a blank page (such as **Useful Documents** created in the recipe *Creating and organizing pages* in *Chapter 2*).

8. Look at the Control Panel and make sure you are in Edit mode.

9. From the Control Panel, pick the **Common Tasks** tab and select the Documents module from the drop-down list.

10. Choose ContentPane from the drop-down list and click on the **Add Module** button.

11. The Documents module will now appear on your blank page and show the current list of available documents. Before we add a document, let's edit the settings of the module.

12. Hover over the Documents module menu and select **Settings**.

13. Scroll down to the **Documents Module Settings**.

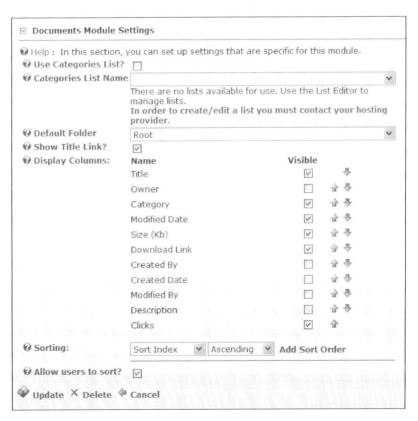

14. Fill in the information as shown above.

15. Click on **Update** to save your changes.

16. Now we can add a document for others to download. Back at the **Documents** page, click on the **Add New Document** link.

17. When the **Edit Documents** page is displayed fill in the information as shown in the above screenshot.

18. Click on **Update** to save your changes.

19. This image file is now available to the users of your portal. They download it by clicking on the **Download** link.

How it works...

The reason why the host user must specify what files are allowed for distribution is because some types of files (like executable files) are more susceptible to viruses and malicious code. By controlling the kinds of files your portal can distribute or receive from users you reduce the chances of this happening.

In this example, we selected **Track Number Of Times This Linked is Clicked?** This is used to keep track of how often users view the document. As we selected **Clicks** as one of the display columns we can see the count when the document is listed on the page.

There's more...

If the users can see the Documents module then they have access to download the documents within it. Limit access to your documents by setting the security on the module or the page as described in the recipe *Granting access to modules* in *Chapter 2*.

Publishing a Newsletter

A good way to keep your users informed with current news and events or alert them to changes in your portal is with a newsletter. In DNN a newsletter is an e-mail that goes out at regular intervals to people registered with your site.

Getting ready

Newsletters are sent out to security groups defined in your site, as well as any individual e-mail addresses you deem necessary. Sending a newsletter requires that your DNN site has been set up to send e-mails. See the recipe *Setting up the SMTP Server with Gmail* in *Chapter 2* for instructions. Also, as we are using the Subscribers role in this example, you should have at least one user with the Subscriber role with a valid e-mail address to receive the newsletter.

How to do it...

1. Log in as the Portal Administrator (`sysadmin` in our examples).

2. Select **Newsletters** from the **Admin** menu.

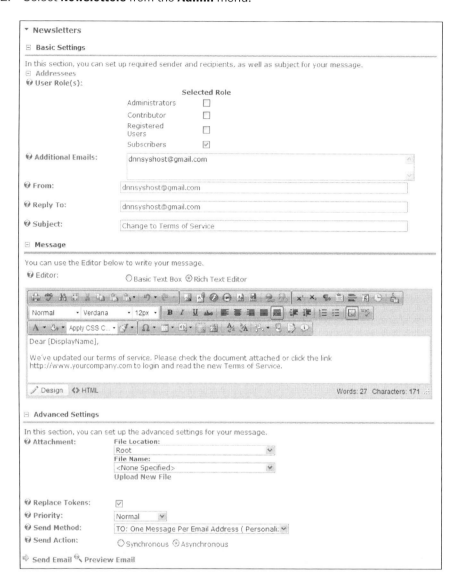

3. Fill in the information as shown in the above screenshot.

4. Click on **Preview Email** to view and confirm the message is correct.

5. Click on **Send Email** to send out your newsletter.

6. As soon as you click the link the newsletter e-mails will go out. In addition, a summary e-mail is sent to the Portal Administrator with the count of e-mails sent.

How it works...

All e-mails are sent either one by one (TO send method) or in a single mail with all recipients' addresses to the members of the role. In the first case, if **Replace Tokens** is checked, you may include user or profile variables (for example, [Profile:City]), which get replaced by values of the recipient's user data.

There's more...

In this example we chose **Asynchronous** as the **Send method** which means the e-mails will send in the background. If we had chosen **Synchronous** then the e-mails would still send immediately, but we would not leave the Newsletter form until all the e-mails have been sent. Asynchronous is best if you plan to send a large quantity of e-mails. Be aware there may be additional delays from the mail server depending on how it is configured to handle batch e-mails.

Creating a calendar of events

Calendars are a great way to organize events for your users. The Events module in DNN offers a very powerful calendar and in this recipe we will explore some of its many features.

In this recipe we'll see how to

- Create a calendar of events
- Create a new event with an image

Getting ready

To follow this recipe you must have the Events module installed on your DNN site. See the recipe *Installing standard DNN modules* in *Chapter 1* for instructions.

How to do it...

1. Log in as the Portal Administrator (sysadmin in our examples).
2. Look at the Control Panel and make sure you are in Edit mode.
3. Navigate to the page that will hold the Events Calendar.
4. From the Control Panel, pick the **Common Tasks** tab and select the **Events** module from the drop-down list.

5. Choose **ContentPane** from the drop-down list and click on the **Add Module** button.

6. Adding the Events module to a page immediately creates a calendar for your users. To add an event to the calendar look at the small icon bar at the top of the calendar. Click on the Add Event icon that looks like **+**.

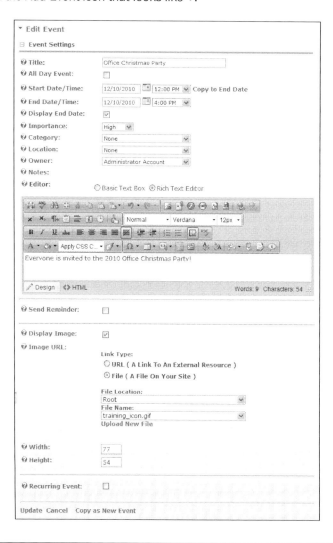

7. When the **Edit Event** form displays, provide the information as shown in the above screenshot.

8. Click on **Update** to save your changes.

9. When you return to the calendar, type `12/20/2010` in the textbox at the top and click on the **Go** button. This will take you to December 2010 and you can see the new event.

10. If you hover the mouse over the event the title and description are displayed. Click on the **Event** to display the full details.

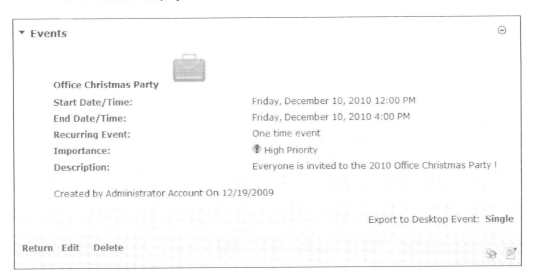

11. Click on **Return** to close the Event form.

There's more

By selecting **Settings** under the module menu you can explore the many features in the Events module, features that allow people to sign up for events or the ability to sell tickets through PayPal.

Creating a Wiki

A Wiki is a special way to publish content where the articles can link to each other and readers are given privileges to edit the content. The name Wiki comes from the Hawaiian word for _Quick_ and the most famous Wiki is probably Wikipedia. This recipe will show you how to create your own Wikipedia for your DNN portal on any topic you like.

For this example we will create a small Wiki with three sample topics:

- ▸ Arduino
- ▸ Physical Computing
- ▸ Transduction

Getting ready...

To follow this recipe you must have the Wiki module installed on your DNN site. See the recipe *Installing standard DNN modules* in *Chapter 1* for instructions.

How to do it...

1. Log in as the Portal Administrator (`sysadmin` in our examples).
2. Look at the Control Panel and make sure you are in Edit mode.
3. Navigate to the page that will hold the **Wiki**.
4. From the Control Panel, pick the **Common Tasks** tab and select the **Wiki** module from the drop-down list.
5. Choose **ContentPane** from the drop-down list and click on the **Add Module** button.
6. To create our first topic, click on the **Add** link along the bottom to display a new page:

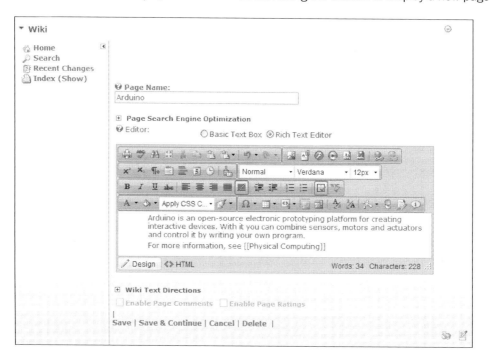

7. Fill in the following information:

    ❏ **Page Name:** Arduino

    ❏ In the Editor:

    Arduino is an open source electronic prototyping platform for creating interactive devices. With it you can combine sensors, motors and actuators and control it by writing your own program.

    For more information, see [[Physical Computing]]

8. Click on **Save** at the bottom. The topic is now displayed with the phrase **Physical Computing** shown as a hyperlink.

9. Click on the new **Physical Computing** link.

10. A new topic is created automatically. Click on the **Edit** link and provide the content:

    ❏ **Page Name:** Physical Computing

    ❏ In the Editor:

    Physical Computing is a term that describes the process of connecting a computer to the physical world and giving it the power to sense and react to its environment.

    The key principle behind physical computer is [[Transduction]]

11. Click on **Save**.

12. Click on the new **Transduction** link, then **Edit** to create a third topic:

    ❏ **Page Name:** Transduction

    ❏ In the Editor:

    Transduction is the conversion of one form of energy to another. A microphone is an example of transduction since it changes sound waves into a changing electrical voltage.

13. Click on **Save**.

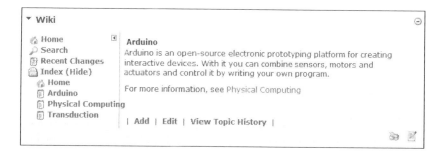

14. Click on **Index (Show)** on the left to display all three topics. You can select a topic from the index shown or by clicking on the links that appear in the topic itself.

15. To directly assign editing privileges to the security roles, hover over the module menu and select **Administration**.

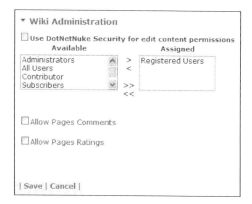

16. Uncheck **Use DotNetNuke Security**.

17. Pick the security role(s) that can edit the topics.

18. Click on the **>** link to assign that role to the Wiki.

19. Click on **Save** to save your changes.

How it works...

A Wiki in DNN is really a collection of topics connected with hyperlinks. You designate a hyperlink in your Wiki topic by enclosing the target page name in double-brackets ([[and]]). Be sure the page name in brackets matches the actual page name of the Topic or the link will not work. You may also specify a different caption for the link by using the tag [[Target Page Name|Caption]]. For example, [[Physical Computing|Click here to see Physical Computing]] will create a link to the Physical Computing topic but the link will say "Click here to see Physical Computing".

Publishing sets of popular links

A very useful feature offered by DNN is the links module. The links module is a set of popular website links you provide for your users. Not only are these links a convenience for your users but also a means of gathering statistics.

Getting ready

To follow this recipe you must have the Links module installed on your DNN site. See the recipe *Installing standard DNN modules* in *Chapter 1* for instructions.

How to do it...

1. Log in as the Portal Administrator (sysadmin in our examples).

2. Look at the Control Panel and make sure you are in Edit mode.

3. Navigate to the page that will hold the list of Links.

4. From the Control Panel, pick the **Common Tasks** tab and select the **Links** module from the drop-down list.

5. Choose **ContentPane** from the drop-down list and click on the **Add Module** button.

6. Click on the **Add Link** link.

7. Fill in the following information as shown in the above screenshot.

8. Click on **Update** to save your changes.

9. Back at the list of links, click on **Add Link** again.

    ❏ **Title:** Digg

    ❏ **Link Type: URL (A Link To An External Resource)**

    ❏ **Location:** http://www.digg.com

    ❏ **Track Number of Times This Link Is Clicked ?** Checked

    ❏ **Log The User, Date, And Time For Every Link Clicked ?** Checked

    ❏ **Open Link In New Browser Windows?** Checked

    ❏ **Description:** Digg News

    ❏ **View Order:** 2

10. Click on **Update** to save your changes.

11. Click on **Add Link** one more time.

    ❏ **Title:** I Can Has Cheezburger?

    ❏ **Link Type: URL (A Link To An External Resource)**

    ❏ **Location:** http://icanhascheezburger.com

- ❑ **Track Number of Times This Link Is Clicked?** Checked
- ❑ **Log The User**, **Date**, **And Time For Every Link Clicked?** Checked
- ❑ **Open Link In New Browser Windows?** Checked
- ❑ **Description**: LOL Cats
- ❑ **View Order**: 3

12. Click on **Update** to save your changes.

13. If you want to change how the links are displayed, hover over the module menu and select **Settings**.

14. Scroll down until you see **Links Settings**.

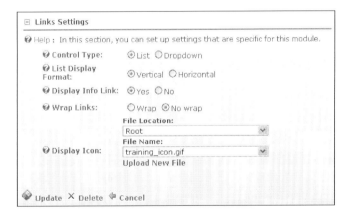

15. You can add an image and display the description with the link by selecting the following:

- ❑ **Display Link Info**: Yes
- ❑ **Display Icon**: Select **Root** and training_icon.gif from the drop-down list

16. Click on **Update** to save the changes to **Settings**.

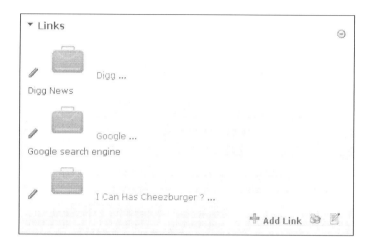

Displaying RSS news feeds

A News Feed is a frequently updated source of information, similar to a blog or news headline that is published by websites such as Google and CNN. DNN offers a module that will display news feeds from the Internet on your portal.

The format of these feeds is called **Really Simple Syndication (RSS)** so these are often called RSS News Feeds.

Getting ready

To follow this recipe you must have the News Feeds module installed on your DNN site. See the recipe *Installing standard DNN* modules in *Chapter 1* for instructions.

To use a RSS news feed you need the web address (the URL) of the feed. In this example, we will display a news feed from a popular technology news site called Digg. The URL for this feed is `http://feeds.digg.com/digg/container/technology/popular.rss`.

How to do it...

1. Log in as the Portal Administrator (`sysadmin` in our examples).
2. Look at the Control Panel and make sure you are in Edit mode.
3. Navigate to the page that will hold the News Feed.
4. From the Control Panel, pick the **Common Tasks** tab and select the **News Feeds (RSS)** module from the drop-down list.

5. Choose **ContentPane** from the drop-down list and click on the **Add Module** button.

6. Now we choose the feeds we want. Click on the **Edit Newsfeeds** link.

7. This will display the **Edit News Feeds (RSS)** page that shows any feeds we have. Click on **Add Feed** to create a new feed.

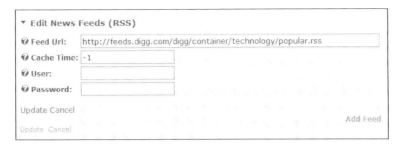

8. Fill in the information as shown in the above screenshot.

9. Click on **Update** to save your changes.

10. Now the new feed appears in the list. Click on **Update** to save your changes and display the feed.

11. You'll see a short status bar then the news stories will appear on your DNN page.

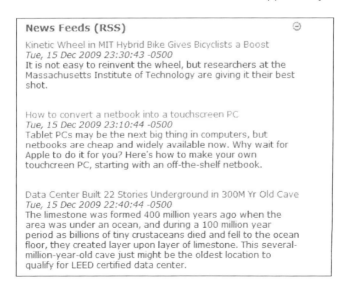

How it works...

RSS is really a set of different XML formats for syndicating news stories. It generally contains a summary of the story along with a link to the full text. One of the nice features in DNN is its ability to aggregate several feeds into a single feed on the page. Just use the **Add Link** to add more feeds. To display a feed in the News feeds module it must adhere to the RSS standard.

There's more...

Feeds often look good if the module is set in the right or left side of your DNN page. Experiment with positioning to see what looks best on your portal.

Configuring RSS news feeds

In the recipe *Displaying RSS news feeds* we saw how to display RSS feeds in your DNN site. In this recipe we will see how to configure the News Feeds module to control how the feeds are formatted and displayed.

Getting ready

To follow this recipe you must have the News Feeds module installed on your DNN site. See the recipe *Installing standard DNN modules* in *Chapter 1* for instructions. You must also have completed the previous recipe:

 ▸ *Displaying RSS news feeds*

This recipe will demonstrate two configuration features:

 ▸ Use the **Settings** to control the number of stories displayed on the page

 ▸ Using a XSL transformation file to display a feed as a news ticker

How to do it...

1. Log in as the Portal Administrator (sysadmin in our examples).
2. Look at the Control Panel and make sure you are in Edit mode.
3. Navigate to the page that holds the News Feed created in the previous recipe.

4. To control the number of stories displayed hover over the module menu and select **Settings**.

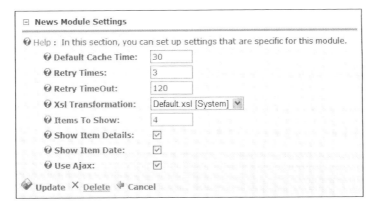

5. Scroll down until you see the section called **News Module Settings**.

6. Find the one labeled **Items to Show**, type 4 for the value.

7. Click on **Update** to save your changes.

8. Now only four news stories are displayed on your DNN page. Another way to display your feeds is a news ticker running along the bottom of your DNN page. To create a news ticker:

    □   Hover over the module menu and select **Move**, then select **Move to BottomPanel** from the submenu. This puts the module along the bottom of your page.

❑ Hover over the module menu again and select **Settings** from the module menu.

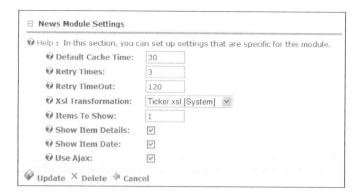

❑ Scroll down until you see the section called **News Module Settings**.

❑ Find **Xsl Transformation** and select **Ticker.xsl [System]** from the drop-down list.

❑ For **Items to Show**, type 1.

❑ Click on **Update**.

There's more...

If you have a favorite news feed but find it won't display correctly using the News feed module, you can take more control of how a feed is displayed by using the XML/XSL module with a similar XSL transformation file. To learn more, see the recipe *Displaying an XML feed* in *Chapter 10*.

Publishing a simple report

DNN provides an excellent reporting module for querying information from the database using **Structured Query Language (SQL)** with results showing in a DNN page. To use the Reports module effectively you need to know the basics of the SQL query language and know which tables in the database to use.

In this recipe we will query one of the standard database tables that come with DNN and display the results on a page.

Getting ready

To follow this recipe you must have the Reports module installed on your DNN site. See the recipe *Installing standard DNN modules* in *Chapter 1* for instructions.

Reports can be a dangerous module for non-administrators. SQL is a powerful query language that can access other tables in the DNN schema and reveal information you may want to keep private.

How to do it...

1. Log in as host user (`syshost` in our examples).

2. Look at the Control Panel and make sure you are in Edit mode.

3. Navigate to a blank page (or create a new page).

4. From the Control Panel, pick the **Common Tasks** tab and select the **Reports** module from the drop-down list.

5. Choose **ContentPane** from the drop-down list and click on the **Add Module** button.

6. Hover over the module menu and select **Settings**.

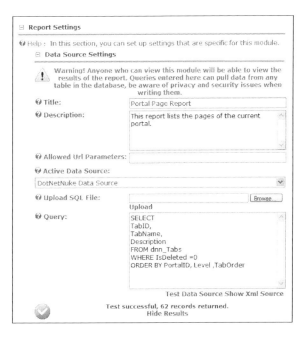

7. Scroll down, find **Report Settings** and fill in the information as shown in the above screenshot.

8. Click on **Test Data Source** to check your SQL.

9. If you see an SQL warning message, click on **OK**. You should see a message **Test Successful**.

10. Leave the rest of the fields as default.

11. Click on **Update** to save your changes.

12. When you return to the reports page, your SQL query will automatically run and the results will be displayed.

▼ Reports

TabID	TabName	Description
7	Host	
16	Host Settings	Manage configuration settings which apply to all portals.
17	Portals	Add, modify, and delete portals.
18	Module Definitions	Install, add, modify and delete modules.
19	File Manager	Manage files.
20	Vendors	Manage vendor accounts, banner advertising and affiliate referrals.
21	SQL	Execute SQL queries against the database.
25	Schedule	Add, modify and delete scheduled tasks to be run at specified intervals.
29	Search Admin	Manage search settings associated with DotNetNuke's search capability.
33	Lists	Manage common lists.
34	Superuser Accounts	Manage host user accounts.
36	Extensions	Install, add, modify and delete extensions, such as modules, skins and language packs.
37	Dashboard	Summary view of application and site settings.
38	What's New	Provides a summary of the major features for each release.

There's more...

For a review of databases and Structured Query Language see the recipes in *Chapter 4*.

There are also different presenters and data sources, which may also be extended by installing additional add-ons.

Publishing a survey questionnaire

A survey is a set of questions and answers published from your portal. You can use it for feedback from your users or just to see what topics seem to be of interest to people.

In this recipe we will build a simple survey called **Future Technologies** to see what people think about the future.

Getting ready

To follow this recipe you must have the Survey module installed on your DNN site. See the recipe *Installing standard DNN modules* in *Chapter 1* for instructions.

How to do it...

1. Log in as the Portal Administrator (sysadmin in our examples).

2. Look at the Control Panel and make sure you are in Edit mode.

3. Navigate to the page that will hold the Survey.

4. From the Control Panel, pick the **Common Tasks** tab and select the **Survey** module from the drop-down list.

5. Choose **ContentPane** from the drop-down list and click on the **Add Module** button.

6. Click on the **Add Question** link.

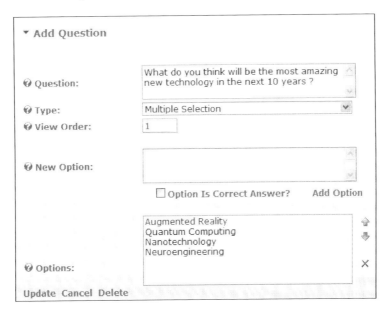

7. Fill in the following information:

   ❑ **Question**: What do you think will be the most amazing new technology in the next 10 years?

   ❑ **Type**: Select **Multiple Selection**

   ❑ **View Order**: 1

   ❑ **New Option**: **Augmented Reality**

8. Repeat this step to create three more options:

   ❑ **Quantum Computing**

   ❑ **Nanotechnology**

   ❑ **Neuroengineering**

9. Click on **Update** to save your survey.

10. Check the **Augmented Reality** and **Quantum Computing** checkboxes and click on **Submit Survey**.

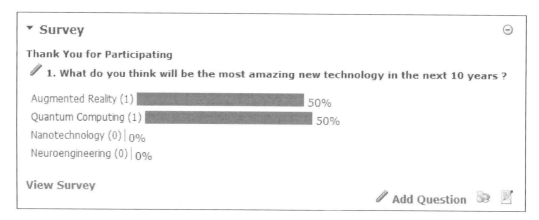

11. You'll now see a graph of all survey responses. As more responses are submitted, the graph will change.

There's more...

If you want your survey to allow only a single answer (a radio button instead of checkboxes) then select **Single Selection** as your **Survey Type**.

For tests, you may also specify the correct answer.

4

Creating your Own Modules

In this chapter we will cover the following topics:

- ▶ Installing Visual Web Developer 2010 Express
- ▶ Viewing the database from Web Developer
- ▶ Installing the DNN 5 Starter Kit
- ▶ Creating a new module with the Starter Kit
- ▶ Creating a database table with keys
- ▶ Creating stored procedures
- ▶ Connecting a module to the database
- ▶ Creating an uninstall script

Introduction

The previous chapters introduced DNN and showed how to add existing modules to your DNN site. In this chapter, we will show how to download and install the tools you need to start writing your own DNN modules. We will also show how to get a jump start by creating a module using the DNN Starter Kit and the steps required to connect it to the database.

Installing Visual Web Developer 2010 Express

In this recipe we will download and install Visual Web Developer 2010 Express — the free .NET development tool.

Getting ready

To follow along with this recipe you must first complete the recipe *Downloading the Microsoft Web Platform Installer* from *Chapter 1*.

How to do it...

1. Start by launching the Microsoft Web Platform Installer.

2. When the list of available products is displayed, click on the **Web Platform** tab.

3. Under the **Tools** section, click on the **Customize** link.

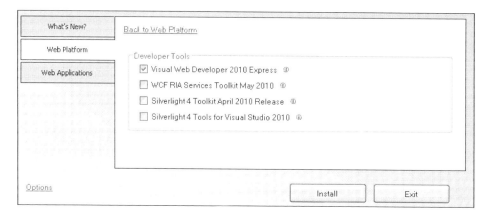

4. Make sure the following product is selected:

   ❑ **Visual Web Developer 2010 Express**

5. Click on the **Install** button to begin the install.

6. The next dialog will list the file you are downloading and prompt **I Decline** or **I Accept**. Click on **I Accept**.

7. The Web Platform installation will begin. You may be prompted one or more times to reboot. Click on **Yes** to reboot your machine and the installation will continue automatically after the reboot.

8. When the install finishes and the **Congratulations** screen shows, click on **Finish**.

9. Close the Web Platform Installer by clicking on **Exit**.

10. To confirm the installation was successful, look under **Start menu | All Programs** and the **Microsoft Visual Web Developer 2010 Express Edition** should appear under the Microsoft Visual Studio 2010 Express folder.

See also

Completing this recipe gives you the tools to start programming, but to develop modules for DNN you will also need to complete the recipe _Installing the DNN 5 Starter Kit_.

Viewing the database from Web Developer

As you will be spending much time in Visual Web Developer, it is useful to create a connection to the database to see the tables, views, and stored procedures that your module will be using.

Getting ready

To follow along with this recipe you need to have installed Visual Web Developer and have access to a local database like the one running your DNN site.

How to do it...

1. Start by launching your preferred development tool (Visual Studio or Visual Web Developer Express).

2. Under the **View** menu, select **Database Explorer** (or **Solution Explorer** in Visual Studio). This will show any database connections you have.

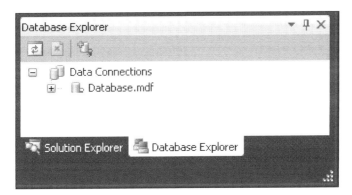

3. Under the **Tools** menu, select **Connect to Database...** or click on the Connect to Database icon.

4. If you are prompted for a **Data source**, select **Microsoft SQL Server (SqlClient)** and click **Continue**. Otherwise skip to the next step.

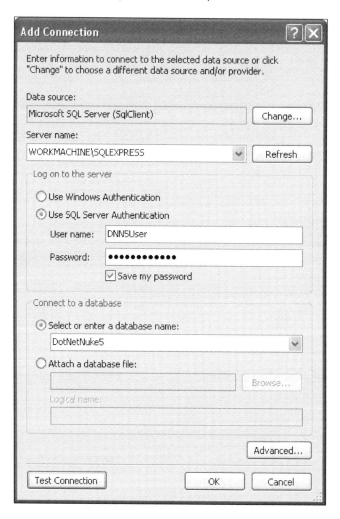

5. When the **Add Connection** dialog displays, if the data source is not **Microsoft SQL Server,** click on the **Change** button next to **Data Source**, select **Microsoft SQL Server,** and click on **OK**.

6. For **Server Name**, click on the drop-down list and select your local SQL Express server or just type machinename\servername as in YOURMACHINENAME\SQLEXPRESS.

7. For the log on, select **Use SQL Server Authentication** (you can also use **Windows Authentication** and skip to step 10).

8. For the **User name** and **Password**, use the username and password that created the database (in *Chapter 1* this was DNN5User and DNN5User2010).

9. Check **Save my Password**.

10. In the **Connect to database** section, select the name of the DotNetNuke database you created when DNN was installed (DotNetNuke5 in these examples).

11. Click on the **Test Connection** button.

12. If you do not see a **Test connection succeeded** message, check if you have typed the correct server name and DNN database name for your site.

13. Click on **OK** to create the database connection.

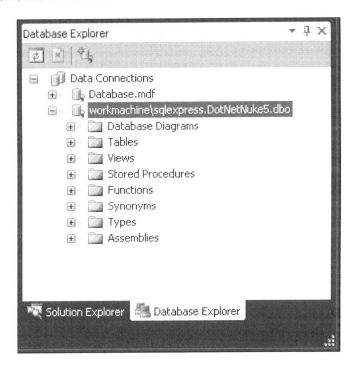

14. Your DNN database will now appear in the **Database Explorer** window. Under the database you will see the tables, views, and stored procedures inside your DNN installation.

Installing the DNN 5 Starter Kit

In this recipe we will download and install the DNN 5 Starter Kit. The Starter Kit will generate a near complete DNN module based only on a module name. The module it creates will still need editing, but it will save us a lot of typing.

Getting ready

The Starter Kit requires Visual Studio or Visual Web Developer Express Edition. To install Visual Web Developer 2010 Express for your development environment see the previous recipe *Installing Visual Web Developer 2010 Express.*

How to do it...

1. Go to `http://dotnetnuke.codeplex.com`.
2. Click on the **Downloads** tab at the top of the page.
3. Look for the **Visual Studio Starter Kit** link on the left side and click on the link.

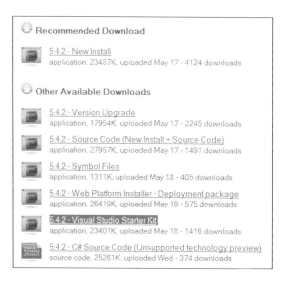

4. When prompted for license terms, click on **I Agree**.

5. When prompted to **Open** or **Save**, click on **Open**.

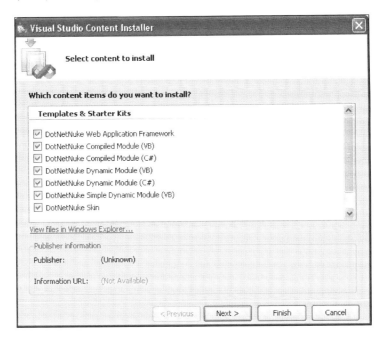

6. The installation file will download and the installation will begin. Leave all the options checked and click on **Next**.

7. If you see a security warning, **No Signature Found**, click on **Yes**.

8. Click on **Finish** to complete the installation.

9. You should see a success message for each of the items installed. Click on **Close** when the installation is done.

How it works...

The Starter Kit is a set of templates for VB.NET and C#.NET. Using the module name you provide, the wizard will generate a complete module along with install and uninstall scripts.

See also

To create a module using the Starter Kit see the following recipe.

Creating a new module with the Starter Kit

In this recipe we demonstrate how to create your first DNN module. We will create a simple module that stores Employee information in the DNN database.

Getting ready

To create your first DNN module you must complete the two previous recipes:

- ▸ *Installing Visual Web Developer 2010 Express*
- ▸ *Installing the DNN 5 Starter Kit*

We will use the Visual Web Developer, but the process is virtually identical in Visual Studio.

How to do it...

1. Launch your preferred development tool (Visual Studio or Visual Web Developer Express).

2. Under the **File** menu, select **New Project...**.

3. In the **New Project** dialog, look under **My Templates** and select **DotNetNuke Compiled Module** for the template. If you do not see DotNetNuke under your templates, see the previous recipe *Installing the DNN 5 Starter Kit*.

4. Type **Employee** for the project name and **Solution name**.

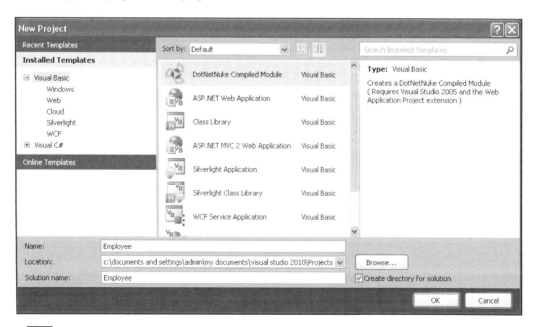

5. Click on **OK** to create the project.

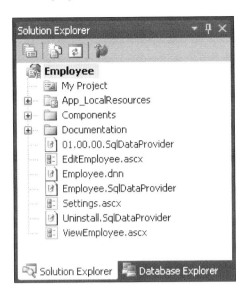

6. Before we begin there is a quick configuration change we need to make. In the upper-right corner of the screen is the **Solution Explorer**. Find the first icon labelled **Employee** and right-click on it to display the pop-up menu.

7. Select **Properties** from the pop-up menu.

8. Blank the field called **Root namespace**.

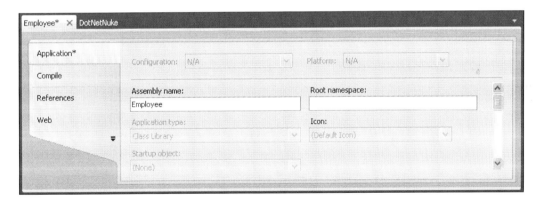

9. Look under the **File** menu and select **Save All** to save your changes.

How it works...

Choosing a good module name is important. The Starter Kit uses the module name to create procedures and generate code. To choose a name for the module decide what is the most important thing the module will do and use a singular word to describe it. For example, *Employee* is a good name for a module that tracks the employees of a company.

There's more...

In this example we kept things simple and called the module **Employee**. In a professional development environment it is a better practice to use your company name or initials as a prefix to your module name (such as `YourCompany.Employee`). This prevents a collision between two modules from different companies that happen to have the same name.

See also

The project wizard creates the files you need for a module, but you must edit these files before the project can deploy to a DNN site. See the other recipes in this chapter to create tables, procedure, and the necessary code changes.

Creating a database table with keys

As DNN is a database driven **Content management system** (**CMS**), it is likely your module will include one or more database *Tables*. A database table is used to hold information for your module. Similar to a spreadsheet, a table consists of columns called `Fields` and rows called `Records`. As we are creating a module called **Employee**, the fields in our table will hold employee information such as first and last name. Each record in the table will hold one employee.

One of the things that makes a database table more powerful than a simple spreadsheet is its ability to automatically validate the information in the records. For example, it is important that each employee record in the table has a unique value that identifies the record (called the `Item ID`). The database can enforce the unique value with a `PRIMARY KEY` (named for the fact that the `Item ID` is the most important key to the employee record).

Fortunately, the Starter Kit has already created the code to create an `Employee` table and the necessary keys. Looking in the Employee project you will find a script called `01.00.00.SqlDataProvider`. This creation script runs when your module is deployed to the DNN site and it has the responsibility for creating the tables, views, keys, and stored procedures that your module needs.

Getting ready

In this recipe we will modify the creation script to create a table called Employee along with the necessary keys. This script will create the table when the module is deployed or you can copy and paste from the script to the database directly so that the table exists while you are developing.

To follow along with this recipe you must have completed the previous recipe *Creating a new module with the Starter Kit*.

How to do it...

1. Start by launching your preferred development tool (Visual Studio or Visual Web Developer Express).

2. Look for **Recent Projects** shown on the left side of the screen. Click on **Employee** to load the project.

3. Look under the **Solution Explorer** on the right side of the screen and double-click on **01.00.00.SqlDataProvider**. This will display the creation script in the editor.

4. At the very top of the file you will a see the CREATE TABLE section. The Starter Kit wizard has already created a single CREATE TABLE statement along with a PRIMARY KEY, an index, and a foreign key to the standard DNN module table. The script from the wizard looks like this:

```
/** Create Table **/

if not exists (select * from dbo.sysobjects where id =
   object_id(N'{databaseOwner}[{objectQualifier}
   YourCompany_Employee]') and OBJECTPROPERTY(id, N'IsTable') = 1)
   BEGIN
      CREATE TABLE
            {databaseOwner}[{objectQualifier}YourCompany_Employee]
      (
         [ModuleID] [int] NOT NULL,
         [ItemID] [int] NOT NULL IDENTITY(1, 1),
         [Content] [ntext] NOT NULL,
         [CreatedByUser] [int] NOT NULL,
         [CreatedDate] [datetime] NOT NULL
      )


      ALTER TABLE {databaseOwner}
[{objectQualifier}YourCompany_Employee]
         ADD CONSTRAINT [PK_{objectQualifier}
         YourCompany_Employee] PRIMARY KEY CLUSTERED  ([ItemID])
      CREATE NONCLUSTERED INDEX
               [IX_{objectQualifier}YourCompany_Employee]
```

```
                                ON {databaseOwner}[{objectQualifier}
                                YourCompany_Employee] ([ModuleID])

            ALTER TABLE {databaseOwner}
             [{objectQualifier}YourCompany_Employee] WITH NOCHECK ADD
             CONSTRAINT [FK_{objectQualifier}
             YourCompany_Employee_{objectQualifier} Modules] FOREIGN
             KEY ([ModuleID]) REFERENCES {databaseOwner}
             [{objectQualifier}Modules] ([ModuleID]) ON DELETE CASCADE
             NOT FOR REPLICATION
          END
       GO
```

5. The first thing we need to do is to change the text `YourCompany` in the script. Instead of `YourCompany`, you can place your actual company name or initials. We do this with a simple search and replace — under the **Edit** menu, look under **Find and Replace** and select **Quick Replace** (or just press *Ctrl+H*).

6. When prompted:

   ❑ **Find What**: `YourCompany`

   ❑ **Replace with**: `ACME`

   ❑ **Look in**: `Current Document`

7. Click on **Replace All**.

8. Next we add the fields we need, into the table. The wizard put `Content` as a single field. We will replace `Content` with our field names. Replace the single line `[Content] [ntext] NOT NULL`, with the following six lines:

```
          [EmpFirstName] [nvarchar](30) NOT NULL,
          [EmpLastName] [nvarchar](30) NOT NULL,
          [ManagerNo] [int] NULL,
          [HireDate] [datetime] NOT NULL,
          [Salary] [float] NOT NULL,
          [DeptNo] [int] NOT NULL,
```

9. Our table creation code should now look like this:

```
/** Create Table **/

if not exists (select * from dbo.sysobjects where id =
  object_id(N'{databaseOwner}[{objectQualifier}ACME_Employee]')
  and OBJECTPROPERTY (id, N'IsTable') = 1)
  BEGIN
    CREATE TABLE {databaseOwner}[{objectQualifier}ACME_Employee]
    (
        [ModuleID] [int] NOT NULL,
        [ItemID] [int] NOT NULL IDENTITY(1, 1),
        [EmpFirstName] [nvarchar](30) NOT NULL,
```

```
        [EmpLastName] [nvarchar](30) NOT NULL,
        [ManagerNo] [int] NULL,
        [HireDate] [datetime] NOT NULL,
        [Salary] [float] NOT NULL,
        [CreatedByUser] [int] NOT NULL,
        [CreatedDate] [datetime] NOT NULL
    )

    ALTER TABLE {databaseOwner}[{objectQualifier}ACME_Employee]
      ADD CONSTRAINT [PK_{objectQualifier}ACME_Employee]
      PRIMARY KEY CLUSTERED    ([ItemID])
    CREATE NONCLUSTERED INDEX
      [IX_{objectQualifier}ACME_Employee] ON
      {databaseOwner}[{objectQualifier}ACME_Employee]
                                    ([ModuleID])

    ALTER TABLE {databaseOwner}[{objectQualifier}ACME_Employee]
      WITH NOCHECK ADD CONSTRAINT
    [FK_{objectQualifier}ACME_Employee_{objectQualifier}Modules]
    FOREIGN KEY ([ModuleID]) REFERENCES
    {databaseOwner}[{objectQualifier}Modules] ([ModuleID])
      ON DELETE CASCADE NOT FOR REPLICATION
  END
GO
```

10. That's all we need to do at this point. This script will run when the module is deployed to the DNN site.

How it works...

The Starter Kit wizard from the *Creating a new module* recipe produced a basic table creation script, but we need to add our own fields before the script is ready to run. The two ALTER TABLE statements that follow the CREATE TABLE statement will make the keys for our table.

The first key is a PRIMARY KEY to enforce ItemId as the unique identifier for our employee records. Normally, we might call such a field EmpId, but the DNN wizard prefers ItemId as the key field and has already filled our other module code with ItemId.

The second key is a FOREIGN KEY, which makes certain that the ModuleId we save in the employee table is a valid ModuleId.

Creating stored procedures

When the Starter Kit wizard creates a module it also builds a script with a standard set of stored procedures for adding, updating, and deleting records in the table driving the new module.

There are several reasons to use stored procedures instead of directly putting the SQL in the project code. For one, stored procedures generally perform better; also the code is easier to maintain than hard-coded SQL and we benefit from the increased encapsulation. If the code is only working with database tables and records, it makes sense to leave it in the database.

In this recipe we will show how to modify the wizard-generated code to perform the actual add, update, and deletes your module needs.

Getting ready

To follow along with this recipe you must have completed these previous recipes:

▶   *Creating a new module with the Starter Kit*

▶   *Creating a database table with keys*

 In this recipe we will again locate and replace any occurrences of the phrase YourCompany. If you have followed the previous recipe this is already done and you can skip right to step 8.

How to do it...

1. Start by launching your preferred Development Tool (Visual Studio or Visual Web Developer Express).

2. Look for **Recent Projects** shown on the left side of the screen. Click on **Employee** to load the project.

3. Look under the **Solution Explorer** on the right side of the screen and double-click on **01.00.00.SqlDataProvider**. This will display the creation script in the editor.

4. Scroll down past the CREATE TABLE part of the script until you see Drop Existing Stored Procedures.

```
/** Drop Existing Stored Procedures **/

if exists (select * from dbo.sysobjects where id =
  object_id(N'{databaseOwner}[{objectQualifier}
  YourCompany_GetEmployees]') and OBJECTPROPERTY
  (id, N'IsProcedure') = 1)
    drop procedure
{databaseOwner}{objectQualifier}YourCompany_GetEmployees
GO

if exists (select * from dbo.sysobjects where id =
  object_id(N'{databaseOwner}[{objectQualifier}
  YourCompany_GetEmployee]') and OBJECTPROPERTY
  (id, N'IsProcedure') = 1)
```

```
    drop procedure
{databaseOwner}{objectQualifier}YourCompany_GetEmployee
GO


if exists (select * from dbo.sysobjects where id =
    object_id(N'{databaseOwner}[{objectQualifier}
    YourCompany_AddEmployee]') and OBJECTPROPERTY
    (id, N'IsProcedure') = 1)
     drop procedure {databaseOwner}{objectQualifier}YourCompany_
                                                      AddEmployee
GO
if exists (select * from dbo.sysobjects where id =
    object_id(N'{databaseOwner}[{objectQualifier}
    YourCompany_UpdateEmployee]') and OBJECTPROPERTY
    (id, N'IsProcedure') = 1)
    drop procedure
{databaseOwner}{objectQualifier}YourCompany_UpdateEmployee
GO


if exists (select * from dbo.sysobjects where id =
    object_id(N'{databaseOwner}[{objectQualifier}
    YourCompany_DeleteEmployee]') and OBJECTPROPERTY
    (id, N'IsProcedure') = 1)
    drop procedure
{databaseOwner}{objectQualifier}YourCompany_DeleteEmployee
GO
```

5. In this Drop section, you will see the code to drop five wizard-generated stored procedures. We want to keep this section, but we need to change the text `YourCompany_` in the script. Instead of `YourCompany`, you can place your actual company name or initials. We do this with a simple search and replace — under the Edit menu look under **Find and Replace** and select **Quick Replace** (or just press *Ctrl+H*).

6. When prompted:

    ❏ **Find What**: `YourCompany`

    ❏ **Replace with**: `ACME`

    ❏ **Look in**: `Current Document`

7. Click on **Replace All**.

8. Now scroll down to the next section of the script `Create Stored Procedures`. In this section we need to add the actual field names from our table. Continuing with the example table from the previous recipes, wherever we see the field `Content`, we have to put in our five fields `EmpFirstName`, `EmpLastName`, `ManagerNo`, `HireDate`, and `Salary`.

9. Start by finding the first procedure called `ACME_GetEmployees`.

10. Where the word `Content` appears in the select statement, change it to:

```
/** Create Stored Procedures **/


create procedure {databaseOwner}{objectQualifier}
                                 ACME_GetEmployees


  @ModuleId int

as

select ModuleId,
       ItemId,
       EmpFirstName,
       EmpLastName,
       ManagerNo,
       HireDate,
       Salary,
       CreatedByUser,
       CreatedDate,
       'CreatedByUserName' = {objectQualifier}Users.FirstName + '
         ' + {objectQualifier}Users.LastName
from {objectQualifier}ACME_Employee
inner join {objectQualifier}Users on
  objectQualifier}ACME_Employee.CreatedByUser =
  {objectQualifier}Users.UserId
where  ModuleId = @ModuleId
GO
```

11. Next, scroll down to the second procedure `ACME_GetEmployee`.

12. Just as before, replace the word `Content` with our five fields. The code should now look like:

```
create procedure {databaseOwner}{objectQualifier}
                                 ACME_GetEmployee


  @ModuleId int,
      @ItemId int

as

select ModuleId,
       ItemId,
       EmpFirstName,
```

```
        EmpLastName,
        ManagerNo,
        HireDate,
        Salary,
        CreatedByUser,
        CreatedDate,
        'CreatedByUserName' = {objectQualifier}Users.FirstName + '
        ' + {objectQualifier}Users.LastName
from {objectQualifier}ACME_Employee
inner join {objectQualifier}Users on
  {objectQualifier}ACME_Employee.CreatedByUser =
  {objectQualifier}Users.UserId
where  ModuleId = @ModuleId
and ItemId = @ItemId
GO
```

13. In the next procedure `ACME_AddEmployee`, we need to change `Content` in three places. In each case, we need to change `Content` to our five fields. The first `Content` is in the parameter list of our procedure. Use the editor to change the text to read:

```
create procedure {databaseOwner}{objectQualifier}
                                ACME_AddEmployee


   @ModuleId       int,
   @EmpFirstName       nvarchar(30),
   @EmpLastName        nvarchar(30),
   @ManagerNo      int,
   @HireDate       datetime,
   @Salary         float,
   @UserID         int
```

14. Now change the first part of the insert statement to read:

```
insert into {objectQualifier}ACME_Employee (
   ModuleId,
   EmpFirstName,
   EmpLastName,
   ManagerNo,
   HireDate,
   Salary,
   CreatedByUser,
   CreatedDate
)
```

15. Change the second part to read:

```
values (
    @ModuleId,
    @EmpFirstName,
    @EmpLastName,
    @ManagerNo,
    @HireDate ,
    @Salary,
    @UserID,
    getdate()
)
```

16. So the entire `procedure` should be:

```
create procedure {databaseOwner}{objectQualifier}
                        ACME_AddEmployee

    @ModuleId        int,
    @EmpFirstName    nvarchar(30),
    @EmpLastName     nvarchar(30),
    @ManagerNo       int,
    @HireDate        datetime,
    @Salary          float,
    @UserID          int

as

insert into {objectQualifier}_Employee (
    ModuleId,
    EmpFirstName,
    EmpLastName,
    ManagerNo,
    HireDate,
    Salary,
    CreatedByUser,
    CreatedDate
)
values (
    @ModuleId,
    @EmpFirstName,
    @EmpLastName,
    @ManagerNo,
    @HireDate ,
    @Salary,
    @UserID,
    getdate()
```

```
)

GO
```

17. The next procedure `ACME_UpdateEmployee` is similar, so we have two places to make changes. Add the five fields to the procedure's parameter list and then add the five fields to the update statement. The procedure should now look like:

```
create procedure
{databaseOwner}{objectQualifier}ACME_UpdateEmployee

    @ModuleId        int,
    @ItemId          int,
    @EmpFirstName        nvarchar(30),
    @EmpLastName         nvarchar(30),
    @ManagerNo       int,
    @HireDate        datetime,
    @Salary          float,
    @UserID          int

as

update {objectQualifier}ACME_Employee
set     EmpFirstName      = @EmpFirstName,
        EmpLastName       = @EmpLastName ,
        ManagerNo      = @ManagerNo,
        HireDate       = @HireDate,
        Salary         = @Salary,
        CreatedByUser = @UserID,
        CreatedDate    = getdate()
where   ModuleId = @ModuleId
and     ItemId = @ItemId

GO
```

18. The final procedure `ACME_DeleteEmployee` does not need to be modified as it does not reference any of the fields.

How it works...

Modules in DNN follow Microsoft's **N-Tier Architecture**. This is a mechanism for separating the logic of the application from the business and database logic. In this recipe we constructed the stored procedures of the database layer.

 You can learn more about the N-Tier architecture from this excellent article by David Chappell and Steve Kirk found at `http://msdn.microsoft.com/en-us/library/ms978384.aspx`.

There's more...

After creating the stored procedures the last step for a new module is to connect it to the database. The recipe *Connecting a module to the database* demonstrates how to create the procedures to support the database and business logic layers.

Connecting a module to the database

To connect the wizard-generated code to the module's database table, we must go through the project code and substitute the placeholder called Content with our fields and data types.

Getting ready

To follow along with this recipe you must have completed these previous recipes:

- ▸ *Creating a new module with the Starter Kit*
- ▸ *Creating a database table with keys*
- ▸ *Creating stored procedures*

How to do it...

1. Start by launching your preferred development tool (Visual Studio or Visual Web Developer Express).

2. Look for **Recent Projects** shown on the left side of the screen. Click on **Employee** to load the project.

3. Look under the **Solution Explorer** on the right side of the screen, expand the folder called **Components** and double-click on DataProvider.vb.

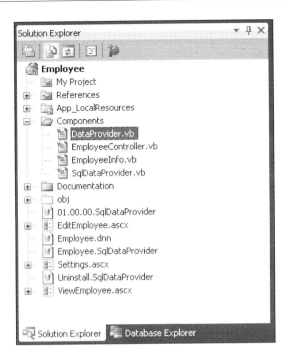

4. Scroll down to the bottom of the file and look for the region of code called `Abstract methods`. We must replace the placeholder `Content` with our actual field names in these two places. Change the code to read:

```
#Region "Abstract methods"

Public MustOverride Function GetEmployees(ByVal ModuleId As
                                Integer) As IDataReader
Public MustOverride Function GetEmployee(ByVal ModuleId As
                Integer,ByVal ItemId As Integer) As IDataReader
Public MustOverride Sub AddEmployee(ByVal ModuleId As Integer,
                            ByVal EmpFirstName As String,
                            ByVal EmpLastName As String,
                            ByVal ManagerNo As Integer,
                            ByVal HireDate As Datetime,
                            ByVal Salary As Double,
                            ByVal UserId As Integer)
Public MustOverride Sub UpdateEmployee(ByVal ModuleId As Integer,
                            ByVal ItemId As Integer,
                            ByVal EmpFirstName As String,
                            ByVal EmpLastName As String,
                            ByVal ManagerNo As Integer,
                            ByVal HireDate As Datetime,
                              ByVal Salary As Double,
                              ByVal UserId As Integer)
```

```
        Public MustOverride Sub DeleteEmployee(ByVal ModuleId As
                                          Integer, ByVal ItemId As
Integer)


#End Region
```

5. Now we repeat the process in the next file. Double-click on `SqlDataProvider.vb` and scroll to the bottom of the file to the `Public Methods` region. We need to change the code in two of the parameter lists and two of the argument lists:

```
#Region "Public Methods"


        Public Overrides Function GetEmployees(ByVal ModuleId As
                                       Integer) As IDataReader
            Return CType(SqlHelper.ExecuteReader(ConnectionString,
                          GetFullyQualifiedName("GetEmployees"),
                          ModuleId), IDataReader)
        End Function

        Public Overrides Function GetEmployee(ByVal ModuleId As
           Integer, ByVal ItemId As Integer) As IDataReader
             Return CType(SqlHelper.ExecuteReader(ConnectionString,
               GetFullyQualifiedName("GetEmployee"), ModuleId,
               ItemId), IDataReader)
        End Function

        Public Overrides Sub AddEmployee(ByVal ModuleId As
           Integer, ByVal EmpFirstName As String,
           ByVal EmpLastName As String, ByVal ManagerNo As
                                                   Integer,
           ByVal HireDate As DateTime,
           ByVal Salary As Double, ByVal UserId As Integer)
            SqlHelper.ExecuteNonQuery(ConnectionString,
                          GetFullyQualifiedName("AddEmployee"),
                          ModuleId, EmpFirstName,
                          EmpLastName, ManagerNo, HireDate,
                          Salary, UserId)
        End Sub

        Public Overrides Sub UpdateEmployee(ByVal ModuleId As
                            Integer, ByVal ItemId As Integer,
                            ByVal EmpFirstName As String,
                            ByVal EmpLastName As String,
                            ByVal ManagerNo As Integer,
                            ByVal HireDate As DateTime,
                            ByVal Salary As Double,
                            ByVal UserId As Integer)
            SqlHelper.ExecuteNonQuery(ConnectionString,
                          GetFullyQualifiedName("UpdateEmployee"),
                          ModuleId, ItemId, EmpFirstName,
                          EmpLastName, ManagerNo, HireDate,
```

```
                              Salary, UserId)
        End Sub

        Public Overrides Sub DeleteEmployee(ByVal ModuleId As
                            Integer, ByVal ItemId As Integer)
            SqlHelper.ExecuteNonQuery(ConnectionString,
                        GetFullyQualifiedName("DeleteEmployee"),
                        ModuleId, ItemId)
        End Sub


    #End Region
```

6. Next we need to change the `EmployeeController` file in two places. Double-click on `EmployeeController.vb` and scroll down a little to the `Public Methods` region.

7. Find the two procedures `AddEmployee` and `UpdateEmployee`. Once again, substitute `Content` for our actual column names and put `EmpFirstName` in the `IF` statement that checks if the record is valid:

```
        Public Sub AddEmployee(ByVal objEmployee As EmployeeInfo)

            If objEmployee.EmpFirstName.Trim <> "" Then
        DataProvider.Instance().AddEmployee(objEmployee.ModuleId,
                                objEmployee.EmpFirstName,
                                objEmployee.EmpLastName,
                                objEmployee.ManagerNo,
                                objEmployee.HireDate,
                                objEmployee.Salary,
                                objEmployee.CreatedByUser)

            End If

        End Sub

        Public Sub UpdateEmployee(ByVal objEmployee As
                                            EmployeeInfo)

            If objEmployee.EmpFirstName.Trim <> "" Then
        DataProvider.Instance().UpdateEmployee(objEmployee.ModuleId,
                                objEmployee.ItemId,
                                objEmployee.EmpFirstName,
                                objEmployee.EmpLastName,
                                objEmployee.ManagerNo,
                                objEmployee.HireDate,
                                objEmployee.Salary,
                                objEmployee.CreatedByUser)

            End If

        End Sub
```

8. So far so good. Now we need to update the `EmployeeInfo` file in two places. Double-click on `EmployeeInfo.vb` and scroll down a little to the `local property declarations` section.

9. Change the one line with `Content` to the five lines of our fields:

```
' local property declarations
Private _ModuleId As Integer
Private _ItemId As Integer
Private _EmpFirstName As String
Private _EmpLastName As String
Private _ManagerNo As Integer
Private _HireDate As DateTime
Private _Salary As Double
Private _CreatedByUser As Integer
Private _CreatedDate As DateTime
Private _CreatedByUserName As String
```

10. In the rest of the file, we need to again remove the `Content` property and replace it with our five fields. Scroll down and find the section with the `Content` property. Now change the code to have our five property procedures:

```
Public Property ItemId() As Integer
    Get
        Return _ItemId
    End Get
    Set(ByVal Value As Integer)
        _ItemId = Value
    End Set
End Property

Public Property EmpFirstName() As String
    Get
        Return _EmpFirstName
    End Get
    Set(ByVal Value As String)
        _EmpFirstName = Value
    End Set
End Property

Public Property EmpLastName() As String
    Get
        Return _EmpLastName
    End Get
    Set(ByVal Value As String)
        _EmpLastName = Value
    End Set
```

```vbnet
End Property

Public Property ManagerNo() As Integer
    Get
        Return _ManagerNo
    End Get
    Set(ByVal Value As Integer)
        _ManagerNo = Value
    End Set
End Property

Public Property HireDate() As Datetime
    Get
        Return _HireDate
    End Get
    Set(ByVal Value As Datetime)
        _HireDate = Value
    End Set
End Property

Public Property Salary() As Double
    Get
        Return _Salary
    End Get
    Set(ByVal Value As Double)
        _Salary = Value
    End Set
End Property


Public Property CreatedByUser() As Integer
    Get
        Return _CreatedByUser
    End Get
    Set(ByVal Value As Integer)
        _CreatedByUser = Value
    End Set
End Property
```

11. Select **Save All** from the **File** menu to save your project files.

How it works...

Completing this recipe creates the procedures used by the database and business logic layers. Using Procedures to connect to the database frees our code from having to call the database directly using SQL. It provides a better separation of the database logic and the business logic.

Creating an uninstall script

When the Starter Kit creates a module it also builds an uninstall script that is run when you uninstall a module from DNN. This script is responsible for removing all the things created by your module: stored procedures, databases, views, tables, and so on.

In this recipe we will take the uninstall script created by the Starter Kit and change the company name to match the company name used in the install script.

Getting ready

To follow along with this recipe you must have completed the previous recipe *Creating a new module with the Starter Kit*

How to do it...

1. Start by launching your preferred development tool (Visual Studio or Visual Web Developer Express).

2. Look for **Recent Projects** shown on the left side of the screen. Click on **Employee** to load the project.

3. Look under the **Solution Explorer** on the right side of the screen and double-click on `Uninstall.SqlDataProvider`. This will display the uninstall script in the editor.

4. The only thing we need to do is change the text `YourCompany_` in the script. Instead of `YourCompany` you can place your actual company name or initials. We do this with a simple search and replace — under the **Edit** menu, look under **Find and Replace** and select **Quick Replace** (or just press *Ctrl+H*).

5. When prompted:

    - **Find What**: `YourCompany`
    - **Replace with**: `ACME`
    - **Look in**: `Current Document`

6. Click on **Replace All**.

7. The script should now appears as follows:

```
/*****************************************************************/
/*****               SqlDataProvider                       *****/
/*****                                                     *****/
/*****                                                     *****/
/***** Note: To manually execute this script you must     *****/
/*****       perform a search and replace operation        *****/
/*****       for {databaseOwner} and {objectQualifier}      *****/
/*****                                                     *****/
/*****************************************************************/


/** Drop FAQs Table **/

ALTER TABLE {databaseOwner}[{objectQualifier}ACME_Employee] DROP
CONSTRAINT [FK_{objectQualifier}Employee_{objectQualifier}Modules]
GO


ALTER TABLE {databaseOwner}[{objectQualifier}ACME_Employee] DROP
CONSTRAINT [PK_{objectQualifier}ACME_Employee]
GO


DROP INDEX {databaseOwner}[{objectQualifier}ACME_Employee].[IX_
{objectQualifier}ACME_Employee]
GO
DROP TABLE {databaseOwner}[{objectQualifier}ACME_Employee]
GO


/** Drop Stored Procedures **/

DROP PROCEDURE {databaseOwner}[{objectQualifier}ACME_GetEmployees]
GO


DROP PROCEDURE {databaseOwner}[{objectQualifier}ACME_GetEmployee]
GO


DROP PROCEDURE {databaseOwner}[{objectQualifier}ACME_AddEmployee]
GO


DROP PROCEDURE {databaseOwner}[{objectQualifier}ACME_
UpdateEmployee]
GO


DROP PROCEDURE {databaseOwner}[{objectQualifier}ACME_
DeleteEmployee]
```

```
GO

/*********************************************************/
/*****                SqlDataProvider                *****/
/*********************************************************/
```

8. Select **Save All** from the **File** menu to save your changes.

How it works...

It is important to keep the uninstall script in synch with the install script. If you add tables or stored procedures to your module, you must remember to supply the code to remove them when the module is uninstalled.

5

Building, Debugging, and Deploying Modules

In this chapter we will cover the following topics:

- ▶ Building a View control
- ▶ Building an Edit control
- ▶ Editing the Manifest File
- ▶ Building for release or debug
- ▶ Deploying a module as a standalone package
- ▶ Downloading the DNN 5 source code
- ▶ Setting up a debugging environment
- ▶ Preparing a module for debugging
- ▶ Setting a breakpoint and stepping through module code
- ▶ Creating a Manifest from an installed module

Introduction

In the previous chapter we saw how to install Web Developer Express and start creating our custom modules. In this chapter we will see how to create working *View* and *Edit* controls, how to deploy custom modules and how to configure the development tool for module debugging.

▶ **Development tools**

The recipes in this chapter and the following chapters work equally well with either Visual Studio 2008 or Visual Web Developer Express 2010. You can use whichever tool you are more familiar with or have access to. In these examples we will use Web Developer Express but for convenience we will use the term Development Tool when referring to Visual Studio or Web Developer.

▶ **WAP vs. WSP**

There are two ways to build a custom module. Which approach to use is based on what you need to do:

❑ You can build it as a **Web Application Project** (**WAP**). This is good if you just want to code, build, and deploy your project. This method was described in the last chapter and most of this chapter.

❑ You can put your module code in with the DNN source code and build the website as one Web Site Project (WSP). This gives the ability to set breakpoints and step through your module code. This method is demonstrated at the end of this chapter.

▶ **Controls in DNN**

Before we get started in earnest, here is a quick overview of what we want to accomplish. When we talk about module development in DNN we are really talking about four key parts:

❑ User Controls: These are the user interface elements of your module. They will be dynamically placed on the pages of your DNN portal based on what part of the module you are viewing. In the examples of this chapter the first control that is displayed is the View user control. The Edit control is displayed when you click on an employee record and the Settings control is displayed when you click on the Settings link.

❑ Assemblies: The code behind the user controls (the `*.vb` files) will be compiled into an assembly (a DLL file) when you build the Employee project. When the module is deployed the assembly will be placed in the portal's `/bin` folder.

❑ Database scripts: As we saw in the previous chapter, modules depend on database tables to hold information. As part of your module you will have an installation script to create your module database tables and an uninstall script to remove them when the module is uninstalled.

❑ Module Manifest: An XML file that tells DNN how the module should be installed. In DNN version five the manifest can include release notes and a license agreement.

Building a View control

Although DNN modules vary in the number and kind of controls they contain, a common approach (and the one generated by the Starter Kit) consists of three user controls:

- ▶ View control: To display the module on the DNN page
- ▶ Edit control: To edit your module data
- ▶ Settings control: To change the settings of your module

When you place a DNN module on a page the View control of the module is responsible for displaying the initial state of the module. In this recipe, we will look at the View control created by the Starter Kit and expand it to include the fields of the sample Employee table.

The View control we will create will display all the Employee records in the table like this:

Getting ready

To follow along with this recipe you must have completed the following recipe from *Chapter 4:*

- ▶ *Creating a new module with the Starter Kit*

How to do it...

1. Start by launching your preferred development tool (Visual Studio or Visual Web Developer Express).
2. Look for Recent Projects shown on the left side of the screen. Click on **Employee** to load the project.
3. Double-click to open the `ViewEmployee.ascx` file.

4. When the module is displayed it will show the Employee records in the Employee table. The Starter Kit has given us a `datalist` control which is used to display records from the database. We need to put our Employee fields into this control. We do this by replacing the `lblContent` label control with label controls for each of our five fields.

```
<%@ Control language="vb"
            Inherits="YourCompany.Modules.Employee.ViewEmployee"
            AutoEventWireup="false" Explicit="True"
            Codebehind="ViewEmployee.ascx.vb" %>
<%@ Register TagPrefix="dnn" TagName="Audit"
            Src="~/controls/ModuleAuditControl.ascx" %>
<asp:datalist id="lstContent" datakeyfield="ItemID" runat="server"
            cellpadding="4">
<itemtemplate>
<table cellpadding="4" width="100%">
<tr>
<td valign="top" width="100%" align="left">
<asp:HyperLink ID="HyperLink1" NavigateUrl='<%#
EditURL("ItemID",DataBinder.Eval(Container.DataItem,"ItemID")) %>'
Visible="<%# IsEditable %>" runat="server"><asp:Image ID="Image1"
Runat=server ImageUrl="~/images/edit.gif" AlternateText="Edit"
Visible="<%#IsEditable%>" resourcekey="Edit"/></asp:hyperlink>
<asp:Label ID="lblEmpFirstName" runat="server" CssClass="Normal"/>
<asp:Label ID="lblEmpLastName" runat="server" CssClass="Normal"/>
<asp:Label ID="lblManagerNo" runat="server" CssClass="Normal"/>
<asp:Label ID="lblHireDate" runat="server" CssClass="Normal"/>
<asp:Label ID="lblSalary" runat="server" CssClass="Normal"/>
</td>
</tr>
</table>
</itemtemplate>
</asp:datalist>
```

5. Next we must add code to populate the `datalist` control. Double-click to open the `ViewEmployee.ascx.vb` file (if you don't see it listed in the Solution Explorer, click on the **Show All Files** icon on the Solution Explorer toolbar — the second one from the left).

The `datalist` control is part of the DNN web controls library. It will display records from the database, but we must tell it what fields from the table to display.

6. Scroll down to the `Page_Load` procedure that was created by the Starter Kit. The procedure is calling the `GetEmployees` function to pull all the employees from the employee table and binding the results to the `datalist` control. We want to change the code so that we only bind if some employees were found. So find the lines highlighted below:

```
Private Sub Page_Load(ByVal sender As System.Object,
          ByVal e As System.EventArgs) Handles MyBase.Load
     Try
          Dim objEmployees As New EmployeeController
          Dim colEmployees As List(Of EmployeeInfo)

          ' get the content from the Employee table
          colEmployees = objEmployees.GetEmployees(ModuleId)

          If colEmployees.Count = 0 Then
              ' add the content to the Employee table
              Dim objEmployee As EmployeeInfo =
                                        New EmployeeInfo
              objEmployee.ModuleId = ModuleId
              objEmployee.EmpFirstName =
                    Localization.GetString
                      ("DefaultContent", LocalResourceFile)
              objEmployee.CreatedByUser = Me.UserId
              objEmployees.AddEmployee(objEmployee)
              ' get the content from the Employee table
              colEmployees =
                        objEmployees.GetEmployees(ModuleId)
          End If

          ' bind the content to the repeater
          lstContent.DataSource = colEmployees
          lstContent.DataBind()

     Catch exc As Exception          'Module failed to load
          ProcessModuleLoadException(Me, exc)
     End Try
End Sub
```

7. Now change the code to look like this:

```
Private Sub Page_Load(ByVal sender As System.Object,
              ByVal e As System.EventArgs) Handles MyBase.Load
   Try
   Dim objEmployees As New EmployeeController
   Dim colEmployees As List(Of EmployeeInfo)

    ' get the content from the Employee table
```

```
colEmployees = objEmployees.GetEmployees(ModuleId)


If colEmployees.Count > 0 Then
    ' bind the content to the repeater
    lstContent.DataSource = colEmployees
    lstContent.DataBind()
End If


  Catch exc As Exception          'Module failed to load
  ProcessModuleLoadException(Me, exc)
  End Try
End Sub
```

8. The last step is to add our five employee fields to the binding event handler that was created by the Starter Kit. Scroll down a little bit until you see the `lstContent_ItemDataBound` procedure:

```
Protected Sub lstContent_ItemDataBound(ByVal sender As Object,
      ByVal e As System.Web.UI.WebControls.DataListItemEventArgs)
      Handles lstContent.ItemDataBound
  Dim strContent As String = ""


  ' add content to template
  If CType(Settings("template"), String) <> "" Then
  strContent = CType(Settings("template"), String)
  Dim objProperties As ArrayList =
                          Common.Utilities.CBO.GetPropertyInfo
                                      (GetType(EmployeeInfo))
  Dim intProperty As Integer
  Dim objPropertyInfo As PropertyInfo
  For intProperty = 0 To objProperties.Count - 1
      objPropertyInfo = CType(objProperties(intProperty),
                                              PropertyInfo)

      strContent = strContent.Replace("
                  [" & objPropertyInfo.Name.ToUpper & "]",
                          DataBinder.Eval(e.Item.DataItem,
                              objPropertyInfo.Name).ToString())
  Next intProperty
   Else
  strContent = DataBinder.Eval(e.Item.DataItem, "Content")
   End If


   ' assign the content
   Dim lblContent As Label = CType(e.Item.FindControl
                                      ("lblContent"), Label)
   lblContent.Text = strContent
End Sub
```

9. Once again, remove the highlighted code and replace it with the following code:

```
Protected Sub lstContent_ItemDataBound(ByVal sender As Object,
        ByVal e As System.Web.UI.WebControls.DataListItemEventArgs)
                                Handles lstContent.ItemDataBound
    ' assign the content
    Dim lblEmpFirstName As Label =
            CType(e.Item.FindControl("lblEmpFirstName"), Label)
    Dim lblEmpLastName As Label =
            CType(e.Item.FindControl("lblEmpLastName"), Label)
    Dim lblManagerNo As Label =
            CType(e.Item.FindControl("lblManagerNo"), Label)
    Dim lblHireDate As Label =
            CType(e.Item.FindControl("lblHireDate"), Label)
    Dim lblSalary As Label =
            CType(e.Item.FindControl("lblSalary"), Label)

    lblEmpFirstName.Text = DataBinder.Eval(e.Item.DataItem,
                                        "EmpFirstName")
    lblEmpLastName.Text = DataBinder.Eval(e.Item.DataItem,
                                        "EmpLastName")
    lblManagerNo.Text = DataBinder.Eval(e.Item.DataItem,
                                        "ManagerNo")
    lblHireDate.Text = DataBinder.Eval(e.Item.DataItem,
                                        "HireDate")
    lblSalary.Text = DataBinder.Eval(e.Item.DataItem, "Salary")
End Sub
```

10. What we've done here is to change code so that when we bind the employees to the `datalist`, the binding handler extracts the employee information and places it into the label fields we created back in step 4.

11. Click on **Save All** from the **File** menu to save your changes.

How it works...

The *View* control comes from two files, the `ViewEmployee.ascx` and the code behind file called `ViewEmployee.ascx.vb`. To complete the control and connect it to our fields we change `ViewEmployee.ascx` to show our fields and `ViewEmployee.ascx.vb` to populate them.

In this recipe we saw an important subroutine called `Page_Load`. The page load routine is called when the page is loaded and as a consequence it is a common place to handle all the setup you need to do before the page is displayed.

There's more...

This recipe shows the simplest way to display data. In *Chapter 6* we will see how to replace the `datalist` control with a more powerful `datagrid` control.

See also

We've taken the first step in changing the module created by the Starter Kit into a module we can deploy to a DNN portal. See the recipe *Building an Edit control* for the next step in the process.

Building an Edit control

In this recipe we will create a basic Edit control from the code generated by the Starter Kit. The Edit control displays a single record from the database using textboxes so we can edit the values. It also includes Update, Cancel, and Delete links to save, cancel, or delete the record.

The Starter Kit creates the control with a single field labeled "Content", a textbox, and a validation control to print a warning message if the record is saved without a value. This is a good start but we want to take out the content field and replace it with the five fields from the sample Employee table creating a control that will look something like this:

In this recipe we'll get a closer look at the `EditEmployee` control and see how it displays a selected employee record using four special pieces:

- ▸ Label: The common control that displays the name of the edit field and includes a small help icon (**?**) to provide more information.
- ▸ TextBox: A standard input control for typing text.
- ▸ Required field validator: A special control that will show an error message if we do not supply a value in the TextBox.
- ▸ Update link button: When clicked will trigger an event we can trap and write code for.

Getting ready

To follow along with this recipe you must have completed the following recipe from *Chapter 4:*

▶ *Creating a new module with the Starter Kit*

How to do it...

1. Start by launching your preferred development tool (Visual Studio or Visual Web Developer Express).

2. Look for Recent Projects shown on the left side of the screen. Click on **Employee** to load the project.

3. Double-click to open the `EditEmployee.ascx` file. The part we need to fix is an HTML table that holds the Employee fields. The Starter Kit created a single row in the HTML table and once again we must substitute the place holder Content with the names of our fields. This form offers a text label, input control, and a validation control, so we need to replace it with a label, an input control, and a validation control for our five fields.

```
<%@ Control language="vb"
          Inherits="YourCompany.Modules.Employee.EditEmployee"
          AutoEventWireup="false" Explicit="True"
          Codebehind="EditEmployee.ascx.vb" %>
<%@ Register TagPrefix="dnn" TagName="Label"
          Src="~/controls/LabelControl.ascx" %>
<%@ Register TagPrefix="dnn" TagName="TextEditor"
          Src="~/controls/TextEditor.ascx"%>
<%@ Register TagPrefix="dnn" TagName="Audit"
          Src="~/controls/ModuleAuditControl.ascx" %>
<table width="650" cellspacing="0" cellpadding="0" border="0"
      summary="Edit Table">
   <tr valign="top">
      <td class="SubHead" width="125"><dnn:label id="lblContent"
          runat="server" controlname="lblContent" suffix=":">
                                   </dnn:label>
      </td>
      <td>
         <dnn:texteditor id="txtContent" runat="server"
                    height="200" width="500" />
         <asp:RequiredFieldValidator ID="valContent"
                 resourcekey="valContent.ErrorMessage"
                 ControlToValidate="txtContent"
            CssClass="NormalRed" Display="Dynamic"
               ErrorMessage="<br>EmpFirstName is required"
                                       Runat="server" />
```

```
      </td>
    </tr>
  </table>
  <p>
      <asp:linkbutton cssclass="CommandButton" id="cmdUpdate"
                  resourcekey="cmdUpdate" runat="server"
                  borderstyle="none" text="Update">
  </asp:linkbutton> 
  <asp:linkbutton cssclass="CommandButton" id="cmdCancel"
              resourcekey="cmdCancel" runat="server"
              borderstyle="none" text="Cancel"
              causesvalidation="False">
  </asp:linkbutton> 
  <asp:linkbutton cssclass="CommandButton" id="cmdDelete"
              resourcekey="cmdDelete" runat="server"
              borderstyle="none" text="Delete"
              causesvalidation="False">
      </asp:linkbutton> 
  </p>
  <dnn:audit id="ctlAudit" runat="server" />
```

4. Change the highlighted code shown above by renaming the controls using
    `EmpFirstName` instead of `Content`. We'll also use a textbox control instead of a
    texteditor control. The code becomes:

```
<tr valign="top">
<td class="SubHead" width="125"><dnn:label id="lblEmpFirstName"
        runat="server" controlname="lblEmpFirstName"
                                              suffix=":">
                    </dnn:label>
</td>
<td>
<asp:TextBox ID="txtEmpFirstName" runat="server"></asp:TextBox>
<asp:RequiredFieldValidator ID="valEmpFirstName"
                    resourcekey="valEmpFirstName. ErrorMessage"
                    ControlToValidate="txtEmpFirstName"
CssClass="NormalRed" Display="Dynamic"
  ErrorMessage="<br>EmpFirstName is required" Runat="server" />
</td>
    </tr>
```

5. That's one field (employee first name). Now comes the hard part — we need to repeat
    this process four more times to create the other four fields. So take the code you just
    edited for First Name, copy it and paste it four times.

6. That gives five rows in the HTML table holding our fields. The last thing we need to do is edit the code to show our employee fields. The entire HTML table should now look like this:

```
<table width="650" cellspacing="0" cellpadding="0" border="0"
summary="Edit Table">
    <tr valign="top">
 <td class="SubHead" width="125"><dnn:label
                                     id="lblEmpFirstName"
        runat="server" controlname="lblEmpFirstName" suffix=":">
                              </dnn:label>
</td>
<td>
<asp:TextBox ID="txtEmpFirstName" runat="server"></asp:TextBox>
<asp:RequiredFieldValidator ID="valEmpFirstName"
                    resourcekey="valEmpFirstName.ErrorMessage"
                    ControlToValidate="txtEmpFirstName"
    CssClass="NormalRed" Display="Dynamic"
      ErrorMessage="<br>EmpFirstName is required" Runat="server" />
</td>
</tr>
```

7. The second row of the table has the employee's last name:

```
<tr valign="top">
<td class="SubHead" width="125"><dnn:label id="lblEmpLastName"
        runat="server" controlname="lblEmpLastName" suffix=":">
                            </dnn:label>
</td>
<td>
<asp:TextBox ID="txtEmpLastName" runat="server"></asp:TextBox>
<asp:RequiredFieldValidator ID="valEmpLastName"
                    resourcekey="valEmpLastName.ErrorMessage"
                    ControlToValidate="txtEmpLastName"
CssClass="NormalRed" Display="Dynamic" ErrorMessage="<br>
                    EmpLastName is required" Runat="server" />
</td>
    </tr>
```

8. The third row of the table has the employee's manager number:

```
<tr valign="top">
    <td class="SubHead" width="125"><dnn:label id="lblManagerNo"
            runat="server" controlname="lblManagerNo" suffix=":">
                            </dnn:label></td>
    <td>
    <asp:TextBox ID="txtManagerNo" runat="server"></asp:TextBox>
    <asp:RequiredFieldValidator ID="valManagerNo"
                    resourcekey="valManagerNo.ErrorMessage"
                    ControlToValidate="txtManagerNo"
```

```
CssClass="NormalRed" Display="Dynamic" ErrorMessage=
                  "<br>ManagerNo is required" Runat="server"/>
</td>
   </tr>
```

9. The fourth row of the table has the employee's hire date:

```
<tr valign="top">
<td class="SubHead" width="125"><dnn:label id="lblHireDate"
       runat="server" controlname="lblHireDate" suffix=":">
                       </dnn:label></td>
<td>
<asp:TextBox ID="txtHireDate" runat="server"></asp:TextBox>
<asp:RequiredFieldValidator ID="valHireDate"
                  resourcekey="valHireDate.ErrorMessage"
                  ControlToValidate="txtHireDate"
CssClass="NormalRed" Display="Dynamic" ErrorMessage=
                  "<br>HireDate is required" Runat="server" />
</td>
   </tr>
```

10. The fifth row of the table has the employee's salary:

```
<tr valign="top">
<td class="SubHead" width="125"><dnn:label id="lblSalary"
       runat="server" controlname="lblSalary" suffix=":">
                       </dnn:label>
</td>
<td>
<asp:TextBox ID="txtSalary" runat="server"></asp:TextBox>
<asp:RequiredFieldValidator ID="valSalary"
                  resourcekey="valSalary.ErrorMessage"
                  ControlToValidate="txtSalary"
CssClass="NormalRed" Display="Dynamic" ErrorMessage=
                  "<br>Salary is required" Runat="server" />
</td>
   </tr>

</table>
```

11. To check the results change the editor mode to **Source**. The page should now look
    as shown in the following screenshot (don't worry if you see errors about missing
    controls. The controls are part of the DNN site and the editor can't see them. To see
    the fields correctly, you need to deploy the module to a test DNN site):

12. Now that the edit form is completed, we need to add the code to populate the fields when the form opens. Double-click to open the `EditEmployee.ascx.vb` file.

13. Scroll down to the `Page_Load` procedure.

14. Look in the middle of the procedure under the comment line "get content".

```
Dim objEmployees As New EmployeeController
Dim objEmployee As EmployeeInfo =
                        objEmployees.GetEmployee(ModuleId,ItemId)
If Not objEmployee Is Nothing Then
    txtContent.Text = objEmployee.EmpFirstName
    ctlAudit.CreatedByUser = objEmployee.CreatedByUserName
    ctlAudit.CreatedDate = objEmployee.CreatedDate.ToString
Else ' security violation attempt to access item not related to
this Module
    Response.Redirect(NavigateURL(), True)
End If
```

15. Here we need to replace the single content line with the five lines to populate our fields. In addition, the Starter Kit has generated two lines used by an audit control. You can also comment out the two audit lines to help the form compile as they are unnecessary:

```
Dim objEmployees As New EmployeeController
Dim objEmployee As EmployeeInfo =
                    objEmployees.GetEmployee(ModuleId,ItemId)
If Not objEmployee Is Nothing Then
txtEmpFirstName.Text = objEmployee.EmpFirstName
    txtEmpLastName.Text = objEmployee.EmpLastName
    txtManagerNo.Text = objEmployee.ManagerNo
    txtHireDate.Text = objEmployee.HireDate
    txtSalary.Text = objEmployee.Salary
    'ctlAudit.CreatedByUser = objEmployee.CreatedByUserName
    'ctlAudit.CreatedDate = objEmployee.CreatedDate.ToString
Else ' security violation attempt to access item not related to
this Module
Response.Redirect(NavigateURL(), True)
End If
```

16. Finally, we must grab the values from the form and save them to the database when the user clicks on **Update**. To do this, we need to change the code that appears in the Update link handler. The link handler is called when a user clicks on the Update link that appears at the bottom of the **Edit Employee** form. This is the code that will save what the user has typed back to the database. What we need to do is replace the single Content field with our five fields. Start by scrolling down to the `cmdUpdate_Click` procedure. Find the single content line:

```
Private Sub cmdUpdate_Click(ByVal sender As Object, ByVal e As
                            EventArgs) Handles cmdUpdate.Click
Try
    Dim objEmployees As New EmployeeController

    Dim objEmployee As EmployeeInfo = New EmployeeInfo

    objEmployee.ModuleId = ModuleId
    objEmployee.ItemId = ItemId
    objEmployee.EmpFirstName = txtContent.Text
    objEmployee.CreatedByUser = Me.UserId
```

17. Substitute the single line for the five lines to get our fields:

```
objEmployee.EmpFirstName = txtEmpFirstName.Text
objEmployee.EmpLastName = txtEmpLastName.Text
objEmployee.ManagerNo = txtManagerNo.Text
objEmployee.HireDate = txtHireDate.Text
objEmployee.Salary = txtSalary.Text
```

18. The whole procedure should now appear as:

```
Private Sub cmdUpdate_Click(ByVal sender As Object, ByVal e As
                           EventArgs) Handles cmdUpdate.Click
    Try
        Dim objEmployees As New EmployeeController

        Dim objEmployee As EmployeeInfo = New EmployeeInfo

        objEmployee.ModuleId = ModuleId
        objEmployee.ItemId = ItemId
        objEmployee.EmpFirstName = txtEmpFirstName.Text
        objEmployee.EmpLastName = txtEmpLastName.Text
        objEmployee.ManagerNo = txtManagerNo.Text
        objEmployee.HireDate = txtHireDate.Text
        objEmployee.Salary = txtSalary.Text
        objEmployee.CreatedByUser = Me.UserId

        If Common.Utilities.Null.IsNull(ItemId) Then
            ' add the content within the Employee table
            objEmployees.AddEmployee(objEmployee)
        Else
            ' update the content within the Employee table
            objEmployees.UpdateEmployee(objEmployee)
        End If

        ' Redirect back to the portal home page
        Response.Redirect(NavigateURL(), True)
    Catch exc As Exception    'Module failed to load
        ProcessModuleLoadException(Me, exc)
    End Try
End Sub
```

19. That completes the changes to the **EditEmployee** form. Click on **Save All** from the **File** menu to save your changes.

See also

We've made a lot of progress in changing the module created by the Starter Kit into a module we can deploy to a DNN portal. See the recipe *Editing the Manifest File* for the next step in the process.

Editing the Manifest File

Before deploying a new module you should review and update the *Manifest* File generated by the Starter Kit.

The Manifest File is an XML file that tells DNN how to install and configure your module for use in a portal. DNN will read this file when you deploy the module and save it in the database. There are five elements in particular we want to edit before deployment.

`<name>`	This is the internal name of the module. Once the module is deployed, you should not change this name without completely uninstalling the module first.
`<friendlyname>`	This is the friendly name for the module. It is displayed when the host lists installed modules and it is the name that appears in the drop down when you are placing a module on a page.
`<description>`	The description of the module that appears in the list of installed modules.
`<module><friendlyname>`	Displayed on the container holding the module.
`<src>`	Gives the path to the user controls.

Getting ready

To follow along with this recipe you must have completed this recipe from *Chapter 4:*

> ▸ *Creating a new module with the Starter Kit*

How to do it...

1. Start by launching your preferred development tool (Visual Studio or Visual Web Developer Express).

2. Look for Recent Projects shown on the left side of the screen. Click on **Employee** to load the project.

3. Double-click to open the `Employee.dnn` file. At the top of the file you should see the following:

```
<dotnetnuke version="3.0" type="Module">
<folders>
<folder>
<name>YourCompany.Employee</name>
<friendlyname>Employee</friendlyname>
<foldername>YourCompany.Employee</foldername>
<modulename>YourCompany.Employee</modulename>
<description>A Employee module</description>
```

```
<version>01.00.00</version>
<businesscontrollerclass>YourCompany.Modules.Employee.
EmployeeController</businesscontrollerclass>
<compatibility></compatibility>
<modules>
<module>
<friendlyname>Employee</friendlyname>
<cachetime>0</cachetime>
        <controls>
```

4. Most of the generated lines are fine, but some of the lines need to be fixed. Start by replacing `YourCompany` with your actual company name with a simple search and replace: Under the **Edit** menu, look under **Find and Replace** and click on **Quick Replace** (or just press *Ctrl+H*).

5. When prompted by the **Find and Replace** dialog, provide the following information:

   ❑ **Find What**: `YourCompany`

   ❑ **Replace with**: `ACME`

   ❑ **Look in**: `Current Document`

6. Click on **Replace All**.

7. Next, update these three lines :

   ❑ Change `<friendlyname>` to `ACME Employees`

   ❑ Change `<description>` to `A list of current ACME employees`

   ❑ Change `<module><friendlyname>` to `Current ACME Employees`

8. The top of the file should now look like this:

```
<dotnetnuke version="3.0" type="Module">
  <folders>
    <folder>
      <name>ACME.Employee</name>
      <friendlyname>ACME Employees</friendlyname>
      <foldername>ACME.Employee</foldername>
      <modulename>ACME.Employee</modulename>
      <description>A list of current ACME employees.</
description>
      <version>01.00.00</version>
<businesscontrollerclass>ACME.Modules.Employee.
EmployeeController
</businesscontrollerclass>
      <compatibility></compatibility>
      <modules>
        <module>
          <friendlyname>Current ACME Employees</friendlyname>
      <cachetime>0</cachetime>
      <controls>
```

9. The next changes we need to make are the folder names where your files will go.

   a. First, change

   ```
   <src>DesktopModules/Employee/ViewEmployee.ascx</src>
   ```

   to

   ```
   <src>DesktopModules/ACME.Employee/ViewEmployee.ascx</src>
   ```

   b. Next, change

   ```
   <src>DesktopModules/Employee/EditEmployee.ascx</src>
   ```

   to

   ```
   <src>DesktopModules/ACME.Employee/EditEmployee.ascx</src>
   ```

   c. Then, change

   ```
   <src>DesktopModules/Employee/Settings.ascx</src>
   ```

   to

   ```
   <src>DesktopModules/ACME.Employee/Settings.ascx</src>
   ```

10. Save your changes by looking under the **File** menu and selecting **Save All**.

Building for release or debug

When you have successfully edited the Starter Kit project as described in the previous recipes you should be able to build the project without errors. You can build projects for release or debugging. In this recipe we will show how to set the development tool for release build or debug build.

How to do it...

1. Start by launching your preferred Development Tool (Visual Studio or Visual Web Developer Express).

2. Look for Recent Projects shown on the left side of the screen. Click on **Employee** to load the project.

3. First, if you are using Web Developer 2010 Express and you don't see the **Build** menu, you can enable it by looking under the **Tools** menu, under the **Settings** menu and selecting **Expert Settings**.

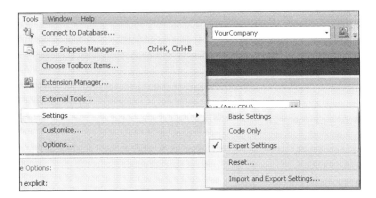

4. Now, look under the **Build** menu and select **Configuration Manager**.

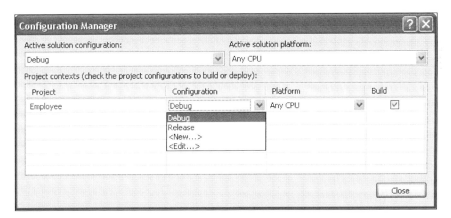

5. You will see your projects listed. To change how the project is built, select either **Debug** or **Release** from the drop-down list.

6. Click on **Close** to save your change.

7. When you build the project the compiled library (the * . dll file) will appear in your project folder under either the /obj/Debug or the /obj/Release folder.

8. Once the project has been rebuilt, you can deploy the DLL file directly to the DNN portal by copying it into the /bin folder of the DNN site.

If you receive compile errors when you build your Employee project for the first time, check that you changed the code as described in the previous recipes. If you still have errors, try commenting out the offending code and see if the project will build.

How it works...

When you are developing your module, it is best to build for debugging so the `*.dll` file contains the information the debugger needs. This is necessary if you intend to step through your module as shown in the recipe *Setting a breakpoint and stepping through module code*. Building for release makes for a smaller and more efficient library and it is best used when your module is complete.

Deploying a module as a standalone package

To deploy a custom module as a standalone package we need to put the correct module files, scripts, and assemblies in a compressed file, log into the DNN site as host and install the module. This is the same process that was used in the recipe *Installing a new extension* back in *Chapter 1*.

The files that need to be deployed will be different for each module you develop. Generally they will be the user interface files (the `*.ascx`), the assembly files (the DLL file), the resource files (*.ascx.resx), the install and uninstall scripts and manifest file and any other files (images, and so on) that your module needs. In this recipe we will deploy the files needed by the Employee module.

Getting ready

To follow along with this recipe you must have completed this recipe from *Chapter 4:*

  ▸   *Creating a new module with the Starter Kit*

How to do it...

1.   From the **Start** menu open **My Documents** and find the folder where you saved the Employee project files (usually it would be `My Documents\Visual Studio 2010 \Projects\Employee\Employee`). The folder should look like this:

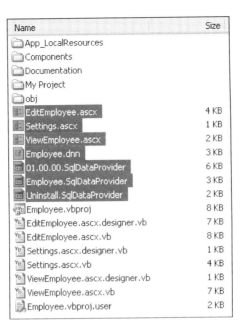

2. Select the following files from this folder:

    ❑   EditEmployee.ascx

    ❑   Settings.ascx

    ❑   ViewEmployee.ascx

    ❑   Employee.dnn

    ❑   01.00.00.SqlDataProvider

    ❑   Employee.SqlDataProvider

    ❑   Uninstall.SqlDataProvider

3. Right-click on these selected files and select **Send To | Compressed (zipped) Folder**. This will create a new ZIP file.

4. Rename the new file Employee_01.00.00_Install.zip.

5. There are more files to add so open the ZIP file and select the folder `App_LocalResources`. Click and drag these three files into the open ZIP file:

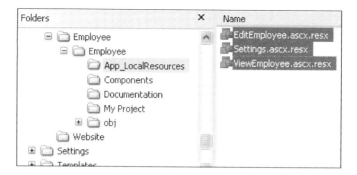

6. Lastly, select the file `\obj\Debug\Employee.dll` (or `\obj\Release\Employee.dll` if you're not debugging) and add it to the ZIP file.

 If you do not see a DLL file for your project in either folder, follow the steps in the previous recipe *Building for release or debug to create the DLL file.*

7. The ZIP file should now contain the following:

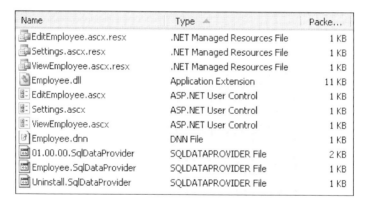

8. To install the module on the DNN site, begin by logging in as the host user (`syshost` in our examples).

9. Look at the Control Panel and make sure you're in Edit mode.

10. Look under the **Host** menu and select **Extensions**.

11. Select **Install Extension Wizard** from the action menu or click on the link at the bottom.

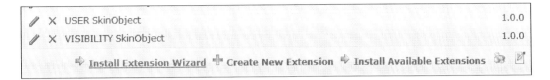

12. The wizard will prompt for the ZIP file (called the extension package).

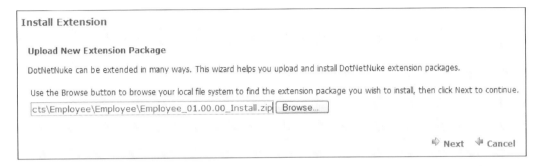

13. Click on the **Browse** button and select the file `Employee_01.00.00_Install.zip`. Click on **Open** then click on **Next**.

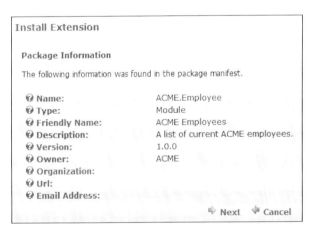

14. The wizard will display your module information. Click on **Next**.

15. The wizard will display your Release Notes. Click on **Next**.

16. At the license page, check **Accept License?** and click on **Next**.

17. Now the install script will run, creating the table and the stored procedures for the module. At the end you should see the message "Installation successful".

18. Click on **Return**.

19. Now navigate to a blank page and add the module to the page (see the recipe *Adding a module to a page* in *Chapter 1* for details) Notice how the name we placed in the `<friendlyname>` element of the Manifest File is the name that appears in the drop-down list.

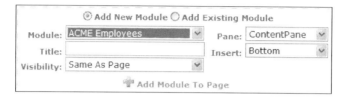

20. Also note how the name we placed in the `<module><friendlyname>` element is the name that appears in the container title:

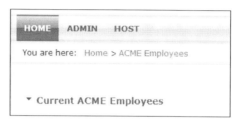

Downloading the DNN 5 source code

To help develop our own modules for DNN we can download the source code so that our compiler has access to the libraries that come with DNN 5. In this recipe we will download the compressed ZIP file and extract it into a folder for our projects.

How to do it...

1. Go to `http://dotnetnuke.codeplex.com`.

2. Click on the **Downloads** tab at the top of the page.

3. Scroll down a little and click on the button labeled **Source Code (New Install + Source Code)**.

4. If you are prompted with licensing terms, click on **I Agree**.

5. When prompted to **Open** or **Save**, click on **Save**.

6. Pick a temporary folder to hold the ZIP file.

7. When the download is complete, extract the files into an easy to remember folder, like `My Documents\DNNSource`.

How it works...

This is an optional recipe. Although you don't need the source files to run a DNN site and they are not required to create modules, they are useful if you want to step through the DNN code while debugging and they offer valuable insights into how DNN was written.

See also

The files downloaded in this recipe are used in the next recipe *Setting up a debugging environment*.

Setting up a debugging environment

Once a module is deployed, how is it debugged? How can you trace step by step through the module code or set a breakpoint?

In this recipe, we will configure the development tool to create a robust testing environment by combining the DNN source code and the module source code as a single solution. Then we can set breakpoints and go step by step through both the module and DNN code.

Note that if you have already used this recipe to create a test environment you can't rebuild the environment by running the recipe again. If you need to reinstall your development environment it is necessary to completely remove the environment before using this recipe to reinstall it.

Getting ready

To follow along with this recipe you must have completed these recipes from *Chapter 4*:

- *Installing Visual Web Developer 2010 Express*
- *Downloading the DNN 5 source code*

How to do it...

1. Start by finding the folder where you downloaded the DNN source files (in these examples it was `My Documents\DNNSource\website`).
2. Locate the file `release.config`. Copy this file and name it `web.config`.
3. Now launch your preferred development tool (Visual Studio or Visual Web Developer Express).
4. From the **File** menu, select **Open Web Site....**.
5. At the **Open Web Site** dialog, select the DNN source folder (`My Documents\DNNSource\website`) and click on **Open**.

6. Once the site loads, build the entire site by looking under the **Debug** menu and selecting **Start Without Debugging** (or press *Ctrl+F5*).

7. All the source code for the site will compile and the site will launch in your browser.

 If you encounter an error on the build, you might need to add an additional reference. For example, in DNN 5.02 source, it was necessary to add a reference to `\Library\Components\Telerik\Telerik.Web.UI.dll` before building.

8. If this is the first time building the site, then it will go through the DNN installation process, just as it did in the recipe *Running the DotNetNuke installation* back in *Chapter 1*. However, this time we will create a new database just for testing our modules.

9. At the first screen it will prompt for installation type. Choose **Typical** and click on **Next**.

10. The next page will test the file permissions. Click on **Test Permissions**. After a pause you should see the message **Your site passed the permissions check**. Click on **Next**.

11. On the next page we choose the database. For debugging we will create a new database NOT an existing DNN database. Select **SQL Server 2005/2008 (Express) File** in the radio button at the top of the page.

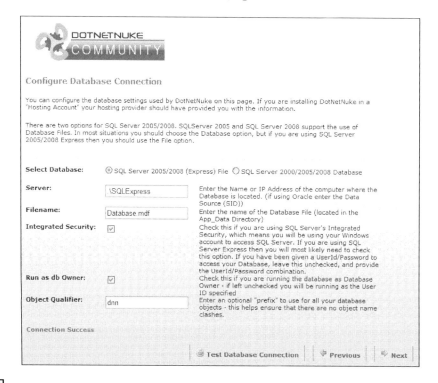

12. Enter the following information:

    ❑ **Server**: `.\SQLExpress`

    ❑ **Filename**: `Database.mdf`

    ❑ **Integrated Security**: Checked

    ❑ **Run as db Owner**: Checked

    ❑ **Object Qualifier**: `dnn`

13. Click on **Test Database Connection**. You should see the message **Connection Success**.

14. Click on Next. You will now see status messages as the database tables and stored procedures are created. At the end should be the message **Installation of Database Complete**.

15. Now the wizard will create two users to start with: the host user who controls the entire DNN installation and the admin user who administers the portals and has more limited privileges.

16. For the **First Name**, keep the default `SuperUser`.

17. For the **Last Name**, type `Account`.

18. For **User Name**, type `syshost` (don't use the standard `host` for the username. It is too well known).

19. Choose a good password and confirm it. Then write it down as you will need it later.

20. Provide your e-mail address to get system messages.

21. You can skip the STMP section. Click on **Next** and provide the details for the Administrator user.

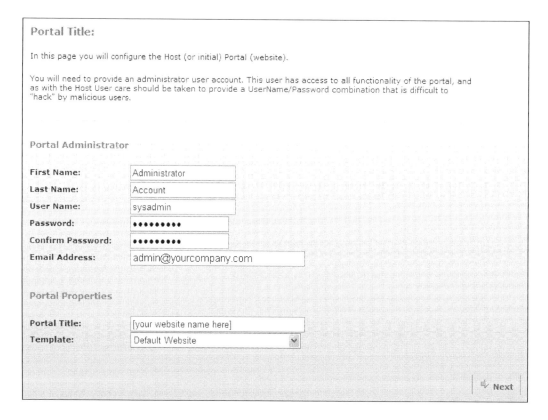

22. For the **First Name**, keep the default `Administrator`.

23. For the **Last Name**, type `Account`.

24. For **User Name**, type `sysadmin` (don't use the standard `admin` for the username. It is too well known).

25. Choose a good password and confirm it. Then write it down as well.

26. Provide your e-mail address to get system messages.

27. Lastly, the wizard will prompt for the basic information for your site. Choose a title for your site and type it into **Portal Title**.

28. Select **Default Website** for the **Template**.

29. Click on Next.

30. When you see the Congratulations screen, click on **Finished** (Goto Site) to complete the installation.

31. After a pause you should see the Welcome screen to your new website. At this point you have successfully created a debugging DNN website.

Preparing a module for debugging

Once we have created a debugging environment, we can add our modules to the DNN website project and debug our module in the DNN environment.

Getting ready

To follow along with this recipe you must have completed these recipes

> *Setting up a debugging environment*

> *Deploying a module as a standalone package*

How to do it...

1. Start by launching your preferred Development Tool (Visual Studio or Visual Web Developer Express).

2. From the **File** menu, select **Open Web Site.....**.

3. At the **Open Web Site** dialog, select the DNN source folder (`My Documents \DNNSource\website`).

4. Now we will add our existing Employee project. Look under the **File** menu and select **Add/Existing Project.....**.

5. Browse to the Employee project folder (probably `My Documents\Visual Studio 2010\Projects\Employee\Employee`) and select the `Employee.vbproj` file.

6. The Employee project will now appear in the **Solution Explorer**. Right-click on the `Employee` folder and select **Properties**.

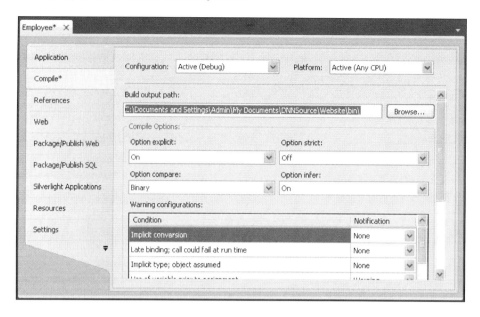

7. Select the **Compile** tab on the left and click on the **Browse** button. Select the `\bin` folder of the DNN source website (for example `My Documents\DNNSource\website\bin`). Click on **OK**.

8. Select the **Web** tab and select **Use the Visual Studio Development Server**.

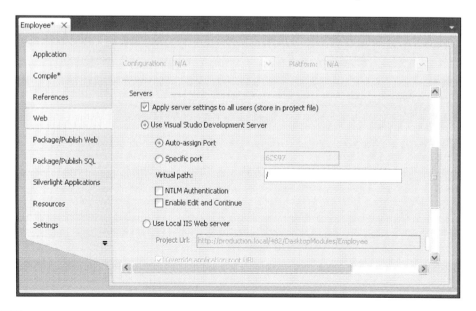

9. Now scroll up to the top of Solution Explorer and right-click on the website. Select **Properties**.

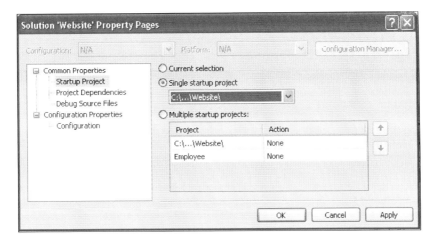

10. Select **Single startup project** from the radio control.

11. Select **Website** from the drop-down list.

12. Click on **OK**.

13. Now we can build the employee project and deploy it to the site. In the **Solution Explorer**, right-click on the Employee folder and select **Build**. You should see the **Build succeeded** message.

14. Follow the steps described in *Deploying a module as a standalone package* to create a ZIP file containing the Employee module.

15. Launch the site by looking under the Debug menu and selecting **Start Without Debugging** (or press *Ctrl+F5*).

16. All the source code for the site will now compile and the site will launch in your browser. After a pause you should see the Welcome screen.

17. Log into the test site as host (`syshost` in this examples).

18. Follow the steps described in *Deploying a module as a standalone package* to install the new ZIP file.

19. The ACME Employee module should now appear in the Control Panel drop-down list. Create a new blank page and add the Employee module to it.

 When you create the new page give access to All Users. Then you can debug your module without having to log in every time.

20. As soon as the Employee module is placed on the page, control will pass to `ViewEmployee.ascx`. If you see errors coming from the Employee module don't worry about it. It will give us something to debug.

21. The Employee module is now part of the website and ready for debugging.

See also

Now that your module is ready to debug, the next three recipes will show three useful debugging techniques: stepping through the code, setting a breakpoint, and using watch variables.

Setting a breakpoint and stepping through module code

In this recipe we will see how to set a breakpoint in the debugging environment and step through the module code. The goal here is to stop the action and take a moment to examine the variables in the module to see what values they hold. Then we can "walkthrough" the code line by line to see how it is running. This is a powerful debugging technique made possible by the features of Visual Studio.

Getting ready

To follow along with this recipe you must have completed these recipes

- *Creating a new module with the Starter Kit*
- *Setting up a debugging environment*
- *Preparing a module for debugging*

How to do it...

1. Start by launching your preferred development tool (Visual Studio or Visual Web Developer Express).

2. From the File menu, select **Open Web Site.....**

3. At the Open Web Site dialog, select the DNN source folder (`My Documents\DNNSource\website`).

4. Look on the right side under the Solution Explorer. You should see the Employee project listed under the website. If you don't see it, make sure you completed the steps of the previous recipe *Preparing a module for debugging*.

5. Double-click on the `ViewEmployee.ascx` file to display it in the editor.

6. Scroll down to the `Page_Load` procedure.

7. Right-click on line 60, choose **Breakpoint**, then choose **Insert Breakpoint** (or press *F9*).

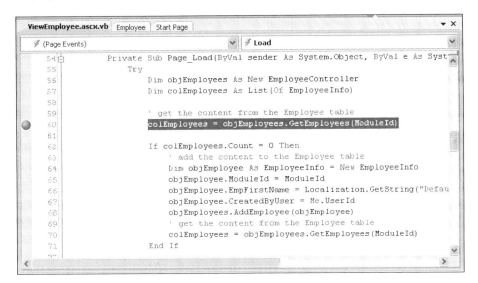

8. Look under the **Debug** menu and select **Start Debugging** (or press *F5*).

9. The website will build. If you haven't debugged the website before, you will be prompted to enable debugging:

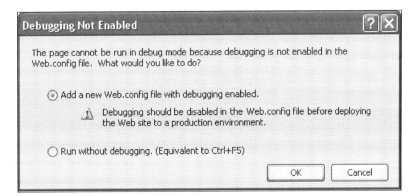

10. Select **Add a new Web.config file with debugging enabled** and click on **OK**.

11. The browser will launch and the Welcome page will display.

12. Navigate to the page with the Employee module.

13. After a pause the program will stop and you will return to the editor. Line 60 will now appear in yellow indicating that control has stopped at this point.

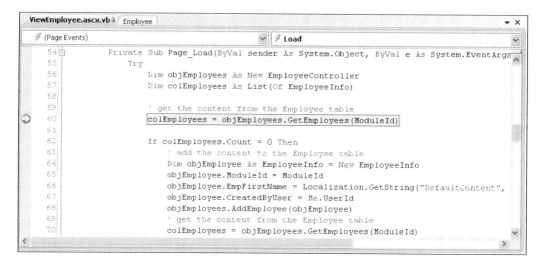

14. You can now step through your module code line by line by selecting **Step Into** from the **Debug** menu (or press *F11*).

15. To step over a procedure or function, select **Step Over** from the **Debug** menu or press *F10.*

16. If you hover over a variable a pop up will display the value held in the variable.

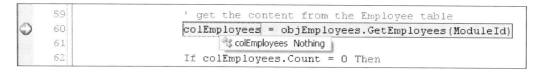

17. You can also select a variable to watch and the value will appear in the Watch window.

18. Right-click on the variable and select **Add Watch**.

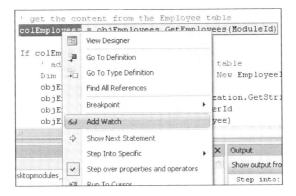

19. The variable and its current value will appear in the **Watch** window.

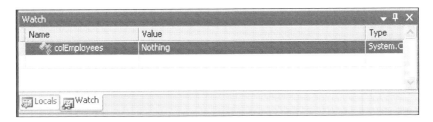

20. To continue running the program, select **Continue** from the **Debug** menu (or press *F5* again).

21. To stop debugging, select **Stop Debugging** from the **Debug** menu (or press *Shift+F5*).

Creating a Manifest from an installed module

In the previous recipe we saw how to modify the manifest file created by the Starter Kit as part of deploying a module. One shortcoming of that approach is that the manifest created by the Starter Kit is not always meant for the latest version of DNN. This is done so that starter modules are usable on the widest range of DNN versions. But if you know that your module will only deploy to the latest version of DNN, you can generate a new, up-to-date manifest file from an installed module.

Getting ready

To follow along with this recipe you must have completed the previous recipe:

▸ *Deploying a module as a standalone package*

How to do it...

1. Begin by logging in as the host user (`syshost` in our examples).

2. Look at the Control Panel and make sure you're in Edit mode.

3. Look under the **Host** menu and select **Extensions**.

4. Find the Employee module and click on the Edit icon next to the name.

5. Scroll to the bottom and click on the link **Create Package**.

6. As we want to create a new manifest, leave **Use Existing Manifest** unchecked and make sure **Review Manifest** is checked.

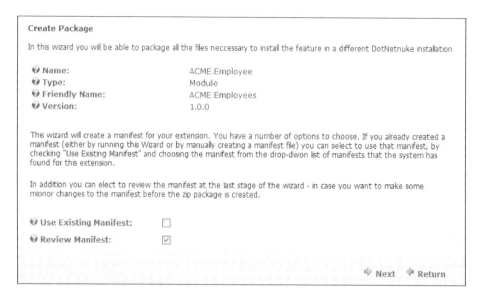

7. Click on **Next**.

8. The wizard will display the files in the module. Leave the files as is and click on **Next**.

9. When prompted for assemblies, type `Employee.dll` in the edit box and click on **Next**.

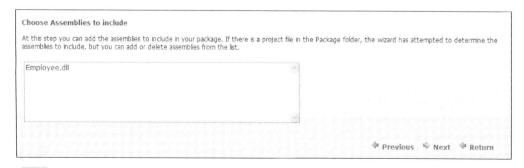

10. The wizard will display the generated manifest file. Click on **Next**.

11. On the **Create Package** screen, adjust the names as follows:

Create Package

The final step is to create the package. To create a copy of the Manifest file check the "Create Manifest File" check box - the file will be created in the Package's folder. Regardless of the setting you use here the manifest will be saved in the database and it will be added to the package.

To create a package check the "Create Package" check box. The package will be created in the relevant Install folder (eg Install/Modules for modules, Install/Skins for skins etc).

❷ **Create Manifest File:**	☑
❷ **Manifest File Name:**	Employee.dnn
❷ **Create Package:**	☑
❷ **Archive File Name:**	Employee_01.00.00_Install.zip

◈ Previous   ◈ Next

12. Click on **Next**.

13. The wizard will display a success message describing where to find the generated files:

Create Package

The Package was created and can be found in the localhost/dotnetnuke/Install/Module folder

14. Click on **Return** to close the wizard.

See also

The newest version of the manifest file offers new options like owner name, e-mail address, and URL. To learn more about these new options see the recipe *Using HTML in the Manifest* in *Chapter 11*.

6

Data Entry Tricks

In this chapter we will cover the following topics:

- Displaying labels from the resource file
- Creating collapsible panels
- Populating a drop-down list from a DNN list
- Populating a drop-down list from a stored procedure
- Displaying a Datagrid with Filter controls
- Adding a Paging control to a Datagrid

Introduction

In this chapter we will look at tools and tricks for basic data entry and data display. We will work with the sample Employee project from *Chapter 4* and expand it to include new data entry controls. We'll see how to use the resource file, populate controls with data from the database, run queries in a stored procedure, and display the results on the page.

- **The Page_Load procedure**

    In the .NET framework when a web form is loaded a special event called `Page_Load` occurs. This event is frequently used to prepare the data for your user controls before they are displayed. In this chapter you will see examples using the `Page_Load` event to populate a drop-down list or prepare a Datagrid. Inside the `Page_Load` routine it is also common to check if the page is being posted back to the server. This tells you if the page is being viewed for the first time and you can populate your controls accordingly.

> **Regions**
>
> Regions are used by Visual Studio to organize code into logical groups. They are not required in your code, but they are recommended. In the recipes of this chapter you will see several regions created by the Starter Kit (such as Private Members or Public Methods) and you will find them helpful when you are trying to find a routine that needs updating.

Displaying labels from the resource file

Data entry forms in DNN often have labels to identify the fields on the page. These are special controls that display text, but also have a "help" icon that displays an explanation when clicked.

But where does this text come from? We could hardcode the text for the labels in the code, but this would limit our ability to update the text easily and we would miss out on the powerful feature of Localization provided by DNN. Localization is a way for DNN to automatically translate labels and system messages based on the language selected by the user. You can learn more about localization from the recipes in *Chapter 9*.

For this recipe we will store the label text and **Help** explanation in the resource file and link them to the labels through a unique ID.

Getting ready

For this recipe we will use the `EditEmployee` control from the sample Employee project. To follow along you must have completed the following recipe from *Chapter 4*:

> * Creating a new module with the Starter Kit

How to do it...

1. Launch the Development Tool and load the Employee project.

2. Double-click to open the `EditEmployee.ascx` file.

3. The recipe *Building an Edit control* in *Chapter 5* created five sets of controls for editing values. Here is an example of the controls to edit Salary. Note the label control `lblSalary`:

```
<tr valign="top">
<td class="SubHead" width="125">
<dnn:label id="lblSalary" runat="server" controlname="lblSalary"
        suffix=":">
</dnn:label>
</td>
```

```
<td>
<asp:TextBox ID="txtSalary" runat="server"></asp:TextBox>
<asp:RequiredFieldValidator ID="valSalary"
                            resourcekey="valSalary.ErrorMessage"
                            ControlToValidate="txtSalary"
CssClass="NormalRed" Display="Dynamic" ErrorMessage=
                            "<br>Salary is required" Runat="server"
/>
</td>
   </tr>
```

4. Each of these five labels will get their value from the Edit resource file. So double-click to open the `EditEmployee.ascx.resx` file inside the `App_LocalResources` folder.

5. Use the resource editor and type a Text and Help message for each of the five fields as follows:

`ControlTitle_edit.Text`: **Edit Employee**

`lblEmpFirstName.Text`: **First Name**

`lblEmpFirstName.Help`: **Enter the first name of the employee**

`lblEmpLastName.Text`: **Last Name**

`lblEmpLastName.Help`: **Enter the last name of the employee**

`lblManagerNo.Text`: **Manager #**

`lblManagerNo.Help`: **Enter the ID number of employee's manager**

`lblHireDate.Text`: **Hire Date**

`lblHireDate.Help`: **Enter employee's date of hire**

`lblSalary.Text`: **Salary**

`lblSalary.Help`: **Enter employee's annual salary**

6. The file should now look like this:

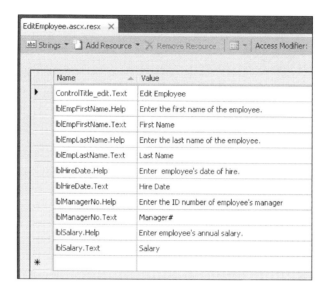

7. Select **Save All** from the **File** menu.

8. To check the results, build and deploy the module to your DNN site (for instructions see the recipe *Deploying a module as a standalone package* in *Chapter 5*).

Creating collapsible panels

Another useful control offered by DNN is the `SectionHead` control that creates a collapsible panel on a data entry form. This panel appears frequently in the DNN modules and is useful when you don't want to waste space on the page with something the user won't always need.

In this recipe we will create a collapsible panel that shows or hides an HTML table containing sample text. In the recipes *Populating a drop-down list from a DNN list* and *Populating a drop-down list from a stored procedure*, we will replace the sample text with real controls to create a more practical example.

Getting ready

To follow along with this recipe you must have completed the following recipe:

- *Creating a new module with the Starter Kit*

How to do it...

1. Start by launching the Development Tool and loading the Employee project.

2. Double-click to open the `ViewEmployee.ascx` file.

3. Look at the top of the file and find the register directives just before the Datalist control:

```
<%@ Control language="vb"
    Inherits="ACME.Modules.Employee.ViewEmployee"
    AutoEventWireup="false" Explicit="True"
    Codebehind="ViewEmployee.ascx.vb" %>
<%@ Register TagPrefix="dnn" TagName="Audit"
    Src="~/controls/ModuleAuditControl.ascx" %>
<asp:datalist id="lstContent" datakeyfield="ItemID" runat="server"
                cellpadding="4">
    <itemtemplate>
```

4. Insert a new register directive just before the Datalist control:

```
<%@ Register TagPrefix="dnn" TagName="SectionHead"
    Src="~/controls/SectionHeadControl.ascx" %>
```

5. The top of the file should now look like:

```
<%@ Control language="vb"
    Inherits="ACME.Modules.Employee.ViewEmployee"
    AutoEventWireup="false" Explicit="True"
    Codebehind="ViewEmployee.ascx.vb" %>
<%@ Register TagPrefix="dnn" TagName="Audit"
    Src="~/controls/ModuleAuditControl.ascx" %>
```

```
<%@ Register TagPrefix="dnn" TagName="SectionHead"
    Src="~/controls/SectionHeadControl.ascx" %>

<asp:datalist id="lstContent" datakeyfield="ItemID" runat="server"
                                    cellpadding="4">
  <itemtemplate>
```

6. Next, we add a simple HTML table and link it to the `SectionHead` control. Insert this code at the top of the file as follows:

```
<%@ Control language="vb"
    Inherits="ACME.Modules.Employee.ViewEmployee"
    AutoEventWireup="false" Explicit="True"
    Codebehind="ViewEmployee.ascx.vb" %>
<%@ Register TagPrefix="dnn" TagName="Audit"
    Src="~/controls/ModuleAuditControl.ascx" %>
<%@ Register TagPrefix="dnn" TagName="SectionHead"
    Src="~/controls/SectionHeadControl.ascx" %>

<dnn:SectionHead ID="dshPanel" runat="server"
    CssClass="Head" ResourceKey="Settings"
              Section="tblPanel" Text="Collapsible Panel">
</dnn:SectionHead>

<table id="tblPanel" cellspacing="2" cellpadding="2" border="0"
    runat="server">
    <tr>
        <td width="20%" class="SubHead">
            [Put a label here]
        </td>
        <td width="25%">
            [Put a control here]
        </td>
        <td width="10%">
             
        </td>
        <td width="20%" class="SubHead">
            [Put a label here]
        </td>
        <td width="25%">
            [Put a control here]
        </td>
    </tr>
</table>

<asp:datalist id="lstContent" datakeyfield="ItemID"
      runat="server" cellpadding="4">
  <itemtemplate>
```

The `SectionHead` control has to know what to hide or show. We tell it by assigning the ID of the table (`tblPanel`) to the `Section` property (`Section="tblPanel"`).

7. When the module is built and deployed it looks like this:

8. You can show and hide the controls by clicking the small minus sign next to the title **Collapsible Panel**.

How it works...

In this example we created a collapsible panel by connecting a `SectionHead` control to an HTML table. The power of this control is that you can put anything inside the table: labels, drop down lists, or images and they will all show or hide together. This works well when you have something that takes up a lot of space on the page, but you don't need to see it all the time.

Populating a drop-down list from a DNN list

This recipe will show how to populate a drop-down list control from a DNN list we create as Host user. Using DNN lists to populate data entry controls means we can update the lists through the site without having to change and redeploy our custom modules.

Getting ready

To follow along with this recipe you must have completed the following recipe:

▶ *Creating a new module with the Starter Kit*

How to do it...

1. Log in as Host user (`syshost` in our examples).
2. Look under the **Host** menu and select **Lists**.

3. Make a new list by clicking on **Add List**.

4. Type the details of our first entry:
    - **List Name**: Salary Range
    - **Parent List**: **None Specified**
    - **Parent Entry**: blank
    - **Entry Text**: $0 or more
    - **Entry Value**: 0
    - **Enable Sort Order**: Checked

5. Click on **Save**.

6. Click on **Add Entry** and create the second list entry:
    - **Entry Text**: $30,000 or more
    - **Entry Value**: 30000

7. Click on **Save**.

8. Click on **Add Entry** and create the third list entry:
    - **Entry Text**: $60,000 or more
    - **Entry Value**: 60000

9. Click on **Add Entry** and create the fourth list entry:
    - **Entry Text**: $100,000 or more
    - **Entry Value**: **100000**

10. Click on **Save**.

11. Now that we have a DNN list, we can use it inside our custom module. Launch the Development Tool.

12. Look for Recent Projects shown on the left side of the screen. Click on **Employee** to load the project.

13. Double-click to open the `ViewEmployee.ascx` file.

14. Look at the top of the file:

```
<%@ Control language="vb"
    Inherits="ACME.Modules.Employee.ViewEmployee"
    AutoEventWireup="false" Explicit="True"
    Codebehind="ViewEmployee.ascx.vb" %>
<%@ Register TagPrefix="dnn" TagName="Audit"
    Src="~/controls/ModuleAuditControl.ascx" %>
<%@ Register TagPrefix="dnn" TagName="Label"
    Src="~/controls/LabelControl.ascx" %>



<asp:datalist id="lstContent" datakeyfield="ItemID"
    runat="server" cellpadding="4">
  <itemtemplate>
```

15. Add the following HTML table code just after the last register directive and before the Datalist:

```
<%@ Register TagPrefix="dnn" TagName="Label" Src="~/controls/
LabelControl.ascx" %>

<table id="tblPanel" cellspacing="2" cellpadding="2" border="0"
    runat="server" >
  <tr>
    <td width="20%" class="SubHead">
        [Put a label here]
```

```
        </td>
        <td width="25%">
            [Put a control here]
        </td>
        <td width="10%">
             
        </td>
        <td width="20%" class="SubHead">
            <dnn:Label ID="lblSalaryRange" runat="server"
                ControlName="ddlddlSalaryRange" Suffix=":">
            </dnn:Label>
        </td>
        <td width="25%">
            <asp:DropDownList ID="ddlSalaryRange"
                runat="server" DataTextField="Text"
                DataValueField="Value" AutoPostBack="true">
            </asp:DropDownList>
        </td>
    </tr>
</table>
```

 If you followed a previous recipe and there is already an HTML table here, just replace it with this new HTML table.

16. Next, open the `ViewEmployee.ascx.vb` file.

17. The first step is to import the `Lists` namespace. Scroll down a little and add the import statement:

```
Imports System.Web.UI
Imports System.Collections.Generic
Imports System.Reflection

Imports DotNetNuke
Imports DotNetNuke.Services.Exceptions
Imports DotNetNuke.Services.Localization
Imports DotNetNuke.Common.Lists
```

18. Next we must bind the DNN list we created to the drop-down list we added to the form. Scroll down to the `Page_Load` procedure and add the following procedure call inside the check for `PostBack`:

```
If Page.IsPostBack = False Then

        BindSalaryDropDown()

End If
```

19. Next, in the `Private Methods` region, we'll add this procedure:

```
Private Sub BindSalaryDropDown()

    Dim objList As New ListController()
    Dim lstSalary As ListEntryInfoCollection =
objList.GetListEntryInfoCollection("Salary Range")

    ddlSalaryRange.DataSource = lstSalary
    ddlSalaryRange.DataTextField = "Text"
    ddlSalaryRange.DataValueField = "Value"

    Try
    ddlSalaryRange.DataBind()

    ' add an extra value to always show a prompt in the drop down

    ddlSalaryRange.Items.Insert(0,
            New ListItem(Localization.GetString("SalaryPrompt",
                                LocalResourceFile), "-1"))
    Catch ex As Exception
    End Try

End Sub
```

 If your module doesn't have a `Private Methods` region, just put this procedure above the `Page_Load` procedure.

20. If you look carefully at the previous example, we are adding a prompt message to the drop-down control along with the Salary list by calling the routine `ddlSalaryRange.Items.Insert()`. The `"-1"` in the insert is the value of this choice rather than an actual salary. In addition, we are following good programming practice and pulling the text of the prompt from the resource file. But this means we need to add the prompt to the resource file along with the labels for the new control. Open the `ViewEmployee.ascx.resx` file (under `/App_LocalResources`) and set the label text and Help prompt:

`lblSalaryRange.Text`: **Salary Range**

`lblSalaryRange.Help`: **Pick the salary range you want to select**

`SalaryPrompt.Text`: **Select Salary Range**

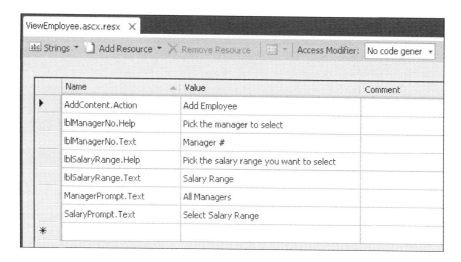

21. Select **Save All** from the **File** menu.

22. To test check the results, build and deploy the module to your DNN site (for instructions see the recipe *Deploying a module as a standalone package* in *Chapter 5*).

23. The drop-down list should contain the values we created along with an additional **Select Salary Range** value from the resource file:

How it works...

We can bind a drop-down list control directly to a DNN list. This allows the host user to add values to the list without having to redeploy the module.

There's more...

As we bind to the list when the page is displayed, you can add more values to the DNN list and they will automatically appear in the drop-down list when the page is refreshed.

Populating a drop-down list from a stored procedure

In this recipe we will see how to populate a drop-down list from a stored procedure. This is similar to binding to a DNN list, but now we can use any data stored in the database for the list.

Getting ready

To follow along with this recipe you must have completed the following recipes:

▸ *Creating stored procedures* (from *Chapter 4*)

▸ *Populating a drop-down list from a DNN list*

How to do it...

1. Start by launching the Development Tool and loading the Employee project.

2. Double-click to open the `ViewEmployee.ascx` file.

3. Find the table and the salary control you added from the previous recipe. Look for the two placeholders and replace them with this label and control code so the HTML table now looks like this:

```
<table id="tblPanel" cellspacing="2" cellpadding="2" border="0"
    runat="server" >
    <tr>
        <td width="20%" class="SubHead">
            <dnn:Label ID="lblManagerNo" runat="server"
                    ControlName="ddlManagerNo" Suffix=":">
            </dnn:Label>
        </td>
        <td width="25%">
```

```
        <asp:DropDownList ID="ddlManagerNo" runat="server"
            DataTextField="ManagerName"
            DataValueField="ItemNo" AutoPostBack="true">
        </asp:DropDownList>
    </td>
    <td width="10%">
         
    </td>
    <td width="20%" class="SubHead">
        <dnn:Label ID="lblSalaryRange" runat="server"
            ControlName="ddlddlSalaryRange" Suffix=":">
        </dnn:Label>
    </td>
    <td width="25%">
        <asp:DropDownList ID="ddlSalaryRange" runat="server"
            DataTextField="Text" DataValueField="Value"
            AutoPostBack="true">
        </asp:DropDownList>
    </td>
    </tr>
</table>
```

4. Now that we have a drop-down control, the next step is to add the routines we need to populate the drop-down control from a stored procedure in the database. Let's start by creating the stored procedure.

5. Double-click to open the `01.00.00.SqlDataProvider` file.

If you have already installed this module once, you can create a new file called `01.00.01.SqlDataProvider` to hold the new procedure. For details see the recipe *Deploying a new module version* in *Chapter 11*.

6. We'll add a new procedure to the script that is very similar to the `GetEmployees` procedure created by the Starter Kit but with a small tweak. In the sample Employee table, there is a field called `ManagerNo` holding the ID of the employee's manager. If the `ManagerNo` is `0` it means the employee is a manager. Therefore to get the list of all managers for the drop-down control the stored procedure needs to select all employees who have a `ManagerNo` of `0`. The code for the procedure looks like this:

```
create procedure {databaseOwner}{objectQualifier}ACME_GetManagers

    @ModuleId int

as

select Emp.ModuleId,
```

```
        Emp.ItemId,
        EmpFirstName,
        EmpLastName,
        ManagerNo,
        HireDate,
        Salary,
        CreatedByUser,
        Emp.CreatedDate,
        'CreatedByUserName' = Usr.FirstName + ' ' + Usr.LastName
from {objectQualifier}ACME_Employee As Emp
inner join {objectQualifier}Users As Usr on Emp.CreatedByUser =
Usr.UserId
where  ModuleId = @ModuleId And ManagerNo = 0


GO
```

7. Next we need to create the routines that will connect the employee controller to this stored procedure. Double-click to open the `DataProvider.vb` file.

8. Scroll down to the bottom of the file and look for the region of code called Abstract methods. Add the following function definition:

```
Public MustOverride Function GetManagers(ByVal ModuleId As
Integer) As IDataReader
```

9. Now, open the `SqlDataProvider.vb` and scroll to the bottom of the file to the Public methods region. Add the new function:

```
Public Overrides Function GetManagers(ByVal ModuleId As Integer)
As IDataReader
    Return CType(SqlHelper.ExecuteReader(ConnectionString,
            GetFullyQualifiedName("GetManagers"),
            ModuleId), IDataReader)

End Function
```

10. Next we need to change the `EmployeeController` file. Double-click on `EmployeeController.vb` and scroll down to the bottom of the Public methods region. Add the following code:

```
Public Function GetManagers(ByVal ModuleId As Integer) As List(Of
EmployeeInfo)

    Return CBO.FillCollection(Of EmployeeInfo)(DataProvider.
Instance().GetManagers(ModuleId))


End Function
```

11. At this point we have the routines that we need to populate the drop-down list, but the finishing touch is to provide a new property in the `EmployeeInfo` object that will give a formatted manager name that will look good in the drop-down control. Double-click on `EmployeeInfo.vb` and scroll down a little to add the following code:

```
' public properties

Public ReadOnly Property ManagerName() As String
    Get
        Return _EmpLastName + ", " + _EmpFirstName
    End Get
End Property
```

12. Now, to hook it all together, we need to go into the `ViewEmployee` code behind and bind the drop-down list to the routines we just created. Double-click to open the `ViewEmployee.ascx.vb` file.

13. Scroll down to the `Page_Load` procedure and find the `BindSalaryDropDown` procedure call from the previous recipe. Add the `BindManagerDropDown` call just before it:

```
If Page.IsPostBack = False Then

    BindManagerDropDown()
    BindSalaryDropDown()

End If
```

14. Scroll up to the `Private methods` region and add this new procedure just before `BindSalaryDropDown`:

```
Private Sub BindManagerDropDown()

    Dim objEmployeeController As New EmployeeController

    ddlManagerNo.DataSource =
        objEmployeeController.GetManagers(ModuleId)
    ddlManagerNo.DataTextField = "ManagerName"
    ddlManagerNo.DataValueField = "ItemId"

    Try
    ddlManagerNo.DataBind()

    ' add an extra value to always show a prompt in the drop down

    ddlManagerNo.Items.Insert(0, New ListItem
        (Localization.GetString("ManagerPrompt",
                                    LocalResourceFile), "-1"))
```

```
    Catch ex As Exception
    End Try
End Sub

Private Sub BindSalaryDropDown()
...
```

15. If you look carefully at the previous example, we are adding a prompt message to the drop-down control along with the manager names by calling the routine `ddlManagerNo.Items.Insert()`. The `"-1"` in the insert is the value of this choice rather than the actual manager number. In addition, we are following good programming practice and pulling the text of the prompt from the resource file. But this means we need to add the prompt to the resource file along with the labels for the new control. Open the `ViewEmployee.ascx.resx` file (under `/App_LocalResources`) and add the following:

    `lblManagerNo.Text`: **Manager #**

    `lblManagerNo.Help`: **Pick the manager to select**

    `ManagerPrompt.Text`: **All Managers**

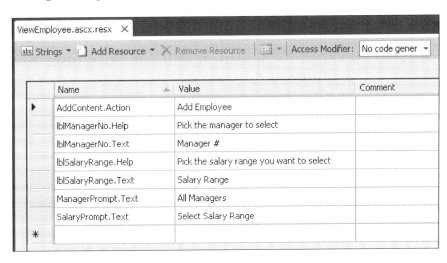

16. One last thing we need to do is add the new stored procedure to the uninstall script to make sure the stored procedure is removed when the module is uninstalled.

17. Open the file `Uninstall.SqlDataProvider`.

18. Scroll to the bottom of the script and add the following:

    ```
    DROP PROCEDURE {databaseOwner}[{objectQualifier}ACME_GetManagers]
    GO
    ```

19. Select **Save All** from the **File** menu.

20. To check the results, build and deploy the module to your DNN site (for instructions see the recipe *Deploying a module as a standalone package* in *Chapter 5*).

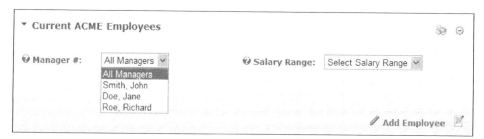

How it works...

HTML tables are often used to arrange controls on a page. In this recipe we have two drop-down lists with labels inside an HTML table. These filters will enable users to control the records that appear in the Datagrid.

See also

You can see how these filters are used in the next recipe.

Displaying a Datagrid with filter controls

In this recipe we will replace the simple Datalist control with a more powerful Datagrid control and add a collapsible panel with filters. This is a useful combination of data entry controls that allows the searching and displaying of module records.

Getting ready

To follow along with this recipe you must have completed the following recipes:

- *Creating collapsible panels*
- *Populating a drop-down list from a DNN list*
- *Populating a drop-down list from a stored procedure*

How to do it...

1. Launch the Development Tool and load the Employee project.
2. Expand the `References` folder and make sure `DotNetNuke.WebControls` is shown.

3. Double-click to open the `ViewEmployee.ascx` file.

4. At the top of the file, add the code to register the `DotNetNuke.UI.WebControls` namespace.

```
<%@ Register TagPrefix="dnn" Namespace="DotNetNuke.UI.WebControls"
    Assembly="DotNetNuke" %>
```

5. Scroll down to the bottom until you see the existing Datalist code:

```
<asp:datalist id="lstContent" datakeyfield="ItemID" runat="server"
    cellpadding="4">
  <itemtemplate>
    <table cellpadding="4" width="100%">
...

<asp:Label ID="lblSalary" runat="server" CssClass="Normal"/>

        </td>
      </tr>
    </table>
  </itemtemplate>
</asp:datalist>
```

6. Delete this code and replace it with the following:

```
<asp:datagrid id="grdResults" AutoGenerateColumns="false"
    width="100%" CellPadding="2" GridLines="None"
    cssclass="DataGrid_Container" Runat="server">
  <headerstyle cssclass="NormalBold" verticalalign="Top"
   horizontalalign="Center"/>
  <itemstyle cssclass="Normal" horizontalalign="Left" />
  <alternatingitemstyle cssclass="Normal" />
  <edititemstyle cssclass="NormalTextBox" />
  <selecteditemstyle cssclass="NormalRed" />
  <footerstyle cssclass="DataGrid_Footer" />
  <pagerstyle cssclass="DataGrid_Pager" />
  <columns>
      <dnn:imagecommandcolumn CommandName="Edit"
          ImageUrl="~/images/edit.gif" EditMode="URL"
          KeyField="ItemID" />
        <dnn:imagecommandcolumn CommandName="Delete"
            ImageUrl="~/images/delete.gif" KeyField="ItemID" />

      dnn:textcolumn datafield="EmpFirstName" headertext="First" />
      <dnn:textcolumn datafield="EmpLastName" headertext="Last"/>
       <dnn:textcolumn datafield="ManagerNo"
                                  headertext="Manager #" />
```

```
        <dnn:textcolumn datafield="FormattedHireDate"
                         headertext="Hire Date"/>
        <dnn:textcolumn datafield="Salary" headertext="Salary"/>

    </Columns>
</asp:datagrid>
```

7. Double-click to open the `01.00.00.SqlProvider` file.

 If you have already installed this module once, you can create a new file called `01.00.01.SqlDataProvider` to hold the new procedure. For details see the recipe *Deploying a new module version* in *Chapter 11*.

8. At the end of the `Drop Existing Procedures` section add:

```
if exists (select * from dbo.sysobjects where id =
                  object_id(N'{databaseOwner}[{objectQualifier}
                     ACME_GetEmployeesByFilter]') and
                     OBJECTPROPERTY (id, N'IsProcedure') = 1)
    drop procedure {databaseOwner}{objectQualifier}
                                     ACME_GetEmployeesByFilter
GO
```

9. Scroll to the bottom and add the following new procedure. It's a modified version of the normal `GetEmployees` procedure that includes filters. If you look closely, we are ignoring the filters if they have a value of `-1`. This is the `-1` we put in the drop-down lists in the previous recipes.

```
CREATE procedure {databaseOwner}{objectQualifier}
                                ACME_GetEmployeesByFilter
    @ModuleID int,
    @MgrFilter int,
    @SalaryFilter  int
AS


/** If we pass -1 for a numeric filter it means ignore the filter
**/


/** create a temp table to hold the Ids of our results  **/

    CREATE TABLE #PageIndex
    (
        IndexID      int IDENTITY (1, 1) NOT NULL,
        ItemId    int
    )
```

```
/** populate the temp temp with the filtered results **/

    INSERT INTO #PageIndex (ItemId)
    SELECT ItemId
     FROM {objectQualifier}ACME_Employee
    WHERE (ModuleId = @ModuleId) AND  (ManagerNo = @MgrFilter OR
                 @MgrFilter = -1) AND (Salary >= @SalaryFilter)
    ORDER BY ItemId DESC

/** remember the count of the results  **/

    SELECT COUNT(*) as TotalRecords
    FROM #PageIndex

/** join the filtered Ids to the employee table to get our fields
**/

select Emp.ModuleId,
       Emp.ItemId,
       EmpFirstName,
       EmpLastName,
       ManagerNo,
       HireDate,
       Salary,
       Emp.CreatedByUser,
       Emp.CreatedDate,
       'CreatedByUserName' = Usr.FirstName + ' ' + Usr.LastName
FROM {objectQualifier}ACME_Employee As Emp
INNER JOIN {objectQualifier}Users As Usr on Emp.CreatedByUser =
Usr.UserId
    INNER JOIN #PageIndex PageIndex
       ON Emp.ItemId = PageIndex.ItemId
    ORDER BY
       PageIndex.IndexID

GO
```

 You can immediately create this stored procedure by pasting this SQL into the SQL page under the **Host** menu on your DNN portal.

10. As we have added a new procedure to the module, we must also add it to the uninstall script so it is taken away when the module is uninstalled. Double-click to open the `Uninstall.SqlDataProvider` file.

11. Scroll down to the bottom and add the following `Drop Procedure`:

```
DROP PROCEDURE {databaseOwner}[{objectQualifier}
                              ACME_DeleteEmployee]
GO


DROP PROCEDURE {databaseOwner}[{objectQualifier}
                              ACME_GetEmployeesByFilter]
GO


/*****************************************************************/
/*****              SqlDataProvider                      *****/
/*****************************************************************/
```

12. Next, double-click to open the `DataProvider.vb` file.

13. Now we need to define the new filter function as an abstract method. This defines the parameters of the function (what filters we will pass) and a return type (a dataset of records found). Scroll to the bottom of the file and add the new function at the end of the `Abstract Methods` region:

```
#Region "Abstract methods"

        Public MustOverride Function GetEmployees(ByVal ModuleId
                                As Integer) As IDataReader
...
        Public MustOverride Sub DeleteEmployee(ByVal ModuleId As
                                Integer, ByVal ItemId As Integer)


        Public MustOverride Function GetEmployeesByFilter(ByVal
ModuleId As Integer, ByVal MgrFilter As Integer, ByVal
SalaryFilter As Integer) As IDataReader

#End Region
```

14. Double-click to open the `SqlDataProvider.vb` file.

15. Now we provide the function body. We're calling the stored procedure and returning the records found as a dataset. Scroll to the bottom of the file and add this new procedure at the end of the `Public Methods` region:

```
Public Overrides Function GetEmployeesByFilter
                            (ByVal ModuleId As Integer,
                            ByVal MgrFilter As Integer,
                            ByVal SalaryFilter As
```

```
                                        Integer) As IDataReader
            Return CType(SqlHelper.ExecuteReader(ConnectionString,
                GetFullyQualifiedName("GetEmployeesByFilter"),
                ModuleId, MgrFilter, SalaryFilter), IDataReader)
    End Function


    #End Region
```

16. Double-click to open the `EmployeeController.vb` file.

17. Next, we are taking the dataset returned from the stored procedure, getting a count of the records found, and converting the results to a collection we can bind to the Datagrid. Scroll to the bottom of the file and add the new procedure at the end of the `Public Methods` region:

```
Public Function GetEmployeesByFilter(ByVal ModuleId As Integer,
                            ByVal MgrFilter As Integer,
                            ByVal SalaryFilter As Integer,
                            ByRef TotalRecords As Integer)
                                            As ArrayList
        Dim dr As IDataReader =
                        DataProvider.Instance.GetEmployeesByFilter
                            (ModuleId, MgrFilter, SalaryFilter)
        Dim retValue As ArrayList = Nothing
        Try
          While dr.Read
              TotalRecords = Convert.ToInt32(dr("TotalRecords"))
          End While
          dr.NextResult()
          retValue = CBO.FillCollection(dr,GetType(EmployeeInfo))
        Finally
          If Not dr Is Nothing Then
              dr.Close()
          End If
        End Try
        Return retValue

End Function
```

18. Double-click to open the `EmployeeInfo.vb` file.

19. Find the `Public Properties` section and add the property `FormattedHireDate` to provide a nicely formatted date.

```
' public properties

Public Property FormattedHireDate() As String
    Get
        Return _HireDate.ToShortDateString
    End Get
    Set(ByVal Value As String)
        _HireDate = CDate(Value)
    End Set
End Property

Public Property ModuleId() As Integer
```

20. Double-click to open the `ViewEmployee.ascx.vb` file.

21. At the top of the file make sure these two imports are there:

```
Imports DotNetNuke.Common.Lists
Imports DotNetNuke.UI.WebControls
```

22. Scroll down to the `Private Methods` region and add this new `BindData` procedure:

```
Private Sub BindData()
    Dim objEmployees As New EmployeeController
    Dim colEmployees As ArrayList

    Dim TotalRecords As Integer

     ' use the filter procedure to retrieve the records

    colEmployees = objEmployees.GetEmployeesByFilter
                    (ModuleId, ddlManagerNo.SelectedItem.Value,
                    ddlSalaryRange.SelectedItem.Value, TotalRecords)

    If colEmployees.Count > 0 Then
        grdResults.Visible = True
        grdResults.DataSource = colEmployees
        grdResults.DataBind()
    Else
        ' hide the controls that need data
        grdResults.Visible = False
    End If

End Sub
```

23. Next, scroll down to the `Page_Load` procedure and add the `BindData()` procedure call:

```
If Page.IsPostBack = False Then

    BindManagerDropDown()
    BindSalaryDropDown()

    BindData()

End If
```

24. The `Page_Init` routine occurs just before the `Page_Load` routine and is frequently used to initialize controls before the `Page_Load`. In this case, we are formatting the Datagrid before we populate it with data. We do this by creating a loop that checks each column of the grid and looks for two things:

    ❑ If the column is an image with the name of "Delete" then we pull a delete confirmation message from the system resource file.

    ❑ If the column is Edit (like the little edit pencil DNN shows next to a record) then we construct a link to the `EditEmployee` form of our module using the `ItemID` from the record.

25. Scroll up a little bit to the `Event Handlers` region and add this procedure at the top:

```
Private Sub Page_Init(ByVal sender As System.Object,
                ByVal e As System.EventArgs)
                                    Handles MyBase.Init

    ' Format the columns of the grid control

    For Each column As DataGridColumn In grdResults.Columns

        ' if the column is the edit or delete icon, build the URL
                                                for the icon
        If column.GetType Is GetType(ImageCommandColumn) Then
            'if it is the delete icon, load the confirmation
                                message from the resource file
            Dim imageColumn As ImageCommandColumn =
                            CType(column, ImageCommandColumn)
            If imageColumn.CommandName = "Delete" Then
                imageColumn.OnClickJS =
                            Localization.GetString("DeleteItem")
            End If

            'Create a URL to pass the selected ItemId to the
                                            EditEmployee form
```

```
                       If imageColumn.CommandName = "Edit" Then
                           Dim formatString As String = EditUrl("ItemId",
                                                      "KEYFIELD", "Edit")
                           formatString = formatString.Replace("KEYFIELD",
                                                                "{0}")
                           imageColumn.NavigateURLFormatString = formatString
                       End If

                   End If

           Next

       End Sub
```

26. Next, we need to connect the delete icon that appears in the Datagrid to a handler routine that will delete the employee record. All we need to do is extract the `ItemId` value from the event we receive, convert it to integer using Int32, and pass it to the `DeleteEmployee` routine created by the Starter Kit. Scroll down and put this procedure just after the `Page_Load` procedure:

```
Private Sub grdResults_DeleteCommand(ByVal source As Object,
            ByVal e As
            System.Web.UI.WebControls.DataGridCommandEventArgs)
            Handles
                                        grdResults.DeleteCommand
    Try
        Dim objEmployeeController As New EmployeeController

        objEmployeeController.DeleteEmployee(ModuleId,
                        Int32.Parse(e.CommandArgument.ToString))

        'redisplay results in the datagrid
        BindData()

    Catch exc As Exception
        ProcessModuleLoadException(Me, exc)
    End Try
End Sub
```

27. Lastly, we want to trap when the filter selections change. Add these two new procedures at the bottom of the `Event Handlers` region:

```
Private Sub ddlManagerNo_SelectedIndexChanged(ByVal sender As
                        System.Object, ByVal e As
                        System.EventArgs) Handles
                        ddlManagerNo.SelectedIndexChanged
    BindData()
End Sub
```

```
Private Sub ddlSalaryRange_SelectedIndexChanged(ByVal sender As
                        System.Object, ByVal e As
                        System.EventArgs) Handles
                        ddlSalaryRange.SelectedIndexChanged
    BindData()
End Sub
```

28. Select **Save All** from the **File** menu.

29. To check the results, build and deploy the module to your DNN site (for instructions see the recipe *Deploying a module as a standalone package* in *Chapter 5*).

How it works...

In this recipe we took the basic module from the Starter Kit and extended it in three ways:

▶ We added the filter controls from the previous recipe

▶ We replaced the Datalist control with a Datagrid control

▶ We created a new database procedure that extends the basic `GetEmployees` procedure with the filters

There's more...

If you look at the stored procedure in this recipe it may seem that it is doing more work than necessary to filter the Employee records (creating a temporary table, and so on). The extra code in the stored procedure is to support paging which we will see in the next recipe.

See also

In the next recipe we will extend the Datagrid even farther by adding a paging control so we can limit our Datagrid results to a manageable size.

Adding a paging control to a Datagrid

In this recipe we will extend the previous recipe by adding paging controls to the Datagrid and filters. DNN offers a very good paging control that will take our filtered search results and break them into multiple pages based on the page size we select.

In this recipe we will add a new drop down on the `ViewEmployee` form to control the size of our pages. Then we will modify our filter procedure to accept and use paging variables.

Getting ready

To follow along with this recipe you must have completed the following recipes:

▶ *Displaying a Datagrid with filter controls*

How to do it...

1. Start by launching the Development Tool and loading the Employee project.
2. Double-click to open the `ViewEmployee.ascx` file.
3. At the top of the file is an HTML table that is holding the filters we created in previous chapters. We need to add another drop-down control that holds the options for the page sizes. Find the HTML table from the previous recipe and change the code as follows:

```
<table id="tblPanel" cellspacing="2" cellpadding="2" border="0"
    runat="server">
    <tr>
        <td width="12%" class="SubHead">
            <dnn:Label ID="lblManagerNo" runat="server"
                ControlName="ddlManagerNo" Suffix=":">
            </dnn:Label>
        </td>
        <td width="18%">
            <asp:DropDownList ID="ddlManagerNo" runat="server"
                DataTextField="ManagerName"
                DataValueField="ManagerNo"
                AutoPostBack="true">
            </asp:DropDownList>
        </td>
        <td width="5%">
             
        </td>
        <td width="12%" class="SubHead">
```

```
        <dnn:Label ID="lblSalaryRange" runat="server"
                ControlName="ddlddlSalaryRange" Suffix=":">
        </dnn:Label>
    </td>
    <td width="18%">
        <asp:DropDownList ID="ddlSalaryRange" runat="server"
            DataTextField="Text" DataValueField="Value"
            AutoPostBack="true">
        </asp:DropDownList>
    </td>
    <td width="5%">
         
    </td>
    <td width="12%" class="SubHead">
            <dnn:Label ID="plRecordsPage" runat="server"
                CssClass="SubHead"
                ResourceKey="Recordsperpage" Suffix=":">
            </dnn:Label>
    </td>

    <td width="18%">
        <asp:DropDownList ID="ddlRecordsPerPage"
            runat="server" AutoPostBack="True">
            <asp:ListItem Value="10">10</asp:ListItem>
            <asp:ListItem Value="25">25</asp:ListItem>
            <asp:ListItem Value="50">50</asp:ListItem>
            <asp:ListItem Value="100">100</asp:ListItem>
            <asp:ListItem Value="250">250</asp:ListItem>
        </asp:DropDownList>
    </td>

</tr>
</table>
```

4. Next, scroll down to the bottom of the file and add this paging control code after the Datagrid:

```
<br />
<dnn:PagingControl ID="ctlPagingControl" runat="server">
</dnn:PagingControl>
<br />
```

5. Double-click to open the `ViewEmployee.ascx.vb` file.

6. For the paging to work, we need to remember what page number is currently selected. To do that we create a private variable to hold the Page Index. The Index starts at 0 (page one) and we pass it to the stored procedure so it can calculate which records should appear on the page. Look at the top of the file and add the `Private Members` region with a single variable declaration. Place it just before the `Private Methods` region:

```
#Region "Private Members"

        Dim PageIndex As Integer = 1

#End Region

#Region "Private Methods"

        Private Sub BindData()
```

7. Scroll down a little to the `BindData()` procedure and make the following changes:

```
Private Sub BindData()
    Dim objEmployees As New EmployeeController
    Dim colEmployees As ArrayList

    Dim TotalRecords As Integer
    Dim PageSize As Integer = Convert.ToInt32(ddlRecordsPerPage.
SelectedValue)

    Dim CurrentPage As Integer = PageIndex
    If CurrentPage > 0 Then CurrentPage = CurrentPage - 1

    ' use the filter procedure to retrieve the records
    colEmployees = objEmployees.GetEmployeesByFilter
                    (ModuleId, ddlManagerNo.SelectedItem.Value,
                        ddlSalaryRange.SelectedItem.Value,
                        CurrentPage, PageSize, TotalRecords)

    If colEmployees.Count > 0 Then
        grdResults.Visible = True
        grdResults.DataSource = colEmployees
        grdResults.DataBind()

        ctlPagingControl.Visible = (PageSize < TotalRecords)
        InitializePaging(ctlPagingControl, TotalRecords, PageSize)
    Else
        ' hide the controls that need data
        grdResults.Visible = False
        ctlPagingControl.Visible = False
    End If

End Sub
```

8. After the `BindData` procedure add this new procedure:

```
Private Sub InitializePaging(ByVal ctlPagingControl As
                            DotNetNuke.UI.WebControls.
                                                    PagingControl,
                            ByVal TotalRecords As Integer,
                            ByVal PageSize As Integer)

    ctlPagingControl.TotalRecords = TotalRecords
    ctlPagingControl.PageSize = PageSize
    ctlPagingControl.CurrentPage = PageIndex
    Dim strQuerystring As String = ""
    If ddlRecordsPerPage.SelectedIndex <> 0 Then
        strQuerystring += "&PageRecords=" +
                                ddlRecordsPerPage.SelectedValue
    End If

    ctlPagingControl.QuerystringParams = strQuerystring
    ctlPagingControl.TabID = TabId
End Sub
```

9. Next, find the `Page_Init` procedure and add this code to the very top:

```
Private Sub Page_Init(ByVal sender As System.Object,
                    ByVal e As System.EventArgs)
                                            Handles MyBase.Init

    If Not Request.QueryString("CurrentPage") Is Nothing Then
        PageIndex = CType(Request.QueryString("CurrentPage"),
                                                        Integer)
    End If

    ' Format the columns of the grid control

    For Each column As DataGridColumn In grdResults.Columns
```

10. Scroll down to the `Page_Load` procedure and add this code inside the `IsPostBack` check, just before the binding calls:

```
If Not Page.IsPostBack Then

    If Not Request.QueryString("PageRecords") Is Nothing Then
        ddlRecordsPerPage.SelectedValue =
                            Request.QueryString("PageRecords")
    End If

    BindManagerDropDown()
    BindSalaryDropDown()

    BindData()

End If
```

11. Finally, scroll down to the bottom of the `Event Handlers` region and add this code to trap when the drop-down list is changed:

```
Private Sub ddlRecordsPerPage_SelectedIndexChanged
        (ByVal sender As System.Object,
         ByVal e As System.EventArgs) Handles
                        ddlRecordsPerPage.SelectedIndexChanged
    PageIndex = 1
    BindData()
End Sub
```

12. Double-click to open the `DataProvider.vb` file.

13. Replace `GetEmployeesByFilter` with this new version that includes paging arguments:

```
Public MustOverride Function GetEmployeesByFilter
                            (ByVal ModuleId As Integer,
                             ByVal MgrFilter As Integer,
                             ByVal SalaryFilter As Integer,
                             ByVal PageIndex As Integer,
                             ByVal PageSize As Integer)
                                    As IDataReader
```

14. Double-click to open the `SqlDataProvider.vb` file.

15. Replace `GetEmployeesByFilter` with this new version:

```
Public Overrides Function GetEmployeesByFilter
                            (ByVal ModuleId As Integer,
                             ByVal MgrFilter As Integer,
                             ByVal SalaryFilter As Integer,
                             ByVal PageIndex As Integer,
                             ByVal PageSize As Integer)
                                    As IDataReader
        Return CType(SqlHelper.ExecuteReader
                        (ConnectionString, GetFullyQualifiedName
                        ("GetEmployeesByFilter"), ModuleId,
                        MgrFilter, SalaryFilter, PageIndex,
                                    PageSize), IDataReader)
End Function
```

16. Double-click to open the `EmployeeController.vb` file.

17. As we have added new arguments for the `GetEmployeesByFiler` routine, change the code as follows:

```
Public Function GetEmployeesByFilter(ByVal ModuleId As Integer,
                            ByVal MgrFilter As Integer,
                            ByVal SalaryFilter As Integer,
                            ByVal PageIndex As Integer,
                            ByVal PageSize As Integer,
                    ByRef TotalRecords As Integer) As ArrayList
```

```
Dim dr As IDataReader =
    DataProvider.Instance.GetEmployeesByFilter
    (ModuleId, MgrFilter, SalaryFilter, PageIndex, PageSize)
Dim retValue As ArrayList = Nothing
Try
    While dr.Read
        TotalRecords = Convert.ToInt32(dr("TotalRecords"))
    End While
    dr.NextResult()
    retValue = CBO.FillCollection(dr, GetType(EmployeeInfo))
Finally
    If Not dr Is Nothing Then
        dr.Close()
    End If
End Try
Return retValue

End Function
```

18. We're using the `Try/Finally` structure to trap any errors that might occur from the stored procedure. If there's a problem, the `Finally` clause will close the data reader for a clean exit.

19. Next, double-click to open the `01.00.00.SqlDataProvider` file.

 If you have already installed this module once, you can create a new file called `01.00.01.SqlDataProvider` to hold the new procedure. For details see the recipe *Deploying a new module version* in *Chapter 11*.

20. To update the stored procedure we need to take the original `GetEmployeesByFilter` procedure from the last recipe and add the code that will provide the paging. It works by saving the filtered results into a temporary table, giving each record an index value, then only returning the records that fall in the range for the selected page. For example, if we are showing ten records per page (`PageSize=10`) and we are looking at page three (which has a `PageIndex` of `2`), the procedure should return records 21-30. Look at the stored procedure code and add the lines highlighted below:

```
CREATE procedure {databaseOwner}
                {objectQualifier}ACME_GetEmployeesByFilter
    @ModuleID int,
    @MgrFilter int,
    @SalaryFilter  int,
    @PageIndex int,
    @PageSize int
AS
```

```
/** If we pass -1 for a numeric filter it means ignore the filter
**/

   DECLARE @PageLowerBound int
   DECLARE @PageUpperBound int

/** Calculate the upper and lower bonds based on the PageIndex and
PageSize  **/

   SET @PageLowerBound = @PageSize * @PageIndex
   SET @PageUpperBound = @PageLowerBound + @PageSize + 1

/** create a temp table to hold the Ids of our results  **/
   CREATE TABLE #PageIndex
   (
      IndexID     int IDENTITY (1, 1) NOT NULL,
      ItemId   int
   )

/** populate the temp temp with the filtered results **/
   INSERT INTO #PageIndex (ItemId)
   SELECT ItemId
    FROM {objectQualifier}ACME_Employee
   WHERE (ModuleId = @ModuleId) AND  (ManagerNo = @MgrFilter OR @
MgrFilter = -1) AND (Salary >= @SalaryFilter)
   ORDER BY ItemId DESC

/** remember the count of the results  **/

   SELECT COUNT(*) as TotalRecords
   FROM #PageIndex

/** join the filtered Ids to the employee table to get our fields
**/

select Emp.ModuleId,
      Emp.ItemId,
      EmpFirstName,
      EmpLastName,
      ManagerNo,
      HireDate,
      Salary,
      Emp.CreatedByUser,
      Emp.CreatedDate,
      'CreatedByUserName' = Usr.FirstName + ' ' + Usr.LastName
FROM {objectQualifier}ACME_Employee As Emp
INNER JOIN {objectQualifier}Users As Usr on Emp.CreatedByUser =
                                                Usr.UserId
   INNER JOIN #PageIndex PageIndex
      ON Emp.ItemId = PageIndex.ItemId
   WHERE ( (PageIndex.IndexID > @PageLowerBound) OR
                                @PageLowerBound is null )
```

```
AND ( (PageIndex.IndexID < @PageUpperBound) OR
                                @PageUpperBound is null )
ORDER BY
    PageIndex.IndexID

GO
```

 If you paste this code directly into the SQL form under the **Host** menu, change the first line to ALTER PROCEDURE... as the procedure already exists.

21. Select **Save All** from the **File** menu.

22. Test the results by rebuilding and redeploying the module. The new records per page control will display and the page control will appear at the bottom if you have more records than will fit (you need at least eleven records in this example to see the paging control).

How it works...

This last recipe brings together all the pieces in this chapter. We have a Datagrid control with filter controls populated from the database. We have a paging control and adjustable page sizes. Lastly, we have a collapsible panel so we can show or hide the filters.

7
Cool Web Controls

In this chapter we will cover the following topics:

- ► Adding web controls to your Toolbox
- ► Showing an e-mail link in a Datagrid
- ► Showing checkboxes in a Datagrid
- ► Showing a thumbnail image in a Datagrid
- ► Creating labels you can edit
- ► Suggest text while typing
- ► Showing data in a Treeview
- ► Using a Tabstrip to separate content
- ► Using a CAPTCHA control for security
- ► Creating a multi-state checkbox

Introduction

One of the powerful features of DNN is the variety of flexible and reusable controls that are available for custom module development. These include many of the web controls seen on the core DNN pages, controls such as editable labels, tree views, CAPTCHA controls, and Tab controls. In this chapter, we will see how to add these web controls to custom modules and tie them to the tables in the database.

In general, using these controls requires four simple steps:

- ► Adding the control code to the View or Edit `.ascx` file
- ► Adding a new property to the info object that will supply the values for the control
- ► Binding the control to the values
- ► Capturing the value from the control and saving to the database (if Edit page)

As the recipes in this chapter focus on web controls and values from the database, it is necessary that you have built and deployed the sample Employee module from *Chapter 6*. We will also extend the Datagrid from the *Chapter 6* and show the different kinds of columns it can display.

Adding web controls to your Toolbox

If you frequently use the visual editor in the development tool to layout your pages, this short recipe will show you how to add the DNN web controls to the Toolbox.

How to do it...

1. Launch the Development Tool.
2. Change the editor to Design mode.
3. Make sure the toolbox is displayed.
4. Right-click on the toolbox and select **Choose Items...**.
5. Click on the **Browse** button.
6. Navigate to the /bin folder within the DNN source (DNNSource/website/bin).

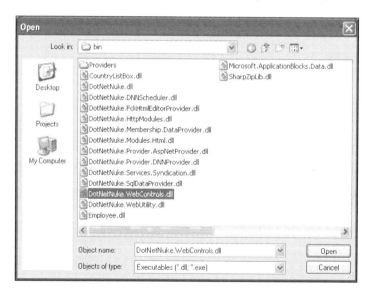

7. Select the DotNetNuke.Webcontrols.dll and click on **Open**.
8. Make sure the DNN controls are checked and click on **OK**.
9. The web controls will now appear under the **General** section of the toolbox when you edit your code.

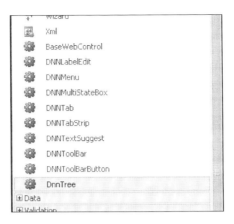

10. Next, we need to add a reference to `DotNetNuke.WebUtility.dll`. Right-click on the **Employee** project in the **Solution Explorer** and select **Add Reference...**.

11. In the pop-up dialog, click on the **Browse** tab and navigate to the folder holding the DNN source files (for example, `My Documents\DNNSource\Website\bin`).

12. Select the file `DotNetNuke.WebUtility.dll` and click on **OK**.

Showing an e-mail link in an Datagrid

As we have seen in the previous chapter, the Datagrid control is perfect for showing records from the database in a neatly formatted table. But the Datagrid can show many other types of information and in this recipe we will see how to display an e-mail hyperlink in a column.

Getting ready

In this recipe, we will extend the Datagrid from the end of *Chapter 6*. To follow along you should successfully have completed and deployed the project *Displaying a Datagrid with filter controls*.

 In this recipe we are using a function to generate an e-mail address for our example. This keeps the recipe simple, but isn't really practical. In a real production environment you would store this in the database as part of the Employee table.

How to do it...

1. Launch the Development Tool and load the **Employee** project.

2. Double-click to open the `ViewEmployee.ascx` file.

3. Locate the Datagrid in the code and add a new column just after the **Salary** column:

```
<dnn:textcolumn datafield="Salary" headertext="Salary"/>

<asp:TemplateColumn HeaderText="Email Contact">
    <itemtemplate>

    <asp:HyperLink id="hlEmail"
            NavigateUrl='<%# "mailto:" & DataBinder.Eval
                        (Container.DataItem,"ContactEmail")
                                                        %>'
            Text='<%# DataBinder.Eval
                        (Container.DataItem,"ContactEmail")
                                                        %>'
            Target="_new"
            runat="server"      />
    </ItemTemplate>
    </asp:TemplateColumn>


    </Columns>
</asp:datagrid>
```

4. Next, open the `EmployeeInfo.vb` file.

5. Find the `Public Properties` section and add the read-only property `EmailAddress` to provide an e-mail address constructed from the employee name:

```
' public properties

Public ReadOnly Property EmailAddress() As String
    Get
        Return _EmpFirstName.Substring(0, 1) +
                        _EmpLastName + "@yourcompany.com"
    End Get
End Property
```

6. Select **Save All** from the **File** menu.

7. To check the results, build and deploy the module to a development portal for testing (for instructions see the recipe *Deploying a module as a standalone package* in *Chapter 5*).

8. Go to the **ACME Employee** page to see the list of employees. The new e-mail hyperlink will appear on the right-hand side.

How it works...

In this recipe we saw the tasks to show an e-mail hyperlink in a Datagrid control:

▸ We took the Datagrid control from the previous recipe and added a new template column holding an e-mail hyperlink control

▸ We added a new property to the `EmployeeInfo` object to provide an e-mail address for the Datagrid

Showing checkboxes in a Datagrid

An element that is useful to display in a Datagrid is a checkbox-like image to indicate the status of the database record. These are not functioning checkboxes but rather a visual indicator showing the data to be true or false.

The control works by having two images, one with a checkmark that is shown when the value is true. The other is an unchecked image that is shown when the value is false.

 This recipe will work with any image indicating true or false. Checkbox-like images are used in other DNN modules so they are familiar to users, but you can experiment with your own images as well.

This recipe has two basic steps:

▸ We will create a new property of the `EmployeeInfo` object called `NewHire`. This property checks the date of hire from the database and returns `true` if the employee was hired less than 30 days ago.

▸ We will add a new column to the Datagrid that evaluates the `NewHire` property and shows one image if the `NewHire` is true and another image if the `NewHire` is false.

Getting ready

In this recipe we will extend the Datagrid that we created in *Chapter 6*. To follow along you should have successfully completed and deployed the project *Displaying a Datagrid with filter controls*.

How to do it...

1. Launch the Development Tool and load the **Employee** project.

2. Double-click to open the `ViewEmployee.ascx` file.

3. The first step is to add a new column to the Datagrid that will show the checkbox images. We will use the `Eval` function to check the `NewHire` function. Locate the Datagrid and add a new column just after the `Salary` column:

```
<dnn:textcolumn datafield="Salary" headertext="Salary"/>

<asp:TemplateColumn HeaderText="New Hire">
  <itemtemplate>
    <asp:Image Runat="server" ID="imgApproved"
               ImageUrl="~/images/checked.gif" Visible='
 <%# DataBinder.Eval(Container.DataItem,"NewHire")="1" %>'/>
    <asp:Image Runat="server" ID="imgNotApproved"
               ImageUrl="~/images/unchecked.gif" Visible=
'<%# DataBinder.Eval(Container.DataItem,"NewHire")="0" %>'/>
  </ItemTemplate>
</asp:TemplateColumn>


</Columns>
</asp:datagrid>
```

4. Next, open the `EmployeeInfo.vb` file.

5. Find the `Public Properties` section and add the read-only property `NewHire` that returns `true` or `false` if the employee was hired in the last 30 days:

```
' public properties

    Public ReadOnly Property NewHire() As Boolean
        Get
            Return (Today() - _HireDate).Days < 30
        End Get
    End Property
```

6. Select **Save All** from the **File** menu.

7. To check the results, build and deploy the module to a development portal for testing (for instructions see the recipe *Deploying a module as a standalone package* in *Chapter 5*).

8. Go to the **ACME Employee** page to see the list of employees. The new checkbox will appear on the right-hand side.

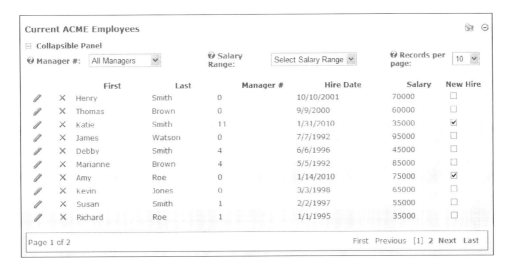

9. Although you cannot click on these checkboxes, they do provide a clear and easy to understand visual status for the records.

How it works...

In this recipe we saw the tasks to show checkbox images in a Datagrid control:

- ▶ We took the Datagrid control from the previous recipe and added a new template column holding two image controls, one checked and the other unchecked.

- ▶ We added a new property to the `EmployeeInfo` object that returns `true` or `false` depending on the database record.

- ▶ We bound the property to the control so that if the property was `true` then the checked image was displayed. If the property was `false` the unchecked image was displayed.

Showing a thumbnail image in a Datagrid

Datagrids are a flexible control that can display a variety of information. In this recipe, we will see how to display a small thumbnail image in the Datagrid based on information in the Employee table.

Getting ready

In this recipe we will extend the Datagrid that we created in *Chapter 6*. To follow along you should have successfully completed and deployed the project *Displaying a Datagrid with filter controls*.

How to do it...

1. First prepare some thumbnail images to display. Generally 64x64 is a good size but you can experiment and see what looks good. To keep it simple, name the images based on the employee name–first initial, and last name with .PNG extension.

ssmith.png   rroe.png   jsmith.png

2. Now we need to upload the images to the DNN site. Log in as Host user (`syshost` in our examples).

3. Look under the **Admin** menu and select **File Manager.** Make sure **Portal Root** appears on the left side:

4. Type **SiteImages** in the folder name textbox and click on **Add Folder**.

5. Click on the **Upload** link.

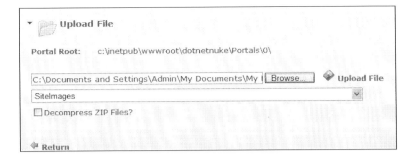

6. Click on the **Browse** button and select a sample image.

7. Click on **Upload File** to upload the image. Repeat for each image you have.

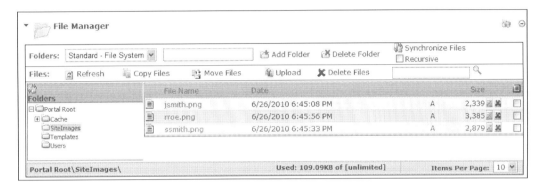

8. With the images available to the site, we put the code in our module to display the images when we display employees.

9. Launch the Development Tool and load the **Employee** project.

10. Double-click to open the ViewEmployee.ascx file.

11. Locate the Datagrid and add a new column just after the **Edit** and **Delete** links:

```
<columns>
    <dnn:imagecommandcolumn CommandName="Edit" ImageUrl=
      "~/images/edit.gif" EditMode="URL" KeyField="ItemID" />
      <dnn:imagecommandcolumn CommandName="Delete" ImageUrl=
        "~/images/delete.gif" KeyField="ItemID" />


    <asp:TemplateColumn HeaderText="Icon">
      <itemtemplate>


      <asp:HyperLink id="imgView"
        ImageUrl='<%# DataBinder.Eval
                          (Container.DataItem,"ImageURL") %>'
```

```
            NavigateUrl='<%# DataBinder.Eval
                          (Container.DataItem,"ImageURL") %>'
            Text='<%# DataBinder.Eval
                          (Container.DataItem,"ContactInfo") %>'
            Target="_new"
            runat="server"/>


        </ItemTemplate>
    </asp:TemplateColumn>


    <dnn:textcolumn datafield="EmpFirstName"
                              headertext="First" />
```

12. Next, open the `EmployeeInfo.vb` file.

13. Find the `Public Properties` section and add the read-only property `ImageURL` that returns the URL of the images we uploaded (based on employee name):

```
' public properties

Public ReadOnly Property ImageURL() As String
    Get
        Return "~\Portals\_default\SiteImages\" +
          _EmpFirstName.Substring(0, 1) + _EmpLastName + ".png"
    End Get
End Property

Public ReadOnly Property ContactInfo() As String
    Get
        Return _EmpFirstName + " " + _EmpLastName + " Hired: " +
                                      FormattedHireDate()
    End Get
End Property
```

14. Select **Save All** from the **File** menu.

15. To check the results, build and deploy the module to a development portal for testing (for instructions see the recipe *Deploying a module as a standalone package* in *Chapter 5*).

16. Go to the **ACME Employee** page to see the list of employees. The employee images will appear on the left side.

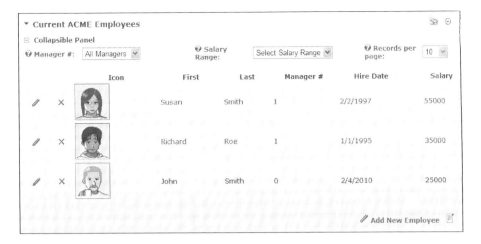

How it works...

In this recipe we saw the tasks to show images in a Datagrid control:

▶ We created a set of images and uploaded them to the DNN site.

▶ We took the Datagrid control from the previous recipe and added a new template column holding an image hyperlink control.

▶ We added a new property to the `EmployeeInfo` object that provided the image URL for the hyperlink.

There's more...

In this recipe the image is displayed in the Datagrid, but there is no navigation attached to it. To see how to create a thumbnail image you can click on and navigate, see the recipe *Controlling navigation with NavigateURL* in *Chapter 12* for more information.

Creating labels you can edit

We have seen the label control in previous recipes, but in this recipe we will see how to create editable labels using the `DNNLabelEdit` control. You can see the `DNNLabelEdit` control at work in the Module titles of the DNN site that allows the administrator to edit the module titles directly on the page.

Getting ready

To follow along with this recipe you must have completed the following recipes:

▸ *Deploying a module as a standalone package*

▸ *Adding web controls to your Toolbox*

One of the important parts of this recipe is that once a label has been changed, we must save the new text somewhere. Fortunately DNN provides a place to save it: in the module settings. The module settings apply to all instances of a module regardless of how many pages they appear on (unlike Tab Module settings which are settings for a particular instance of a module). To access the module settings we use the routine `UpdateModuleSetting`, pass our module ID, a setting name, and setting value.

How to do it...

1. Launch the Development Tool and load the **Employee** project.

2. Double-click to open the `EditEmployee.ascx` file.

3. Make sure the following register directive is at the top of the file:

```
<%@ Register tagprefix="DNN" assembly="DotNetNuke.WebControls"
             namespace="DotNetNuke.UI.WebControls" %>
```

4. Find the HTML table holding the label and text controls and note the existing label control for the employee first name:

```
<table width="650" cellspacing="0" cellpadding="0" border="0"
        summary="Edit Table">
<tr valign="top">
    <td class="SubHead" width="125">
    <dnn:label id="lblEmpFirstName" runat="server"
            controlname="lblEmpFirstName" suffix=":">
     </dnn:label>
    </td>
<td>
<asp:TextBox ID="txtEmpFirstName" runat="server"></asp:TextBox>
```

5. Delete the original label control and replace it with this new label code. The source code will now look like this:

```
<table width="650" cellspacing="0" cellpadding="0" border="0"
        summary="Edit Table">
<tr valign="top">
    <td class="SubHead" width="125">
    <DNN:DNNLabelEdit ID="dleEmpFirstName" runat="server" >[click
                                                here to edit]
    </DNN:DNNLabelEdit>
```

```
            </td>
<td>
<asp:TextBox ID="txtEmpFirstName" runat="server"></asp:TextBox>
```

6. This is enough to let us edit the label, but we want to save the text changes as well. To do that we must handle the event when a label is retyped and save the information. Begin by opening the `EditEmployee.ascx.vb` file.

7. Create a new event handler by pasting this code at the end of the **Event Handlers** region:

```
Private Sub dleEmpFirstName_UpdateLabel(ByVal sender As Object,
      ByVal e As DotNetNuke.UI.WebControls.DNNLabelEditEventArgs)
                               Handles dleEmpFirstName.UpdateLabel


      Dim modCtrl As New
                    DotNetNuke.Entities.Modules.ModuleController
      Dim strLabel As String = e.text.tostring()


      ' save the updated label text in the module settings


      modCtrl.UpdateModuleSetting(ModuleId, "EmpFirstName",
                                                    strLabel)



    End Sub
```

8. Lastly, add the following code to the `Page_Load` procedure:

```
If Page.IsPostBack = False Then


      ' load the label text from the module settings


      Dim strLabelText As String = CType(Settings("EmpFirstName"),
                                                          String)


      ' if no text was saved in module settings, set it to [click
                                                     here to edit]
      If strLabelText Is Nothing Then
         ' pull the default label text from the resource file
         strLabelText = Localization.GetString("lblEmpFirstName",
                                                  LocalResourceFile)
      End If
      dleEmpFirstName.Text = strLabelText
```

9. Select **Save All** from the **File** menu.

10. To check the results, build and deploy the module to a development portal for testing (for instructions see the recipe *Deploying a module as a standalone package* in Chapter 5).

11. Go to the **ACME Employee** page and click on the edit icon (the little pencil) next to an employee to display the **Edit Employee** page.

12. Clicking on the label will unlock it and allow you to type a new label. When you leave the page the text is automatically saved. When you return, the label will show the new text.

How it works...

In this recipe we saw the tasks to create a DNNLabelEdit control:

▶ We placed the control in the .ascx file

▶ In the code behind the file we added an event handler to save the label text when it changes

▶ We changed the Page_Load procedure to read the label text from the database

Suggest text while typing

The DNNTextSuggest control is a textbox that watches user input and suggests text as the user types. This behavior is frequently seen in search engines and other websites.

This control works by having a list of possible text phrases that it can search through as the user types. In this recipe, we will demonstrate this control by using the list of U.S. geographical states that is part of the DNN site along with a new field on the **Edit Employee** page.

Getting ready

To follow along with this recipe you must have completed the following recipes:

▶ *Deploying a module as a standalone package*

▶ *Adding web controls to your Toolbox*

How to do it...

1. Launch the Development Tool and load the **Employee** project.

2. In the **Solution Explorer**, look under the references and make sure your project includes a reference to `DotNetNuke.WebUtility.dll`.

3. Double-click to open the `EditEmployee.ascx` file.

4. Make sure the following register directive is at the top of the file:

```
<%@ Register tagprefix="DNN" assembly="DotNetNuke.WebControls"
             namespace="DotNetNuke.UI.WebControls" %>
```

5. We're going to add a new row to the HTML table holding the Employee fields. Find the HTML table and insert the following code just before the `</TABLE>` tag.

```
<tr valign="top">
    <td class="SubHead" width="200"><dnn:label id="lblSalary"
                        runat="server" controlname="lblSalary"
                                                   suffix=":">
                        </dnn:label>
    </td>
    <td>
    <asp:TextBox ID="txtSalary" runat="server"></asp:TextBox>
    <asp:RequiredFieldValidator ID="valSalary"
                        resourcekey="valSalary.ErrorMessage"
                                ControlToValidate="txtSalary"
    CssClass="NormalRed" Display="Dynamic"
      ErrorMessage="<br>Salary is required" Runat="server" />
    </td>
</tr>

  <tr valign="top">
    <td class="SubHead" width="200">
        <dnn:label id="lblState" runat="server"
                controlname="lblState" suffix=":">
        </dnn:label>
    </td>
    <td>
        <DNN:DNNTextSuggest ID="txtState" runat="server">
        </DNN:DNNTextSuggest>
    </td>
  </tr>

</table>
```

6. Next, open the `EditEmployee.ascx.vb` file.

7. Check the top the file and make sure it has the following imports:

```
Imports DotNetNuke.UI.WebControls
Imports DotNetNuke.Common.Lists
```

8. Scroll down to the `Private Methods` region and add this procedure:

```
#Region "Private Methods"

Private Sub SuggestText(ByVal objNodes As DNNNodeCollection,
                        ByVal strTypedText As String)

    Dim nodeStates As DNNNode
    Dim objList As New ListController()
    Dim lstStates As ListEntryInfoCollection =
            objList.GetListEntryInfoCollection("Region",
                                               "Country.US")
    Dim state As ListEntryInfo

    'loop through the collection and add it to the result set

    For Each state In lstStates
    If txtState.MaxSuggestRows = 0 Or objNodes.Count <
                                  (txtState.MaxSuggestRows + 1)
Then
        ' add the state to the list of suggestions
        nodeStates = New DNNNode(state.Text)
        nodeStates.ID = state.Value
        objNodes.Add(nodeStates)
    End If
    Next

End Sub
```

9. Next, we must trap when text is typed into the control. Scroll down to the bottom of the `Event Handlers` region and add the following procedure:

```
Private Sub txtState_UpdateLabel(ByVal sender As Object, ByVal e
            As DotNetNuke.UI.WebControls.DNNTextSuggestEventArgs)
                               Handles txtState.PopulateOnDemand

    ' call the suggestion procedure and pass the text typed into
                                                    the control
    SuggestText(e.Nodes, e.Text)

End Sub

#End Region
```

10. Lastly, as we included a new label control, open the `EditEmployee.ascx.resx` file (under `/App_LocalResources`) and set the label text and Help prompt:

    `lblState.Text`: **Home State**

    `lblState.Help`: **Type the name of the employee's home state.**

lblState.Text	Home State	
lslState.Help	Type the name of the employee's home state.	

11. Select **Save All** from the **File** menu.

12. To check the results, build and deploy the module to a development portal for testing (for instructions see the recipe *Deploying a module as a standalone package* in *Chapter 5*).

13. Go to the **ACME Employee** page and click on the edit icon (the little pencil) next to an employee to display the **Edit Employee** page.

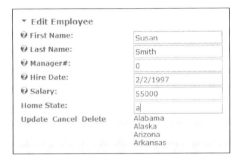

14. The new **Home State** field appears at the bottom. Unlike the other text fields, as you type the name of a **Home State**, the suggestion list will appear below the box. Click on the state name in the list and it will appear in the text box.

How it works...

In this recipe we saw the tasks to create a `DNNTextSuggest` control:

► We placed the control in the `.ascx` file

► In the code behind file we added a new procedure called `SuggestText`

► The `SuggestText` procedure loaded the list of U.S. geographical states from the DNN core and created a list of suggestions

► We added an event handler on the `DNNTextSuggest` control to display the list of suggestions when text is typed

In this recipe we saw how the `SuggestText` web control works and how it is used to prompt for a text value. To keep the recipe simple it did not include the necessary code to load and save the value to the database. For a quick review of adding fields to the database and routines to load and save values, see the recipe *Connecting a module to the database* in *Chapter 4*.

Showing data in a Treeview

A Treeview control is used when you have information arranged in a hierarchy like the organizational chart of a company. The Treeview control will show each level in the hierarchy with an icon to drill-down or expand to the next level.

Getting ready

To follow along with this recipe you must have completed the following recipes:

▶ *Deploying a module as a standalone package* (from *Chapter 5*)

▶ *Displaying a Datagrid with filter controls*

▶ *Adding web controls to your Toolbox*

The Treeview control requires that the employees in the Employee table have been assigned to managers. Here is the data that was used in this recipe:

ItemID	EmpFirstName	EmpLastName	ManagerNo	HireDate	Salary	CreatedByUser	CreatedDate
1	John	Smith	0	2/4/2010 12:00:...	25000	1	2/4/2010 9:33:0...
13	Richard	Roe	0	1/1/1995 12:00:...	35000	1	2/1/2010 7:25:2...
14	Susan	Smith	0	2/2/1997 12:00:...	55000	1	2/1/2010 12:00:...
23	Kevin	Jones	1	3/3/1998 12:00:...	65000	1	2/1/2010 12:00:...
24	Amy	Roe	1	4/4/1999 12:00:...	90000	1	2/12/2010 8:27:...
25	Marianne	Brown	13	5/5/1992 12:00:...	30000	1	2/12/2010 8:28:...
26	Debby	Smith	14	6/6/1996 12:00:...	90000	1	2/12/2010 8:27:...
NULL	NULL	NULL	NULL	NULL	NULL	NULL	NULL

In this example, the employees are arranged in a simple two-level hierarchy. If your ManagerNo is 0 it means you are a manager. Otherwise the manager number on your record is the ItemID of your manager. So John Smith is a manager (his `ManagerNo=0`) and he manages Kevin Jones and Amy Roe (as their ManagerNo is John Smith's ItemID).

How to do it...

1. Launch the Development Tool and load the **Employee** project.

2. In the **Solution Explorer**, look under the references and make sure your project includes a reference to `DotNetNuke.WebUtility.dll`.

3. Double-click to open the `ViewEmployee.ascx` file.

4. Start by adding a new register directive at the top of the file:

```
<%@ Register tagprefix="DNN" assembly="DotNetNuke.WebControls"
             namespace="DotNetNuke.UI.WebControls" %>
```

5. Next, we'll create a simple tree control by placing the following code at the bottom of the file, right after the paging control:

```
<dnn:PagingControl ID="ctlPagingControl" runat="server">
</dnn:PagingControl>
<br />

<DNN:DnnTree ID="treeManager" runat="server"
    CollapsedNodeImage="~\images\plus.gif"
    ExpandedNodeImage="~\images\minus.gif">
</DNN:DnnTree>
```

6. Next, open the `ViewEmployee.ascx.vb` file.

7. Look at the top of the file and make sure the following imports are there:

```
Imports System.Data.SqlClient
Imports DotNetNuke.UI.WebControls
```

8. We must create a procedure to populate the tree control with records from the database. Find the `Private Methods` region at the top of the file and add the following new procedures:

```
#Region "Private Methods"

Private Sub PopulateTreeControl()

    ' set the images to use for the nodes
    treeManager.ImageList.Add("..\images\icon_hostusers_16px.gif")
    treeManager.ImageList.Add("..\images\icon_users_16px.gif")

    ' reset the tree control
    treeManager.TreeNodes.Clear()

    Dim objParentNode As TreeNode
```

```
' get the list of all managers and create a parent node for
                                                    each one

    Dim objEmployeeController As New EmployeeController
    Dim drMgr As SqlDataReader
    drMgr = objEmployeeController.GetManagersDR(ModuleId)

    If drMgr.HasRows Then
Do While drMgr.Read()

    objParentNode = New TreeNode()

    objParentNode.Text = drMgr("EmpLastName") + ", " +
        drMgr("EmpFirstName")
    objParentNode.ImageIndex = 0 ' manager image
    objParentNode.ClickAction = eClickAction.Expand ' when
                                click on a manager, expand
    objParentNode.HasNodes = True
    treeManager.TreeNodes.Add(objParentNode)

    PopulateEmployeeNodes(objParentNode, drMgr("ItemId"))
Loop

    End If

    drMgr.Close()

End Sub

Private Sub PopulateEmployeeNodes(ByRef objParentNode As TreeNode,
                                ByVal ParentItemId As Integer)

    Dim objChildNode As TreeNode

    ' get the list of all employee with the given manager

    Dim objEmployeeController As New EmployeeController
    Dim colEmployees As ArrayList
    Dim objEmployeeInfo As EmployeeInfo
    Dim TotalRecords As Integer
    colEmployees = objEmployeeController.GetEmployeesByFilter
                (ModuleId, ParentItemId, -1, 0, 1000,
                                        TotalRecords)
```

```
        If colEmployees.Count > 0 Then
        ' add a node to the parent that was passed

        For intEmp = 0 To colEmployees.Count - 1
            objEmployeeInfo = CType(colEmployees(intEmp), EmployeeInfo)
            objChildNode = New TreeNode(objEmployeeInfo.EmpLastName +
                                ", " + objEmployeeInfo.EmpFirstName)
            objChildNode.ImageIndex = 1 ' employee image
            objParentNode.TreeNodes.Add(objChildNode)
        Next intEmp


        End If


    End Sub

    #End Region
```

9. What we are doing here is calling a new `GetManagersDR` function for the first level of the tree, then calling the `GetEmployeesByFilter` function from *Chapter 6* to get the list of employees for each manager.

10. Next, we need to call these new procedures when the page loads, so scroll down to the `Page_Load` procedure and add the following code inside the `IsPostBack` check:

```
If Page.IsPostBack = False Then

    If Not Request.QueryString("PageRecords") Is Nothing Then
    ddlRecordsPerPage.SelectedValue =
                            Request.QueryString("PageRecords")
    End If

    BindManagerDropDown()
    BindSalaryDropDown()

    BindData()

    PopulateTreeControl()
End If
```

11. Next, open the `EmployeeController.vb` file.

12. The last step is to create the new `GetManagersDR` function. This is just like the `GetManagers` function from *Chapter 6*, but this time the function returns the list of managers as a DataReader. Add the following code to the bottom of the `Public Methods` region:

```
Public Function GetManagersDR(ByVal ModuleId As Integer) As
    SqlDataReader
    Return DataProvider.Instance().GetManagers(ModuleId)
End Function
```

```
#End Region
```

13. Select **Save All** from the **File** menu.

14. To check the results, build and deploy the module to a development portal for testing (for instructions see the recipe *Deploying a module as a standalone package* in *Chapter 5*).

15. Go to the **ACME Employee** page to see the list of employees in a tree control.

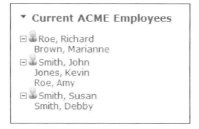

How it works...

In this recipe we saw the tasks to organize database records in a hierarchy tree control:

▶ We placed the control in the `.ascx` file

▶ We defined the images to use for the expand and collapse indicators

▶ In the code behind file we changed the `Page_Load` procedure to populate the tree

▶ We created a `PopulateTreeControl` procedure with two parts:

    ❑ Query the database for the employee managers

    ❑ For each manager add them to the tree and query the database for the employees they manage

Using a TabStrip to separate content

There are many times when you have a lot of information to display, but not enough space on the page. The TabStrip control maximizes the available space by separating the content into tabs and displaying one tab at a time.

To demonstrate this control we're going to take the five fields of the **Edit Employee** page and split them onto two different tabs.

Getting ready

To follow along with this recipe you must have completed the following recipes:

- *Adding web controls to your Toolbox*
- *Deploying a module as a standalone package* (from *Chapter 5*)

How to do it...

1. Launch the Development Tool and load the **Employee** project.

2. In the **Solution Explorer**, look under the references and make sure your project includes a reference to `DotNetNuke.WebUtility.dll`.

3. Double-click to open the `EditEmployee.ascx` file.

4. Make sure the following register directive is at the top of the file:

    ```
    <%@ Register tagprefix="DNN" assembly="DotNetNuke.WebControls"
                 namespace="DotNetNuke.UI.WebControls" %>
    ```

5. We will replace the existing HTML table containing the employee fields with a TabStrip control table holding the name fields under the first tab and the information fields under the second tab. Replace the existing HTML table with the following highlighted code:

    ```
    <DNN:DNNTabStrip
        ID="tsEmployee"
        runat="server"
        TabRenderMode="All"
        CssTabContainer="LoginTabGroup"
        CssContentContainer="LoginContainerGroup"
        DefaultContainerCssClass="LoginContainer"
        DefaultLabel-CssClass="LoginTab"
        DefaultLabel-CssClassHover="LoginTabHover"
        DefaultLabel-CssClassSelected="LoginTabSelected"
        visible="true" >
        <dnn:DNNTab Label-Text="Employee Name" ID="tab1">
    ```

```
                <table width="650" cellspacing="0" cellpadding="0"
                            border="0" summary="Edit Table">
            <tr valign="top">
                <td class="SubHead" width="125"><dnn:label
                    id="lblEmpFirstName" runat="server"
                    controlname="lblEmpFirstName" suffix=":">
                                        </dnn:label>
                </td>
                <td>
                <asp:TextBox ID="txtEmpFirstName" runat="server">
                </asp:TextBox>
                <asp:RequiredFieldValidator ID="valEmpFirstName"
                        resourcekey="valEmpFirstName.ErrorMessage"
                            ControlToValidate="txtEmpFirstName"
                CssClass="NormalRed" Display="Dynamic"
                  ErrorMessage="<br>EmpFirstName is required"
                    Runat="server" />
                </td>
            </tr>


            <tr valign="top">
                <td class="SubHead" width="125"><dnn:label
                    id="lblEmpLastName" runat="server"
                    controlname="lblEmpLastName" suffix=":">
                                        </dnn:label>
                </td>
                <td>
                <asp:TextBox ID="txtEmpLastName" runat="server">
                </asp:TextBox>
                <asp:RequiredFieldValidator ID="valEmpLastName"
                        resourcekey="valEmpLastName.ErrorMessage"
                            ControlToValidate="txtEmpLastName"
                CssClass="NormalRed" Display="Dynamic"
                  ErrorMessage="<br>EmpLastName is required"
                    Runat="server" />
                </td>
            </tr>
        </table>
    </dnn:DNNTab>
    <dnn:DNNTab Label-Text="Information" ID="tab2">
        <table width="650" cellspacing="0" cellpadding="0"
                            border="0" summary="Edit Table">


        <tr valign="top">
```

```
                <td class="SubHead" width="125"><dnn:label
                    id="lblManagerNo" runat="server"
                    controlname="lblManagerNo" suffix=":">
                                            </dnn:label>
                </td>
                <td>
                <asp:TextBox ID="txtManagerNo" runat="server">
                </asp:TextBox>
                <asp:RequiredFieldValidator ID="valManagerNo"
                        resourcekey="valManagerNo.ErrorMessage"
                                ControlToValidate="txtManagerNo"
                CssClass="NormalRed" Display="Dynamic"
                        ErrorMessage="<br>ManagerNo is required"
                        Runat="server" />
                </td>
        </tr>

        <tr valign="top">
                <td class="SubHead" width="125"><dnn:label
                    id="lblHireDate" runat="server"
                    controlname="lblHireDate" suffix=":">
                                                </dnn:label>
                </td>
                <td>
                <asp:TextBox ID="txtHireDate" runat="server">
                </asp:TextBox>
                <asp:RequiredFieldValidator ID="valHireDate"
                            resourcekey="valHireDate.ErrorMessage"
                                ControlToValidate="txtHireDate"
                CssClass="NormalRed" Display="Dynamic"
                  ErrorMessage="<br>HireDate is required"
                      Runat="server" />
                </td>
        </tr>

        <tr valign="top">
                <td class="SubHead" width="125"><dnn:label
                        id="lblSalary" runat="server"
                        controlname="lblSalary" suffix=":">
                                            </dnn:label>
                </td>
                <td>
                <asp:TextBox ID="txtSalary" runat="server">
                </asp:TextBox>
                <asp:RequiredFieldValidator ID="valSalary"
```

```
                              resourcekey="valSalary.ErrorMessage"
                                ControlToValidate="txtSalary"
              CssClass="NormalRed" Display="Dynamic"
              ErrorMessage="<br>Salary is required" Runat="server" />
              </td>
          </tr>

          </table>
      </dnn:DNNTab>
  </dnn:DNNTabStrip>
  <br /><br />

  <p>
      <asp:linkbutton cssclass="CommandButton" id="cmdUpdate"
                    resourcekey="cmdUpdate" runat="server"
                    borderstyle="none" text="Update">
      </asp:linkbutton> 
```

 The appearance of the tab strip is controlled by the styles we apply to it (CssTabContainer, CssContentContainer, DefaultLabel-CssClass, DefaultLabel-CssClassHover, and DefaultLabel-CssClassSelected). In this example we used the same styles as the DNN Login page so we have a similar look and feel. The styles are defined in the /portals/_default/default.css by default.

6. Select **Save All** from the **File** menu.

7. To check the results, build and deploy the module to a development portal for testing (for instructions see the recipe *Deploying a module as a standalone package* in *Chapter 5*).

8. Go to the **ACME Employee** page and click on the edit icon (the little pencil) next to an employee to display the **Edit Employee** page.

9. When you edit the employee record you will see the fields have been separated into two separate tabs. Clicking on **Employee Name** displays the first tab with the name fields:

10. Clicking on **Information** reveals the remaining fields:

How it works...

In this recipe we saw the tasks to use a TabStrip control:

▸ We placed the control in the .ascx file

▸ We separated the existing content onto separate tabs

There's more...

Although the TabStrip is a technique for maximizing your screen "real estate" it is not to be confused with paging that we saw in *Chapter 6*. TabStrips are used in the ASCX file and save space by dividing content onto different tabs. Paging saves space by dividing groups of database records as they are retrieved from the database.

Using a CAPTCHA control for security

CAPTCHA is a technique for detecting when a real person is typing at the keyboard. It works by presenting a word or phrase in an image that has been scrambled enough that a computer cannot read it but a person can.

 Older DNN versions had bugs in the CAPTCHA control. To follow along with this recipe you should make sure your DNN version is 5.1 or later.

In this recipe we will show how to add a CAPTCHA control to a data entry form that will block automated processes from updating a record.

 CAPTCHA is an acronym that stands for "Completely Automated Public Turing test to tell Computers and Humans Apart". You can learn more about CAPTCHA at `http://www.captcha.net`.

Getting ready

To follow along with this recipe you must have completed the following recipes:

- *Adding web controls to your Toolbox*
- *Deploying a module as a standalone package* (from *Chapter 5*)

How to do it...

1. Launch the Development Tool and load the **Employee** project.

2. In the Solution Explorer, look under the references and make sure your project includes a reference to `DotNetNuke.WebUtility.dll`.

3. Double-click to open the `EditEmployee.ascx` file.

4. Make sure the following register directive is at the top of the file:

   ```
   <%@ Register tagprefix="DNN" assembly="DotNetNuke.WebControls"
               namespace="DotNetNuke.UI.WebControls" %>
   ```

5. Scroll down to the bottom of the file and note where the table holding the edit controls ends and the links to save, cancel, or delete are shown:

   ```
   </table>
   <p>
       <asp:linkbutton cssclass="CommandButton" id="cmdUpdate"
                   resourcekey="cmdUpdate" runat="server"
                   borderstyle="none" text="Update">
       </asp:linkbutton> 
   ```

6. Put the following code just after the HTML table and before the links:

   ```
   </table>

   <p>
   <dnn:CaptchaControl ID="btnCaptcha" CaptchaHeight="40"
                                      CaptchaWidth="150"
   ErrorStyle-CssClass="NormalRed" cssclass="Normal" runat="server"
                                      resourcekey="Captcha"
   ErrorMessage="The typed code is case sensitive, must match the
               image and cannot be left blank. Please try again."/>
   </p>

   <p>
       <asp:linkbutton cssclass="CommandButton" id="cmdUpdate"
                   resourcekey="cmdUpdate" runat="server"
                   borderstyle="none" text="Update">
       </asp:linkbutton> 
   ```

7. Next, open the `EditEmployee.ascx.vb` file.

8. As the CAPTCHA control validates before allowing changes, we need to modify the update process to check if the CAPTCHA value has been given before performing the update. Scroll down to the `cmdUpdate_Click` procedure.

9. At the top of the procedure add the first part of an `IF` statement: and place the rest at the bottom of the procedure. The entire procedure should now look like this:

```vb
Private Sub cmdUpdate_Click(ByVal sender As Object,
            ByVal e As EventArgs) Handles cmdUpdate.Click
    Try

        If btnCaptcha.IsValid Then

            Dim objEmployees As New EmployeeController

            Dim objEmployee As EmployeeInfo =
                            New EmployeeInfo

            objEmployee.ModuleId = ModuleId
            objEmployee.ItemId = ItemId
            objEmployee.EmpFirstName =
                            txtEmpFirstName.Text
            objEmployee.EmpLastName = txtEmpLastName.Text
            objEmployee.ManagerNo = txtManagerNo.Text
            objEmployee.HireDate = txtHireDate.Text
            objEmployee.Salary = txtSalary.Text

            objEmployee.CreatedByUser = Me.UserId

            If Common.Utilities.Null.IsNull(ItemId) Then
                ' add the content within the Employee
                                                    table
                objEmployees.AddEmployee(objEmployee)
            Else
                ' update the content within the Employee
                                                    table
                objEmployees.UpdateEmployee(objEmployee)
            End If

            ' Redirect back to the portal home page
            Response.Redirect(NavigateURL(), True)

        End If

    Catch exc As Exception    'Module failed to load
        ProcessModuleLoadException(Me, exc)
    End Try
End Sub
```

10. Select **Save All** from the **File** menu.

11. To check the results, build and deploy the module to a development portal for testing (for instructions see the recipe *Deploying a module as a standalone package* in *Chapter 5*).

12. Go to the **ACME Employee** page and click on the edit icon (the little pencil) next to an employee to display the **Edit Employee** page. At the bottom of the page the CAPTCHA control will appear.

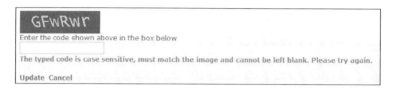

13. When you click on the **Update** link to save any changes to the record it will check that you have filled in the correct CAPTCHA value. If the value doesn't match the image an error message is displayed and the record is not saved.

How it works...

In this recipe we saw the tasks to use a CAPTCHA control:

▶ We placed the control in the .ascx file and set the properties

▶ We modified the normal update procedure to check the CAPTCHA control and only save if the correct value was entered

See also

Other control properties you can set:

Property	Meaning
CaptchaChars	The set of characters that could be used to create the CAPTCHA.
CaptchaHeight	The height of the CAPTCHA image.
CaptchaLength	Total maximum number of characters to use in the CAPTCHA.
CaptchaWidth	The width of the CAPTCHA image.
CssClass	The CSS class for the control.
Text	The prompt Text that is used.

Creating a multi-state checkbox

A checkbox control normally has two possible values (or states): checked and unchecked. The DNN Multi-State checkbox control is used in situations when you want to show a visual indicator for the state of the control but you need more then checked and unchecked.

You can see an example of this with the DNN page security where you grant, deny, or ignore access to a DNN page:

In this recipe we will add a four-state checkbox to the **Edit Employee** page representing the Bonus Level of the employee (None, Small, Medium, and Large) represented by color-coded star icons.

Getting ready

To follow along with this recipe you must have completed the following recipes:

▶ *Adding web controls to your Toolbox*

▶ *Deploying a module as a standalone package* (from *Chapter 5*)

How to do it...

1. Launch the Development Tool and load the **Employee** project.

2. In the Solution Explorer, look under the references and make sure your project includes a reference to `DotNetNuke.WebUtility.dll`.

3. Double-click to open the `EditEmployee.ascx` file.

4. Make sure the following register directive is at the top of the file:

```
<%@ Register tagprefix="DNN" assembly="DotNetNuke.WebControls"
            namespace="DotNetNuke.UI.WebControls" %>
```

5. Scroll down to the bottom of the file and locate the table holding the edit controls. Add a new table row by inserting the following code:

```
<tr valign="top">
    <td class="SubHead" width="125"><dnn:label id="lblBonus"
                    runat="server" controlname="msbBonus"
                                                    suffix=":">
                            </dnn:label>
    </td>
    <td>


    <dnn:DNNMultiStateBox ID="msbBonus" runat="server"
        ImagePath="~/images/">
      <States>
        <dnn:DNNMultiState Key="1" ImageUrl="unchecked.gif"
            DisabledImageUrl="lock.gif" />
        <dnn:DNNMultiState Key="2" ImageUrl="ratingminus.gif"
            DisabledImageUrl="lock.gif" />
        <dnn:DNNMultiState Key="3" ImageUrl="ratingzero.gif"
            DisabledImageUrl="lock.gif" />
        <dnn:DNNMultiState Key="4" ImageUrl="ratingplus.gif"
            DisabledImageUrl="lock.gif" />
      </States>
    </dnn:DNNMultiStateBox>


    </td>
</tr>

</table>
```

6. Next, open the `EditEmployee.ascx.vb` file.

7. Check the top of the file and make sure it has the following imports:

```
Imports DotNetNuke.UI.WebControls
```

8. To set the checkbox when the employee information is displayed, scroll down to the `Page_Load` procedure and add the following code after the existing set values code:

```
txtHireDate.Text = objEmployee.HireDate
txtSalary.Text = objEmployee.Salary

msbBonus.SelectedStateKey = objEmployee.BonusLevel
```

9. Next, scroll down a little more to the `cmdUpdate_Click` procedure and add the following line of code:

```
objEmployee.HireDate = txtHireDate.Text
objEmployee.Salary = txtSalary.Text

objEmployee.BonusLevel = msbBonus.SelectedState.Key

objEmployee.CreatedByUser = Me.UserId

If Common.Utilities.Null.IsNull(ItemId) Then
```

10. Lastly, we need to create a new property that will convert the salary of the employee to a bonus level. Open the `EmployeeInfo.vb` file and add the following code:

```
' public properties

Public Property BonusLevel() As Integer
    Get
        ' use integer division to get 0,1,2,3...
        Return (_Salary \ 30000)
    End Get
    Set(ByVal Value As Integer)
        _Salary = Value * 30000
    End Set
End Property
```

11. As we included a new label control with our new multi-state checkbox, open the `ViewEmployee.ascx.resx` file (under `/App_LocalResources`) and set the label text and Help prompt:

`lblBonus.Text`: **Bonus Level**

`lblBonus.Help`: **Click on the icon to set the salary bonus level.**

lblBonus.Help	Click on the icon to set the salary bonus level.
lblBonus.Text	Bonus Level

12. Select **Save All** from the **File** menu.

13. To check the results, build and deploy the module to a development portal for testing (for instructions see the recipe *Deploying a module as a standalone package* in *Chapter 5*).

14. Go to the **ACME Employee** page and click on the edit icon (the little pencil) next to an employee to display the **Edit Employee** page. The **Bonus Level** will appear at the bottom.

15. Clicking on the **Bonus Level** star icon will change the bonus level which will raise or lower the salary when you update the employee record.

How it works...

In this recipe we saw the tasks to use a multi-state checkbox:

▶ We placed the control in the .ascx file and defined how many states it has

▶ For each state we picked an image

▶ On the page load we set the current state

▶ When a record was updated we saved the state to the database

There's more...

In this example we used existing images from the DNN site, but you are free to upload and use custom images as well. For a quick review of how to upload images to the portal see the recipe *Showing a thumbnail image in a Datagrid* earlier in this chapter.

See also

Other control properties you can set:

Property	Meaning
ImagePath	The path on the server to the folder containing the images for the different checkbox states.
ImageUrl	The name of the image file to display for the state.
Text	A text message to display next to the image.
ToolTip	A message displayed when you hover over the image.

8

Basic Skinning

In this chapter we will cover the following topics:

- ▶ Downloading and installing a skin
- ▶ Creating a simple HTML skin
- ▶ Creating a simple ASCX skin
- ▶ Deploying your skins and containers
- ▶ Exploring skin objects
- ▶ Creating a simple HTML container
- ▶ Creating a basic ASCX container
- ▶ Creating custom container images
- ▶ Styling a container with images
- ▶ Styling a menu with images

Introduction

In DNN, skinning is a term that refers to the process of customizing the look and feel of the DNN portal. One of the powerful features of DNN is that the functionality of the portal is separated from the presentation of the portal. This means we can change the appearance of the portal without affecting how the portal works.

To create a skin in DNN we will work with three kinds of files: HTML, ASCX, and CSS. The HTML or ASCX file describes the layout of the page and the CSS file provides the styling. If you have worked with HTML and CSS before than you will be able to immediately get started. However, if you are familiar with ASCX (and as a DNN developer that is likely) you can achieve the same results faster than HTML. In the recipes, we will show primarily ASCX skinning with some brief examples of HTML skinning.

▸ **Skin Objects**

Before we start looking at the recipes, we need a quick word about Skin Objects. Skin Objects are used in both HTML and ASCX skin files as placeholders for different kinds of dynamic functionality. In HTML skins, you place text tokens such as [CURRENTDATE] in your code and when the code is parsed by the skin engine it will insert the matching skin object. If you are working in ASCX, you register skin objects as controls that you place directly in your code.

DNN offers many different skin objects such as CurrentDate, Logo, Login link, and others and we'll see many of these in action in the recipes of this chapter.

Downloading and installing a skin

Often the easiest way to start skinning is to download an existing skin package and see the different files used for skinning. In this recipe we will download an excellent skin created by Jon Henning from a site called CodePlex that demonstrates the most common skin objects and layouts.

Another reason for starting with an existing skin is that it allows incremental development. We can start with a fully functional skin, deploy it to our DNN portal and then edit the source files right on the server. In this way the changes we make are immediately displayed and problems are easily spotted and fixed. However, as applying a skin can affect the entire site, it is best to create and test skins on a development DNN site before using them on a production site.

Finally, it should also be noted that as a skin is really just another type of extension in DNN, you are already familiar with some of these steps.

How to do it...

1. Open your favorite web browser and go to the site
   http://codeendeavortemplate.codeplex.com/.

2. Click on **Downloads** in the toolbar.

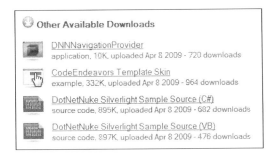

3. Scroll down a little and click on the **CodeEndeavors Template Skin** link.

4. When prompted with the License Agreement, click **I Agree**.

5. The File download dialog will ask if you want to **Open** or **Save**. Click on **Save** and select a temporary folder to hold the ZIP file.

6. That's all we need from the CodePlex site, so close the browser.

7. To install the skin on the DNN site, begin by logging in as the SuperUser.

8. Look at the Control Panel and make sure you're in Edit mode.

9. Look under the **Host** menu and select **Extensions**.

10. Scroll to the bottom and click on the link **Install Extension Wizard**.

11. The wizard will prompt for the ZIP file (called the extension package).

12. Click on the **Browse** button and select the file you just downloaded (for example `CodeEndeavors.TemplateSkin.install.v01.01.07.00.zip`). Click on **Open** then click on **Next**.

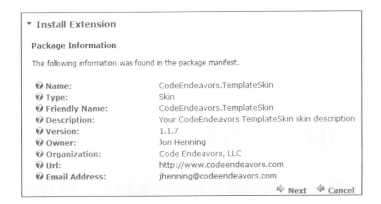

13. The wizard will display the Extension information. Click on **Next**.

14. The wizard will display the Release Notes. Click on **Next**.

15. On the license page, check **Accept License?** and click on **Next**.

16. Now the install script will run, creating the skin. At the end you should see the message "Installation successful".

17. Click on **Return**.

18. To make the skin active, select **Skins** under the **Admin** menu.

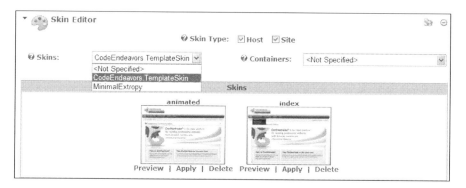

19. From the **Skins** drop-down lists, select **CodeEndeavors.TemplateSkin.**

20. For this chapter, we will use the **Index** skin for our examples. Click on the **Apply** link under the **index** skin to make it active.

21. To see the skin files, you can look in the root folder of the DNN instance under `\Portals\_default\Skins\CodeEndeavors.TemplateSkin`.

22. Here is a summary of the key files you are likely to see in a skin like this:

File name	Description
animated.ascx	An ASCX skin file.
container.ascx	An ASCX container file.
index.html	An HTML skin file.
skin.css	The stylesheet for the skin.
container.css	The stylesheet for the container.
TemplateSkin.dnn	The manifest file for the skin package.
thumbnail_animated.jpg	A preview image of the ASCX skin.
thumbnail_container.jpg	A preview image of the ASCX container.
thumbnail_index.jpg	A preview image of the HTML skin.
license.txt	The text of the license agreement.
releasenotes.txt	The text of the release notes.
version.txt	The version number.
Images folder	A folder holding the graphic images supporting a skin or container.

See also

To learn more about the different skin files and how to create them, see the other recipes in this chapter.

Creating a simple HTML skin

For developers or designers familiar with HTML and CSS, DNN offers a way to create skins without having to know the details of ASCX. The DNN skinning engine can parse an HTML skin and create the ASCX file for the portal.

In this recipe we will create a simple HTML skin and CSS file on a test DNN portal. This will let us preview the skin as it is developed. We will also demonstrate how to use Skin Objects in HTML.

 It is very important that skins contain a DIV element with an ID of "ContentPane". This is used by DNN to show the default site content and is required in all skins.

Getting ready

Here is a diagram of the page layout we will create using HTML:

Menu	User Login
ContentPane	RightPane

HTML provides the layout for the skin but to provide the functionality we will use Skin Objects. Skin Objects are text tokens that will become ASCX controls when the skin is parsed by the skin engine. This process is invisible to the developer. We just need to place the desired text token in the HTML.

In this recipe we will use the following skin object tokens and DIVs:

Skin Object	Description
[MENU]	Displays the DNN menu.
[USER]	Displays who is currently logged in and offers a link to the User Profile page.
[LOGIN]	Offers a Login/Logout link.
ContentPane DIV	Required. This is where the contents of the portal are displayed.
RightPane DIV	Optional. A place to display content on the right side of the page.

How to do it...

1. Start by locating the default skin folder within your test DNN portal (`\Portals\_default\Skins`).

2. Next, create a new folder to hold the skin files. Call this folder `SampleHTMLSkin`.

3. Launch the Development Tool.

4. From the **File** menu, select **New File...**.

5. In the **New File** dialog, select **HTML Page** and click on **Open**.

6. This will give you a basic HTML file. Next, we need to add a simple HTML table to lay out our page. To create the layout shown in the sample diagram, our HTML table code should look like this:

```
<!DOCTYPE html PUBLIC "-//W3C//DTD XHTML 1.0 Transitional//EN"
  "http://www.w3.org/TR/xhtml1/DTD/xhtml1-transitional.dtd">
<html xmlns="http://www.w3.org/1999/xhtml" >
<head>

<link id="skin_css" href="skin.css" type="text/css"
      rel="stylesheet" />

    <title>Untitled Page</title>

</head>
<body>

    <table width="100%">
        <tr>
            <td width="60%">
                [MENU]
            </td>
            <td width="40%">
                [USER]
                   |   
                [LOGIN]
            </td>
        </tr>
        <tr>
            <td>
```

```
                <div id="ContentPane" runat="server"></div>
        </td>
        <td>
                <div id="RightPane" runat="server"></div>
        </td>
    </tr>


    </table>

</body>
</html>
```

7. Here we created an HTML table with two columns and two rows corresponding to the layout diagram. Then we placed the Skin Objects and DIVs in the table.

8. Select **Save HTMLPage1.htm As...** from the **File** menu.

9. Browse to the `SampleHTMLSkin` folder and save the file as `SampleHTMLSkin.htm`.

10. Next, we need to create the CSS file for the skin. From the **File** menu, select **New File...**.

11. At the **New File** dialog, select **Style Sheet** and click on **Open**.

12. Replace the contents of the file with:

```
/* General Styles */
body                            {background: #CCCCCC; height:
100%; margin: 0px; padding: 0px;}
a, a:link, a:visited, a:active  {color: #800000; text-decoration:
none; font-family: Verdana, Arial, Helvetica, sans-serif; font-
weight: normal;}
a:hover                         {color: #C00; text-decoration:
none;}


/* Styles for Controlling the Layout */
.template_style                 {width: 960px; margin: auto;}
.content                        {background: white; border-left:
solid 1px #EAEAEA; border-right: solid 1px #EAEAEA; padding: 10px;
margin: 0 5px 0 5px;}
```

13. Select **Save StyleSheet1.css As...** from the **File** menu.

14. Browse to the `SampleHTMLSkin` folder and save the file as `skin.css`.

15. One more useful thing to do is create a preview image of the skin. This is a little hard to do as we haven't even created the skin yet, but you can use a simple draw program (such as MS Paint) to create an image of what you plan the skin to look like. Something like this:

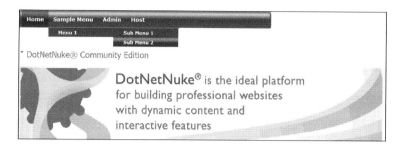

16. Save the image file as `SampleHTMLSkin.jpg`.

17. To see how the new skin will look on our site, start by logging in as the SuperUser.

18. Look under the **Admin** menu and select **Skins**.

19. Select `SampleHTMLSkin` from the drop-down list.

20. As this is an HTML skin, we can't preview it until we parse it. Click on the link **Parse Skin Package**.

21. The new **SampleHTMLSkin** will now appear:

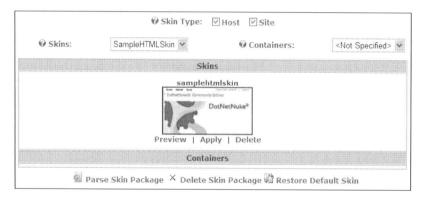

22. To see how the skin looks, click on the **Preview** link.

23. It's not much but you can see that the HTML table layout has correctly placed the menu on the top left and the **Login/Logout** link is in the top right. The content appears in the ContentPane on the bottom left where we put it and the empty RightPane is on the bottom right.

24. To see exactly what the skin installation did, look in the folder containing the skin. Right next to the `SampleHTMLSkin.htm` file you created, the parser created `SampleHTMLSkin.ascx` and a `thumbnail_samplehtmlskin.jpg` (if you included an image for the skin).

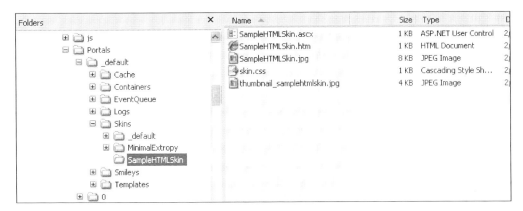

25. To see how to deploy this skin to a production portal, see the recipe *Deploying your skins and containers*.

How it works...

When the skin is deployed, the skin engine will automatically parse the skin package and generate the required `SampleHTMLSkin.ascx` file. If you are still developing the skin and editing the `SampleHTMLSkin.htm` file on the server, you must click on the **Parse Skin Package** link before the changes will appear in the portal.

If you are familiar with HTML and want to start learning to create ASCX skins, you can look at the ASCX skin that the parser generates to see how the HTML is converted. You can even edit the ASCX file directly to see how your changes affect the skin.

There's more...

In this recipe we used an HTML table to position the Skin Objects. Although this might be a familiar technique for HTML developers, we can achieve much greater control over the positioning of objects by using the CSS file. In addition, it is also possible to use more complicated tokens and pass parameters to them. You can see examples of this in the Chapter 13, *Advanced Skinning*.

Creating a simple ASCX skin

Although you can develop skins in HTML and parse them into ASCX, many developers prefer to work directly in ASCX. This has the advantage that changes in the file can be immediately displayed rather than needing parsing first. Which approach you choose often depends on your background. If you are more familiar with ASCX you may find it easier than using HTML. However, if you do switch to ASCX make sure the original HTML file is removed, otherwise your changes may be overwritten by anyone reparsing the original HTML file.

There are a few small differences when developing ASCX-based skins. When using Skin Objects' controls in ASCX, you first place a register directive for the control at the top of the file before referencing it in the body of the ASCX file. After the control has been registered, you can use it as many times as desired providing you give each one a unique ID.

Here is a diagram of the page layout we will create:

Menu	User Login
ContentPane	RightPane

How to do it...

1. Start by locating the default skin folder within your test DNN portal (`\Portals\_default\Skins`).

2. Next, create a new folder to hold the skin files. Call this folder `SampleASCXSkin`.

3. Launch the Development Tool.

4. From the **File** menu, select **New File...**.

5. In the **New File** dialog, select **Web User Control** and click on **Open.**

6. The first step is to place the following directive at the top of the file:

```
<%@ Control language="vb" AutoEventWireup="false" Explicit="True"
        Inherits="DotNetNuke.UI.Skins.Skin" %>
```

 Older skins (before 5.x) did not inherit from `DotNetNuke.UI.Skins.Skin`, so if you need to convert an older skin to 5.x, you will need to add this.

7. The next step is to add a register directive for each Skin Object we plan to use:

```
<%@ Register TagPrefix="dnn" TagName="NAV"
        Src="~/Admin/Skins/Nav.ascx" %>
<%@ Register TagPrefix="dnn" TagName="USER"
        Src="~/Admin/Skins/User.ascx" %>
```

```
<%@ Register TagPrefix="dnn" TagName="LOGIN"
             Src="~/Admin/Skins/Login.ascx" %>
```

8. To create the navigation menu we'll add a `DIV` and insert the `NAV` control:

```
<div >
    <dnn:NAV runat="server" id="dnnNAV"
             ProviderName="DNNMenuNavigationProvider"
             IndicateChildren="false"
             ControlOrientation="Horizontal" />
    </div>
```

9. Then add the code to create the User and Login/Logout links :

```
<div id="login_style" class="user">
    <dnn:USER runat="server" id="dnnUSER"  CssClass="user" />
      |  
    <dnn:LOGIN runat="server" id="dnnLOGIN"  CssClass="user" />
</div>
```

10. Lastly, we create the content panes using an HTML table, but enclose it in a `DIV`:

```
<div class="content">
    <table width="100%" border="0" cellspacing="0" cellpadding="0">
        <tr>
        <td valign="top" id="LeftPane" class="LeftPane"
            runat="server" visible="false">
        </td>
        <td valign="top" id="ContentPane" class="ContentPane"
            runat="server" visible="false">
        </td>
        <td valign="top" id="RightPane" class="RightPane"
            runat="server" visible="false">
        </td>
        </tr>
    </table>
</div>
```

11. The entire file should now look like this:

```
<%@ Control language="vb" AutoEventWireup="false" Explicit="True"
            Inherits="DotNetNuke.UI.Skins.Skin" %>

<%@ Register TagPrefix="dnn" TagName="NAV"
            Src="~/Admin/Skins/Nav.ascx" %>
<%@ Register TagPrefix="dnn" TagName="USER"
            Src="~/Admin/Skins/User.ascx" %>
<%@ Register TagPrefix="dnn" TagName="LOGIN"
```

```
                            Src="~/Admin/Skins/Login.ascx" %>
      <div >
         <dnn:NAV runat="server" id="dnnNAV"
                  ProviderName="DNNMenuNavigationProvider"
                  IndicateChildren="false"
                  ControlOrientation="Horizontal" />
      </div>

      <div id="login_style" class="user">
         <dnn:USER runat="server" id="dnnUSER"  CssClass="user" />
           |  
         <dnn:LOGIN runat="server" id="dnnLOGIN"  CssClass="user" />
      </div>

      <div class="content">
         <table width="100%" border="0" cellspacing="0" cellpadding="0">
           <tr>
           <td valign="top" id="LeftPane" class="LeftPane"
              runat="server" visible="false">
           </td>
           <td valign="top" id="ContentPane" class="ContentPane"
              runat="server" visible="false">
           </td>
           <td valign="top" id="RightPane" class="RightPane"
              runat="server" visible="false">
           </td>
           </tr>
         </table>
      </div>
```

12. Select **Save WebUserControl1.ascx As...** from the **File** menu.

13. Browse to the SampleASCXSkin folder and save the file as SampleASCXSkin.
    ascx.

14. To create the CSS file select **New File...** from the **File** menu.

15. In the **New File** dialog, select **Style Sheet** and click on **Open**.

16. Replace the contents of the file with:

```
/* General Styles */
body                           {background: #CCCCCC; height:
100%; margin: 0px; padding: 0px;}
a, a:link, a:visited, a:active  {color: #800000; text-decoration:
none; font-family: Verdana, Arial, Helvetica, sans-serif; font-
weight: normal;}
```

```
a:hover                                {color: #C00; text-decoration:
none;}

/* Styles for Controlling the Layout */
.template_style                        {width: 960px; margin: auto;}
.content                               {background: white; border-left:
solid 1px #EAEAEA; border-right: solid 1px #EAEAEA; padding: 10px;
margin: 0 5px 0 5px;}

/* Control Styles */
#login_style                           {float: right; padding: 10px 17px
0px 10px;}

/* Pane Styles */
.ContentPane                           {padding: 0px;margin: 0px;}
.MiddlePane                            {padding: 0px 0px 0px 10px; width:
10em; margin: 0px;}
.LeftPane                              {padding: 0px 10px 0px 0px; width:
10em; margin: 0px;}
.RightPane                             {padding: 0px 0px 0px 10px; width:
10em;margin: 0px;}

/* User Styles */
.user, a.user:link, a.user:active, a.user:visited {color: #800000;
font-size: 12px;}
a.user:hover {color: #C00;}
```

17. With these styles we are positioning the Login link on the right side, defining the Panes and setting the color and size of the User link.

18. Select **Save StyleSheet1.css As...** from the **File** menu.

19. Browse to the `SampleASCXSkin` folder and save the file as `skin.css`.

20. One more useful thing to do is create a preview image of the skin. This is a little hard to do as we haven't even created the skin yet, but you can use a simple drawing program (such as MS Paint) to create an image of what you plan the skin to look like. Something like this:

21. Save the image file as `SampleASCXSkin.jpg`.

22. To see how the new skin will look on our site, start by logging in as the SuperUser.

23. Look under the **Admin** menu and select **Skins**.

24. The new **SampleASCXSkin** will now appear:

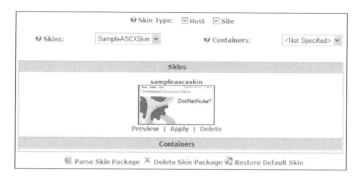

25. To see how the skin looks, click on the **Preview** link.

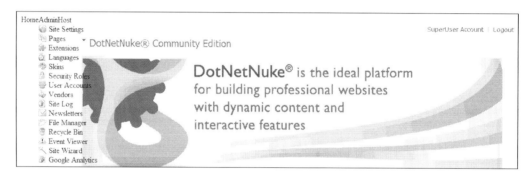

26. It's not much but it correctly includes the Skin Objects and a very simple layout. The other recipes in this chapter will show how to add styling elements and additional Skin Objects.

See also

This sample ASCX skin will be the starting point for the recipes *Exploring Skin Objects* and *Styling a menu with images*.

Deploying your skins and containers

Like a module, skins must be packaged and deployed to your DNN server. Once deployed, they will appear on the **Skins** page under the **Admin** menu for preview and applying to the portal.

In previous recipes we saw how to create new skins directly on a test DNN portal. This allows you to edit the files and immediately see the results just by refreshing your browser. But once a skin has been fully developed, this recipe will show you how to package your skin into a portable ZIP file using the package wizard.

Once created, you can install the skin package on the DNN site by logging in as SuperUser then uploading the ZIP file and installing the skin package as an extension. The skin is installed in the `\Portals\_default\Skins` folder.

 As of DNN 5.x, only the SuperUser can deploy skins. This was done as a security precaution as skins can now contain user-written code.

Getting ready

For this recipe you will need skin files to deploy. We will use the skin files from the previous recipe *Creating a simple ASCX skin*.

How to do it...

1. Begin by logging in as the SuperUser.

2. Look under the **Host** menu and select **Extensions**.

3. The first step is to look under the installed extensions and find the **SampleASCXSkin** under the **Skins** section. If you see it, skip to step 8, otherwise you must create the extension first. Start by selecting **Create Extension** from the action menu (or click on the link at the bottom of the page).

4. Choose **Skin** from Extension Type drop down and fill out the form as shown:

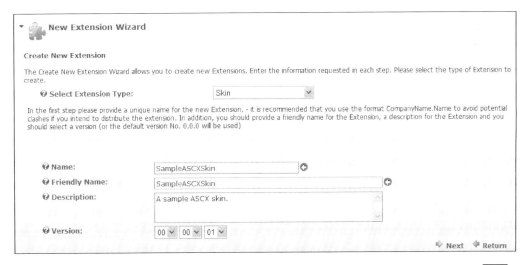

5. Click on **Next**.

6. Provide the owner information and click on **Next**.

7. The **SampleASCXSkin** skin will now appear in the list of extensions.

8. Click on the **Edit** icon next to the name.

9. Scroll to the bottom and click on the link **Create Package**.

10. The **Create Package** screen will display. Click on **Next**.

11. On the next screen you will see the files of the skin. Click on **Next**.

12. Next, the manifest is displayed. Click on **Next**.

13. The wizard will now generate a file name for the ZIP file using the owner name and the skin name. Click on **Next**.

14. The wizard will now complete with a summary page. You will now find a ZIP file in the `/Install/Skin` folder. Click on **Return** to close the wizard.

15. Once the file is packaged in a ZIP file you can upload and install it as described in the recipe *Downloading and installing a skin*.

Exploring Skin Objects

In the previous recipes we saw examples of Skin Objects inserting DNN functionality like the Login link and the menu through text tokens (in HTML) or controls (in ASCX). In this recipe we will expand the sample ASCX skin and demonstrate additional Skin Objects you can use.

Getting ready

To follow along with this recipe you must have completed the following recipe:

▶ *Creating a simple ASCX skin*

Here is a diagram of the new page layout we will create:

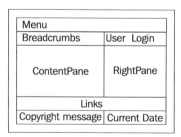

How to do it...

1. Start by locating the default skin folder within your test DNN portal (`\Portals\_default\Skins`).

2. Next, create a new folder to hold the skin files. Call this folder `DetailedASCXSkin`.

3. Launch the Development Tool.

4. Open the `SampleASCXSkin.ascx` file from the *Creating a simple ASCX skin* recipe.

5. Add the following register directive after the existing directives:

```
<%@ Register TagPrefix="dnn" TagName="BREADCRUMB"
             Src="~/Admin/Skins/BreadCrumb.ascx" %>
<%@ Register TagPrefix="dnn" TagName="TEXT"
             Src="~/Admin/Skins/Text.ascx" %>
<%@ Register TagPrefix="dnn" TagName="LINKS"
             Src="~/Admin/Skins/Links.ascx" %>
<%@ Register TagPrefix="dnn" TagName="COPYRIGHT"
             Src="~/Admin/Skins/Copyright.ascx" %>
<%@ Register TagPrefix="dnn" TagName="CURRENTDATE"
             Src="~/Admin/Skins/CurrentDate.ascx" %>
```

6. Next, replace the existing `Login_Style` DIV with a new DIV encompassing both Login and User links:

```
<%--By placing the SkinObjects inside a parent DIV they share the
same style--%>

<div class="bread_bg">
    <div id="bread_style">
        <dnn:TEXT runat="server" id="dnnTEXT"
            CssClass="breadcrumb_text" Text="You are here"
            ResourceKey="Breadcrumb" />
         <span>
  <dnn:BREADCRUMB runat="server" id="dnnBREADCRUMB"
CssClass="Breadcrumb"
            RootLevel="0" Separator=" > " />
</span>
    </div>
    <div id="login_style" class="user">
        <dnn:USER runat="server" id="dnnUSER"  CssClass="user" />
          |  
        <dnn:LOGIN runat="server" id="dnnLOGIN" CssClass="user" />
    </div>
</div>
```

7. Lastly, leave the `ContentPane` DIV as it is and add these new DIVs right below it:

```
<div class="bot_bg links">
    <dnn:LINKS runat="server" id="dnnLINKS" CssClass="links"
        Level="Root" Separator="    |
               " />

</div>

<div class="bot_pad">
    <div id="copy_style" class="footer">
        <dnn:COPYRIGHT runat="server" id="dnnCOPYRIGHT"
            Align CssClass="footer" />
    </div>
    <div id="date_style" class="footer">
        <dnn:CURRENTDATE runat="server" id="dnnCURRENTDATE"
            Align CssClass="footer" />
    </div>
</div>
```

 Separating the Copyright and Date into separate DIVs allow us to put one in the lower-left corner and one in the lower-right corner of the page.

8. Select **Save SampleASCXSkin.ascx As...** from the **File** menu.

9. Browse to the `DetailedASCXSkin` folder and save the file as `DetailedASCXSkin.ascx`.

10. These new Skin Objects will need styles. Open the `skin.css` file from the *Creating a simple ASCX skin* recipe.

11. Add the following styles to the bottom of the `skin.css` file:

```
/*breadcrumbs*/
.Breadcrumb, a.Breadcrumb:link, a.Breadcrumb:active,
a.Breadcrumb:visited {color: #800000; font-size: 13px;}
a.Breadcrumb:hover              {color: #C00;}

.bread_bg                       {background-color: #EAEAEA; font-
family: Verdana, Arial, Helvetica, sans-serif; border-left: solid
1px #EAEAEA; border-right: solid 1px #EAEAEA; margin: 0 5px 0 5px;
height: 30px;}
#bread_style                    {float: left; padding: 10px 0px
0px 17px; color: #000000; font-size: 13px;}

/* for the bottom of the page */
```

```
.bot_bg                                   {background-color: #EAEAEA;
border-left: solid 1px #EAEAEA;border-right: solid 1px #EAEAEA;
border-bottom: solid 1px #EAEAEA; padding: 10px;    margin: 0 5px 0
5px;}
.bot_pad                                  {font-family: Verdana, Arial,
Helvetica, sans-serif; margin-bottom: 20px; padding: 0 30px 0
20px;}

#terms_style                              {float: left;}
#copy_style                               {float: left;}
#date_style                               {float: right; padding: 0px 0px 0px
10px; }

/*links*/
.links                                    {text-align: center;}
.links, a.links:link, a.links:active, a.links:visited {font-
weight: bold; color: #800000; font-size: 11px;}
a.links:hover                             {color: #C00;}

/* Sets the font size and text color of the footer at the bottom
of the page */
.footer, a.footer:link, a.footer:active, a.footer:visited {color:
#800000; font-size: 12px;}
a.footer:hover                            {color: #C00;}
```

12. With these styles we are positioning the Breadcrumb links just below the menu on the left. The Login and User links remain on the right side, ContentPane and RightPane stay the same, and the new Links, Copyright, and CurrentDate controls are arranged along the bottom of the page.

13. Select **Save skin.css As...** from the **File** menu.

14. Browse to the DetailedASCXSkin folder and save the file as skin.css.

15. To see how the new skin will look on the site, log in as the SuperUser.

16. Look under the **Admin** menu and select **Skins**.

17. The new **DetailedASCXSkin** will now appear:

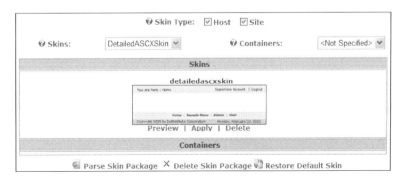

18. Click on **Preview** to see how the skin looks:

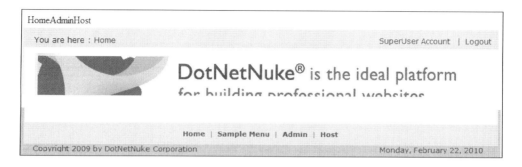

19. See how the breadcrumbs (**You are here:**) appear on the left under the menu, user and login are on the right, and links along the bottom and the copyright message and current date appear in the bottom corners.

There's more...

If you're curious to see which Skin Objects are available on your DNN site, you can log in as the SuperUser and select **Extensions** under the **Host** menu. This will list all the skin objects and their version number.

 Some skin objects may not be installed by default and will not appear in this list until installed.

Creating a simple HTML container

While skins set the styling of the entire page, DNN also allows skinning at the module container level. You can think of a container as the area around the module content. It includes the title of the module as well as the hover menu and the action links that usually appear beneath the content.

In this recipe we will create a simple container using HTML. We will also introduce some of the Skin Objects available to containers.

Containers have their own tokens that are different than those used in skins. This recipe will use the following tokens:

Token	Description
[ACTIONS]	Creates the module hover menu.
[TITLE]	The title of the module.
[VISIBILITY]	Provides the ability to expand or collapse the container.
[PRINTMODULE]	Links for the Admin that map to different ModuleActionTypes (Print Module in this example).

Here is a diagram of the container we will create:

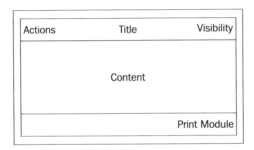

How to do it...

1. Start by locating the default container folder within your test DNN portal (\Portals_default\Containers).

2. Next, create a new folder to hold the container files. Call this folder HTMLContainer.

3. Launch the Development Tool.

4. From the **File** menu, select **New File....**

5. At the **New File** dialog, select **HTML Page** and click on **Open**.

6. This will give you a basic HTML file. Next we need to add links to the CSS files we need.

```
<!DOCTYPE html PUBLIC "-//W3C//DTD XHTML 1.0 Transitional//EN"
"http://www.w3.org/TR/xhtml1/DTD/xhtml1-transitional.dtd">
<html xmlns="http://www.w3.org/1999/xhtml" >
<head>
    <title>Untitled Page</title>

    <link id="container_css" href="container.css" type="text/css"
        rel="stylesheet" />
```

```
</head>
<body>


</body>
</html>
```

7. Next, we need to add the HTML table that will control the layout of the container:

```
<body>


<div class="container_bkg">
    <TABLE cellPadding="0" width="100%" border="0">
      <TR>
       <TD width="25"></TD>
       <TD align="center" >[ACTIONS]</TD>
       <TD width="100%" align="center" >[TITLE]</TD>
       <TD align="center" >[VISIBILITY]</TD>
       <TD width="25"></TD>
      </TR>
      <TR>
       <TD width="25"> </TD>

       <TD id="ContentPane" colspan="3" align="center"
           runat="server" >
       </TD>

       <TD width="25"> </TD>
      </TR>
      <TR>
       <TD width="25"></TD>
       <TD colspan="3" align="right">[PRINTMODULE]</TD>
       <TD width="25"></TD>
      </TR>
    </TABLE>
</div>


</body>
```

8. The entire file should now look like this:

```
<!DOCTYPE html PUBLIC "-//W3C//DTD XHTML 1.0 Transitional//EN"
"http://www.w3.org/TR/xhtml1/DTD/xhtml1-transitional.dtd">
<html xmlns="http://www.w3.org/1999/xhtml" >
<head>
```

```
              <title>Untitled Page</title>

                  <link id="container_css" href="container.css"
                        type="text/ css" rel="stylesheet" />

    </head>
    <body>

    <div class="container_bkg">
        <TABLE cellPadding="0" width="100%" border="0">
          <TR>
            <TD width="25"></TD>
            <TD align="center" >[ACTIONS]</TD>
            <TD width="100%" align="center" >[TITLE]</TD>
            <TD align="center" >[VISIBILITY]</TD>
            <TD width="25"></TD>
          </TR>
          <TR>
            <TD width="25"> </TD>

            <TD id="ContentPane" colspan="3" align="center"
                runat="server" >
            </TD>

            <TD width="25"> </TD>
          </TR>
          <TR>
            <TD width="25"></TD>
            <TD colspan="3" align="right">[PRINTMODULE]</TD>
            <TD width="25"></TD>
          </TR>
        </TABLE>
    </div>

    </body>
    </html>
```

9. Select **Save HTMLPage1.htm As...** from the **File** menu.

10. Browse to the `HTMLContainer` folder and save the file as `HTMLContainer.htm`.

11. These new Skin Objects will need styles. From the **File** menu, select **New File...**.

12. In the **New File** dialog, select **Style Sheet** and click on **Open**.

13. Replace the contents of the file with:

```
/* General Styles */
.TitleLabel{color:GrayText;font-size: 15px;}
.container_bkg {background-color:#DAE7F2;border:solid
                                   1px #4F839F;}
```

14. Select **Save StyleSheet1.css As...** from the **File** menu.

15. Browse to the `HTMLContainer` and save the file as `container.css`.

16. You can also make a preview image of the new container, something like:

17. Save the image file as `HTMLContainer.jpg`.

18. To see how the new container will look on our site, start by logging in as the SuperUser.

19. Look under the **Admin** menu and select **Skins**.

20. Select the **HTMLContainer** from the **Containers:** drop-down list.

21. Click on the **Parse Skin Package** link.

22. The new **HTMLContainer** will now appear:

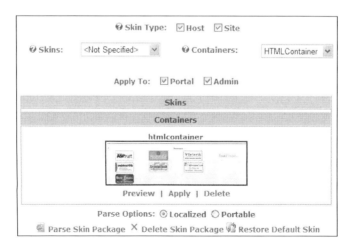

23. To see how the container looks, click on the **Preview** link.

24. It's a simple container but looking at a module like **Sponsors**, you can see the hover menu on the left and the module title centered over the container with a light blue background.

Creating a basic ASCX container

Just as skins can be created using HTML or ASCX, containers too can be developed either way. In this recipe we will see a simple ASCX container.

Here is a diagram of the container we will create:

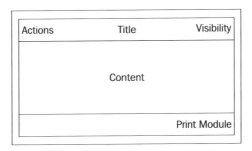

How to do it...

1. Start by locating the default container folder within your test DNN portal (`\Portals\_default\Containers`).

2. Next, create a new folder to hold the container files. Call this folder `ASCXContainer`.

3. Launch the Development Tool.

4. From the **File** menu, select **New File...**.

5. In the **New File** dialog, select **Web User Control** and click on **Open.**

6. The first step is to place the following directive at the top of the file:

```
<%@ Control language="vb"
        CodeBehind="~/admin/Containers/container.vb"
        AutoEventWireup="false" Explicit="True"
        Inherits="DotNetNuke.UI.Containers.Container" %>
```

7. The next step is to add a register directive for each Skin Object we plan to use:

```
<%@ Register TagPrefix="dnn" TagName="ACTIONS"
            Src="~/Admin/Containers/SolPartActions.ascx" %>
<%@ Register TagPrefix="dnn" TagName="TITLE"
            Src="~/Admin/Containers/Title.ascx" %>
<%@ Register TagPrefix="dnn" TagName="VISIBILITY"
            Src="~/Admin/Containers/Visibility.ascx" %>
<%@ Register TagPrefix="dnn" TagName="PRINTMODULE"
            Src="~/Admin/Containers/PrintModule.ascx" %>
```

8. To create the structure of the container we will use an HTML table to lay out the Skin Objects:

```
<div class="container_bkg">
   <TABLE cellPadding="0" width="100%" border="0">
     <TR>
       <TD width="25"></TD>
       <TD align="center" ><dnn:ACTIONS runat="server"
                               id="dnnACTIONS" />
       </TD>
       <TD width="100%" align="center"><dnn:TITLE runat="server"
                                         id="dnnTITLE" />
       </TD>
       <TD align="center" ><dnn:VISIBILITY runat="server"
                               id="dnnVISIBILITY" />
       </TD>
       <TD width="25"></TD>
     </TR>
     <TR>
       <TD width="25"> </TD>

       <TD id="ContentPane" colspan="3" align="center"
           runat="server" >
       </TD>

       <TD width="25"> </TD>
     </TR>
     <TR>
       <TD width="25"></TD>
       <TD colspan="3" align="right">
         <dnn:PRINTMODULE runat="server" id="dnnPRINTMODULE" />
       </TD>
       <TD width="25"></TD>
     </TR>
   </TABLE>
</div>
```

9. The entire file should now look like this:

```
<%@ Control language="vb"
    CodeBehind="~/admin/Containers/container.vb"
    AutoEventWireup="false" Explicit="True"
    Inherits="DotNetNuke.UI.Containers.Container" %>

<%@ Register TagPrefix="dnn" TagName="ACTIONS"
            Src="~/Admin/Containers/SolPartActions.ascx" %>
<%@ Register TagPrefix="dnn" TagName="TITLE"
            Src="~/Admin/Containers/Title.ascx" %>
<%@ Register TagPrefix="dnn" TagName="VISIBILITY"
            Src="~/Admin/Containers/Visibility.ascx" %>
<%@ Register TagPrefix="dnn" TagName="PRINTMODULE"
            Src="~/Admin/Containers/PrintModule.ascx" %>

<div class="container_bkg">
    <TABLE cellPadding="0" width="100%" border="0">
      <TR>
        <TD width="25"></TD>
        <TD align="center" ><dnn:ACTIONS runat="server"
                            id="dnnACTIONS" /></TD>
        <TD width="100%" align="center"><dnn:TITLE runat="server"
                                    id="dnnTITLE" />
        </TD>
        <TD align="center" ><dnn:VISIBILITY runat="server"
                            id="dnnVISIBILITY" />
        </TD>
        <TD width="25"></TD>
      </TR>
      <TR>
        <TD width="25"> </TD>

        <TD id="ContentPane" colspan="3" align="center"
            runat="server" >
        </TD>

        <TD width="25"> </TD>
      </TR>
      <TR>
        <TD width="25"></TD>
        <TD colspan="3" align="right">
         <dnn:PRINTMODULE runat="server" id="dnnPRINTMODULE" />
        </TD>
        <TD width="25"></TD>
      </TR>
    </TABLE>
</div>
```

10. Select **Save WebUserControl1.ascx As...** from the **File** menu.

11. Browse to the `ASCXContainer` folder and save the file as `ASCXContainer.ascx`.

12. Next we create the CSS file by selecting **New File...** from the **File** menu.

13. In the New File dialog, select **Style Sheet** and click on **Open.**

14. Replace the contents of the file with:

```
/* General Styles */
.TitleLabel{color:GrayText;font-size: 15px;}
.container_bkg {background-color:#DAE7F2;border:solid 1px
#4F839F;}
```

15. Select **Save StyleSheet1.css As...** from the **File** menu.

16. Browse to the `ASCXContainer` folder and save the file as `container.css`.

17. You can also make a preview image of the new container, something like:

18. Save the image file as `ASCXContainer.jpg`.

19. To see how the new container will look on our site, start by logging in as the SuperUser.

20. Look under the **Admin** menu and select **Skins**.

21. Select the **ASCXContainer** from the **Containers:** drop-down list.

22. The new **ASCXContainer** will now appear:

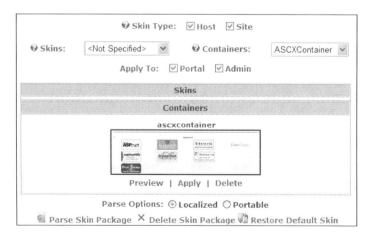

23. To see how the container looks, click on the **Preview** link.

24. It's a simple container but looking at a module like **Sponsors**, you can see the hover menu on the left and the module title centered over the container with a light blue background.

Creating custom container images

Containers can do more than just act as placeholders for module content. By expanding the container skin to include images we can create more elaborate containers limited only by our creativity.

Styling a DNN container using images is a two-part process. First we must create the images we need and save them as a set of graphic files. Then we must design the container to position the images around the container. In this recipe we will see how to create the custom images for styling a container. In the next recipe *Styling a container with images* we'll see how to position these images to create the final container.

Getting ready

Here is a diagram that shows what the final container will look like. We need to create the five images highlighted in red. As you can see in this diagram, we need only create images for the distinctive elements. CSS can fill in the gaps by repeating the background image as necessary to fit the size of the container.

Creating images for a container is a four-step process:

- ▸ Decide which sides of the container will use images. In this example we will create images for the top and bottom container edges and leave the left and right sides as a simple border line.

- ▸ Decide the size of the images. A container border can be very narrow or very wide. In this example we will create a 27 pixel wide border with the images.

- ▸ Decide which images will tile to support variable-sized containers. As containers can stretch or shrink, we need to use an image that can tile. That is, the image can be repeated as many times as necessary to fill the width of the container. In this example, we will pick one image to tile across the top and another to tile along the bottom. As the sides will be just a border line we won't need to worry about tiling vertically.

- ▸ Choose a drawing application (such as MS Paint) to create the images and save them to a temporary folder. You can use a variety of formats—in this example we will save the images as GIF files to save space.

How to do it...

1. Start by launching your favorite drawing application (such as MS Paint).

2. Set the image dimensions to 98 pixels wide and 27 pixels high. There's nothing special about these dimensions, they just look good for this particular design.

3. Draw the image for the upper-left corner of the container. This image will be the background for the title of the module, so it needs to be an image that can tile horizontally as the length of a container title varies.

4. Save the image as a GIF file called `ContainerUL.gif`.

5. Next, create a new image with dimensions 80 by 27 pixels. This image marks the end of the module title and the beginning of the top container border. It does not tile and is used in this example to connect the upper-left corner to the border image that runs across the top of the container.

6. Save the image as a GIF file called ContainerUC1.gif.

7. The next image is the top border of the container and will tile horizontally as the width of the container changes. Set the attributes to be 12 by 27 pixels.

8. Save the image as a GIF file called ContainerUC2.gif.

9. For the border along the bottom of the container, we need two more images. The first is the lower-left corner. Make this image 90 by 27. This image will tile across the bottom for the width of the container.

10. Save the image as a GIF file called ContainerLL.gif.

11. The last image is for the lower-right corner. This image doesn't tile. Make it 100 by 27 pixels.

12. Save the image as a GIF file called ContainerLR.gif.

13. At this point you should have five images in a temporary folder that look something like this:

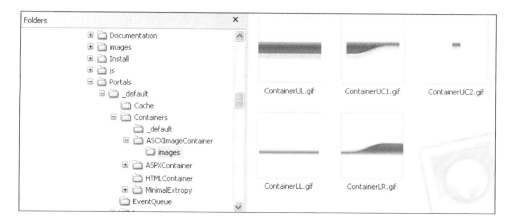

There's more...

In this recipe we saw how to create images for a container and a little bit on how the images can form the borders of a container. In the next recipe we will see how to create the container that will use these images.

Styling a container with images

As we saw in the previous recipe, the first step to styling a container with images is to create the images. In this recipe, we will take the second step and expand the simple ASCX container by adding the images that will create a graphic border around the container. We will also demonstrate changing the font and text color.

Getting ready

To follow along with this recipe you must have completed the following recipes:

▸ *Creating a simple ASCX container*

▸ *Creating custom container images*

How to do it...

1. Start by locating the default container folder within your test DNN portal (`\Portals\_default\Containers`).

2. Next, create a new folder to hold the container files. Call this folder `ASCXImageContainer`.

3. Create a new folder inside to hold the images: `ASCXImageContainer\images`.

4. Copy the five images you created in the previous recipe to this new folder. You should now have the following files:

   ❑ `ContainerUL.gif`: The upper-left corner of the container

   ❑ `ContainerUC1.gif`: The first upper center image

   ❑ `ContainerUC2.gif`: The second upper center image

   ❑ `ContainerLL.gif`: The lower-left corner

   ❑ `ContainerLR.gif`: The lower-right corner

5. With the images in the correct folder, launch the Development Tool.

6. To create the ASCX file, select **New File...** from the **File** menu.

7. In the **New File** dialog, select **Web User Control** and click on **Open**.

8. The first step is to place the following directive at the top of the file:

```
<%@ Control language="vb"
      CodeBehind="~/admin/Containers/container.vb"
      AutoEventWireup="false" Explicit="True"
      Inherits="DotNetNuke.UI.Containers.Container" %>
```

9. Next, place necessary register directives for the Skin Objects we need to support the container:

```
<%@ Register TagPrefix="dnn" TagName="ACTIONS"
          Src="~/Admin/Containers/SolPartActions.ascx" %>
<%@ Register TagPrefix="dnn" TagName="ICON"
          Src="~/Admin/Containers/Icon.ascx" %>
<%@ Register TagPrefix="dnn" TagName="TITLE"
          Src="~/Admin/Containers/Title.ascx" %>
<%@ Register TagPrefix="dnn" TagName="VISIBILITY"
          Src="~/Admin/Containers/Visibility.ascx" %>
<%@ Register TagPrefix="dnn" TagName="ACTIONBUTTON1"
          Src="~/Admin/Containers/ActionButton.ascx" %>
<%@ Register TagPrefix="dnn" TagName="ACTIONBUTTON2"
          Src="~/Admin/Containers/ActionButton.ascx" %>
<%@ Register TagPrefix="dnn" TagName="ACTIONBUTTON3"
          Src="~/Admin/Containers/ActionButton.ascx" %>
<%@ Register TagPrefix="dnn" TagName="ACTIONBUTTON4"
          Src="~/Admin/Containers/ActionButton.ascx" %>
<%@ Register TagPrefix="dnn" TagName="ACTIONBUTTON5"
          Src="~/Admin/Containers/ActionButton.ascx" %>
```

10. To position the images, we start with an encompassing table to set the style of the container, then include a table for the top of the container, a place for the ContentPane, then another table to hold the images for the bottom of the container:

```
<table width="100%" border="0" align="center" cellpadding="0"
    cellspacing="0" class="ASCXImage_Master">
  <tr>
    <td class="ontainerUC2">

        <table height="27" border="0" cellpadding="0"
            cellspacing="0">
          <tr>
            <td valign="top" class="ContainerUL">
              <dnn:ACTIONS runat="server" id="dnnACTIONS" />
            </td>
            <td valign="top" class="ContainerUL">
              <dnn:ICON runat="server" id="dnnICON" />
            </td>
            <td valign="top" class="ContainerUL"> 
             <dnn:TITLE runat="server" id="dnnTITLE"
                  CssClass="ASCXImage_Title"/>
            </td>
            <td valign="top" class="ContainerUC1"> </td>
            <td valign="bottom" class="ContainerUC2"> </td>
          </TR>
        </table>

        <table width="100%" border="0" align="center"
            cellPadding="0" cellSpacing="0">
          <tr>
            <td class="ASCXImage_Content">
             <div runat="server" id="ContentPane">
             </div>
            </td>
          </TR>
        </table>
        <table width="100%" height="21" border="0" cellpadding="0"
            cellspacing="0">
          <tr>
            <td valign="middle" class="ContainerLL"> </td>
            <td valign="middle" class="ContainerLR"> </td>
          </tr>
        </table>
    </td>
  </tr>
</table>
```

11. Finally, we create the table to hold the action buttons that sit outside of the border images:

```
<table width="100%" height="25" border="0" cellpadding="2"
     cellspacing="0">
   <tr valign="bottom">
        <td align="left" nowrap>
         <dnn:ACTIONBUTTON1 runat="server"
             id="dnnACTIONBUTTON1"
             CommandName="AddContent.Action"
             DisplayIcon="True" DisplayLink="True" />
        </td>
        <td height="22" align="right" nowrap>
        <dnn:ACTIONBUTTON2 runat="server"
             id="dnnACTIONBUTTON2"
             CommandName="SyndicateModule.Action"
             DisplayIcon="True"
             DisplayLink="False" /> 
             <dnn:ACTIONBUTTON3
             runat="server" id="dnnACTIONBUTTON3"
             CommandName="PrintModule.Action"
             DisplayIcon="True"
             DisplayLink="False" /> 
             <dnn:ACTIONBUTTON4
             runat="server" id="dnnACTIONBUTTON4"
             CommandName="ModuleSettings.Action"
             DisplayIcon="True"
             DisplayLink="False" />
             <dnn:ACTIONBUTTON5
             runat="server" id="dnnACTIONBUTTON5"
             CommandName="ModuleHelp.Action"
             DisplayIcon="True" DisplayLink="False" />
        </td>
   </tr>
</table>
```

12. Select **Save WebUserControl1.ascx As...** from the **File** menu.

13. Browse to the `ASCXImageContainer` folder and save the file as `ASCXImageContainer.ascx`.

14. Next we create the CSS file by selecting **New File...** from the **File** menu.

15. In the **New File** dialog, select **Style Sheet** and click on **Open**.

16. Replace the contents of the file with:

```
/* Set the containing width and border color */
.ASCXImage_Master { width: 100%; background-color: transparent;
BORDER: #A0A0A0 1px solid;  padding: 0px; }
/* Set the title font */
.ASCXImage_Title { font-family: Impact; font-size: 12px; color:
#ffffff; font-weight: normal; }

/* Set the padding */
.ASCXImage_Content { padding-left: 5px; padding-right: 5px;
padding-top: 5px; padding-bottom: 0px; font-size: 15px; color:
#404040; }

/* Set the images to draw the box around the container */

.ContainerUL { background: url(images/ContainerUL.gif) repeat-x;
height: 27px; }
.ContainerUC1 { background: url(images/ContainerUC1.gif) no-
repeat; width: 80px; height: 27px; }
.ContainerUC2 { background: url(images/ContainerUC2.gif) repeat-x;
height: 27px; }
.ContainerLL { background: url(images/ContainerLL.gif) repeat-x;
height: 27px; }
.ContainerLR { background: url(images/ContainerLR.gif) no-repeat;
width: 100px; height: 27px; }
```

17. Select **Save StyleSheet1.css As...** from the **File** menu.

18. Browse to the `ASCXImageContainer` folder and save the file as `container.css`.

19. You can also make a preview image of the new container, something like:

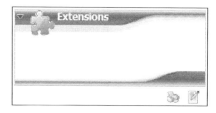

20. Save the image file as `ASCXImageContainer.jpg`.

21. To see how the new container will look on our site, start by logging in as the SuperUser.

22. Look under the **Admin** menu and select **Skins.**

23. Select the **ASCXImageContainer** from the **Containers:** drop-down list.

24. The new **ASCXContainer** will now appear:

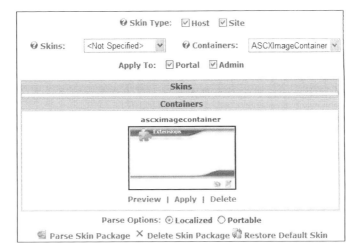

25. To see how the container looks, click on the **Preview** link.

26. We can see that the images form a border around the container with the module title on the left side next to the hover menu. In addition, you can see the action buttons we created in step 11 appearing below the container. Also note how the image for the top and bottom line automatically fill to the full width of the container.

Styling a menu with images

In this recipe, we will take the simple ASCX skin and show how to skin a menu by combining the menu control with background images.

Skinning a DNN menu using images has two parts: the first is a set of images that form the background of the menu; the second is the text that appears in the menu as provided by the menu control.

In this recipe we will examine in detail the professional-looking menu created for the template skin. We will see all the pieces that go into a menu, how to create background images for them and how to style the text. When all the pieces are in place we'll have a menu looking like this:

Getting ready

To follow along with this recipe you must have completed the following recipes:

- *Downloading and installing a skin*
- *Creating a simple ASCX skin*

How to do it...

1. Start by locating the default skin folder within your test DNN portal (`\Portals\_default\Skins`).

2. Next, create a new folder to hold the skin files. Call this folder `ASCXMenuSkin`.

3. Create a new folder inside to hold the images `ASCXMenuSkin\images`.

4. Find the folder holding the template skin from the recipe *Downloading and installing a skin*.

5. Locate and copy these images into the `ASCXMenuSkin\images` folder.

   - `menu_bg.png`
   - `menu_hov.png`
   - `menu_left.png`
   - `menu_right.png`
   - `submenu_hov.png`

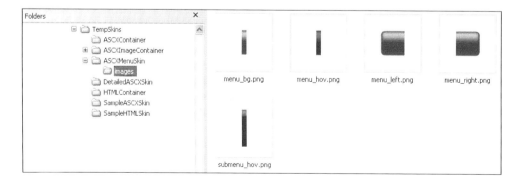

6. With the images in place, we can now open the sample ASCX created in the recipe *Creating a simple ASCX skin* and expand it to use the menu images.

7. Launch the Development Tool.

8. Select **Open File...** from the **File** menu.

9. Browse to the `SampleASCXSkin` folder and select the `SampleASCXSkin.ascx` file.

10. Find the menu Skin Object between the register and the login DIV:

```
<%@ Register TagPrefix="dnn" TagName="LOGIN" Src="~/Admin/Skins/
Login.ascx" %>

<div >
    <dnn:NAV runat="server" id="dnnNAV"
        ProviderName="DNNMenuNavigationProvider"
        IndicateChildren="false"
        ControlOrientation="Horizontal" />
</div>

<div id="login_style" class="user">
```

11. Replace the `DIV` containing the menu with this CSS-styled `DIV`:

```
<%@ Register TagPrefix="dnn" TagName="LOGIN" Src="~/Admin/Skins/
Login.ascx" %>

<div class="menu_style">
    <dnn:NAV runat="server" id="dnnNAV"
        ProviderName="DNNMenuNavigationProvider"
        IndicateChildren="false"
        ControlOrientation="Horizontal"
        CSSControl="mainMenu" />
</div>
<div id="login_style" class="user">
```

12. Select **Save SampleASCXSkin.ascx As...** from the **File** menu.

13. Browse to the `ASCXMenuSkin` folder and save the file as `ASCXMenuSkin.ascx`.

14. As the real work is in the CSS file, we need to define the styles that will provide the images, fonts, and colors to the menu. Select **Open File...** from the **File** menu.

15. Browse to the `SampleASCXSkin` folder and select the `skin.css` file.

16. Scroll down to the bottom of the file and begin by adding the following classes:

```
/* step 1: the main menu */

.mainMenu                       {font-family: Verdana, Arial,
Helvetica, sans-serif; cursor: pointer; font-size: 13px; font-
weight: bold;}
.mainMenu_bg                    {background: url(images/menu_
bg.png) repeat-x top left; margin: 0 19px 0 7px; height: 40px;}
.mainMenu_left                  {background: url(images/menu_left.
```

```
png) no-repeat top left;}
.mainMenu_right                    {background: url(images/menu_
right.png) no-repeat top right;}
.mainMenu .root                    {text-align: center; line-height:
40px; padding: 12px 12px 12px 12px; color: White;}
```

17. If you save your files at this point and then view the skin from the portal, the menu would look like:

18. The next piece to add is the menu hover and active menu. These are the images that will display when the mouse hovers over the main menu text or when the menu is active. It is a narrow image, but `repeat-x` will cause it to expand horizontally to fill the length of the menu text. Add this code to the bottom of the CSS file:

```
/* Main menu hover */
.mainMenu .hov{ color:#fff; background:url(images/menu_hov.png)
   repeat-x top left;}


/* Main menu selected */
.mainMenu .sel, .mainMenu .bc {
color:#FFF;
background:url(images/menu_hov.png) repeat-x top left;
}
```

19. This creates an image that displays when the mouse hovers over the menu item and we will use the same image when the menu is active:

20. The last step is to provide the styles for the submenus. Add the following code to the bottom of `skin.css` file:

```
/* general submenu css */


.mainMenu .m                      {width: 160px; font-size: 11px;
font-weight: bold; z-index: 1000; line-height: 2em;}
.mainMenu .m .mi                  {background-color: #242424;}
.mainMenu .m .icn                 {padding-left: 5px; width: 20px;}
.mainMenu .m .mi *                {color: white; margin-right: 5px;}
/* change * to .txt with latest webcontrols */
.mainMenu .m .sel, .mainMenu .m .bc {background: url(images/
submenu_hov.png) repeat-x top left;}
```

```
.mainMenu .m .hov                    {background: url(images/submenu_
hov.png) repeat-x top left;}
```

21. This creates the images for when the mouse hovers over the submenus:

22. Select **Save skin.css As...** from the **File** menu.

23. Browse to the `ASCXMenuSkin` folder and save the file as `skin.css`.

24. You can also make a preview image of the new container, something like:

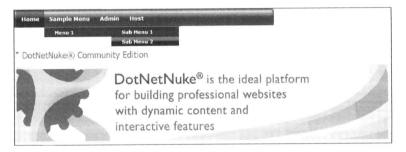

25. Save the image file as `ASCXMenuSkin.jpg`.

26. To see how the new skin will look on the site, log in as the SuperUser.

27. Look under the **Admin** menu and select **Skins.**

28. Select the **ASCXMenuSkin** from the **Skins:** drop-down list.

29. The new **ASCXMenuSkin** will now appear:

30. This is a very simple example, but it shows the basics of skinning a menu.

How it works...

In DNN skins, styles can be applied to HTML elements like DIVs, table TDs, and SPANs. In this recipe we added additional DIVs and styles to set the font and style of the menu text and to create graphic background and edge pieces.

9

Working with Foreign Languages

- ▶ Downloading and installing a language pack
- ▶ Creating a bilingual site with a single portal
- ▶ Editing the language resource file
- ▶ Creating your own module translations
- ▶ Determining controls that need translations
- ▶ Localizing labels, titles, panels, and links
- ▶ Localizing a drop-down list with a stored procedure
- ▶ Localizing a drop-down list with a DNN list
- ▶ Localizing a stored procedure
- ▶ Localizing a DataGrid control

Introduction

As the world gets smaller everyday the ability for a website to support multiple languages becomes more important. Fortunately, DNN provides foreign language support through a process called Localization.

DNN localization is built on the foundations of the .NET framework localization tools. As one language is often used in more than one country, foreign languages in .NET are organized by a locale code which is a combination of the language code and the country code. For example, the code `fr-CA` represents French spoken in Canada. `Fr-FR` represents French spoken in France.

Using locale codes instead of language or country codes allows a more precise translation. French spoken in France is different than French spoken in Canada just as English spoken in the UK is different then English spoken in the United States.

▸ **Static translation vs Content translation**

DNN supports the localizing of static text in the user interface, things such as labels, buttons, system messages, and e-mails. In the current version it does not yet support automatic localizing of content. This means there is automatic translation of Datagrid headers, for example, but not the contents of the Datagrid.

In this chapter we will see recipes that show how to use the DNN localization tools and API. We will also see how you can modify your custom modules to change the content based on the currently selected locale.

▸ **Resource files**

Building on the foundation of ASP.NET, DNN uses Windows resource files to hold the string translations for each locale. The file uses XML tags to provide a simple key and value lookup mechanism. The localization API is how we read the translation strings from the resource file.

Downloading and installing a language pack

A language pack is a collection of resource files for a given locale. Most of these are provided by third parties, often by volunteers. The `www.dotnetnuke.com` site provides links to the most common language packs that are available. If you want your DNN site to support multiple languages your first task is to find, download, and install the language packs you need.

How to do it...

1. Open your favorite web browser and go to the site `http://www.dotnetnuke.com`.

2. In the menu at the top of the page, select **Language Packs** from the **Development** menu.

3. Scrolling down you will see many different language packs that are available. These are mostly created by individuals and the links here lead to many different sites. For this example, click on the **French – Canada (fr-CA)** link.

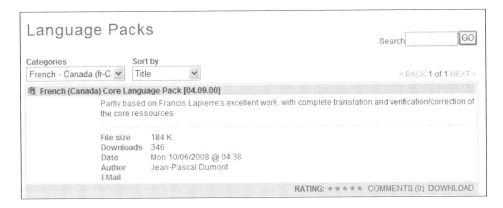

4. The details of the selected pack will display. Click on the **DOWNLOAD** link in the lower-right corner.

5. A dialog will appear prompting if you want to **Open** or **Save** the file. Click on **Save** and choose a temporary folder for this ZIP file.

6. When the download completes you can close the browser. The next step is to upload and install the language pack to the DNN site. If you haven't installed an extension before, see the recipe *Installing a new extension* in *Chapter 1*.

7. You can confirm the successful installation of the language pack by selecting **Extensions** from the **Host** menu. All installed languages packs will display near the middle of the page between the lists of containers and modules.

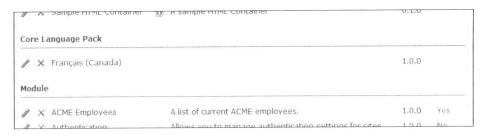

Creating a bilingual site with a single portal

The easiest way to create a bilingual DNN site is to install and enable multiple languages on your default portal. This is a good option if your portal will generally stay the same between the two languages (same menu layout, same general content, same skin, and same administrator user).

Getting ready

To follow along with this recipe you must have completed the previous recipe:

▸ *Downloading and installing a language pack*

How to do it...

1. To have a bilingual portal you must first have downloaded and installed the desired language packs as described in the recipe *Downloading and installing a language pack*.

2. Select **Languages** from the **Admin** menu. The installed language packs for your portal are shown:

3. To pick the language or languages for your portal click on the **Enabled** checkbox next to the language. After a pause the **Update** and **Cancel** links will display.

4. Click **Update** to save your changes.

5. If you enable more than one language, the Language Selector control will appear on the portal pages (depending on the skin your portal uses). Clicking on the different national flag icons will change the current language of the portal. Trying clicking on the Canadian flag.

6. Notice how the label on the logout link has changed from **Logout** to **Déconnexion**.

See also

In this recipe we saw how enabling a language pack will automatically localize certain shared resources. See the other recipes in this chapter to learn how to localize other resources.

Editing the language resource file

DNN provides the ability to edit the language resources installed on your portal. This means you can modify the labels, systems messages, and other text that appears on the pages. Not only does this provide support for multiple languages, but it also means you can customize these messages with your own text (for example, changing "Login" to "Sign On").

With DNN there are three levels of language resource support:

 ▶ Shared (Application): These are translation strings shared throughout the controls in DNN, text such as "Update", "Cancel", or common system message strings.

 ▶ Local: These are translation strings unique to a user control.

 ▶ Global: These are translation strings for shared components that fall somewhere between Application and Local.

In addition, DNN provides resource files at the Portal, Host, or System level. For example, this means even within the same language, you can have different strings displayed on different portals on your site.

In this recipe, we will see how to modify the shared resources file by logging in as SuperUser and changing the text of the **Results Per Page** control used in the sample Employee project.

Getting ready

To follow along you must have completed the following recipe from *Chapter 6*:

 ▶ *Displaying a Datagrid with filter controls*

How to do it...

1. Log in as SuperUser (syshost in our examples).

2. Look under the **Admin** menu and select **Languages.** The installed language packs for your portal are shown.

3. We'll edit the English language in this example. Click on the edit icon (the little pencil) next to English under Portal.

4. The **Language Editor** page will display:

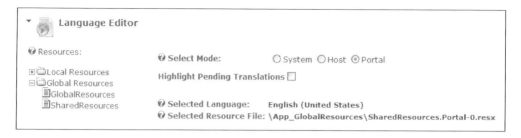

5. Expand **GlobalResources** on the left side and click on **SharedResources** to display the shared resource strings.

6. Scroll down through all the entries in the resource file until you find **Records Per Page** (the list is alphabetical, so it's near the bottom).

7. On the right side you'll see the original text. On the left is where we type the new text. Change the text on the left side as follows:

❑ Recordsperpage.Help: **Choose the maximum number of results to display on a page**.

❑ Recordsperpage.Text: **Results Per Page**

8. Click on **Save Resource File** (at the very bottom).

9. As the portal supports two languages, let's repeat the process and make the same changes to the French Canadian locale.

10. At the list of installed languages, click on the edit icon (the little pencil) next to **Français (Canada)** under Portal.

11. When the language editor displays, click on **SharedResources** on the left.

12. Scroll down through all the entries in the language file until you find **Enregistrements par page**.

13. Change the text on the left side as follows:

❑ Recordsperpage.Help: **Choisissez le nombre maximum de résultats à afficher sur une page.**

❑ Recordsperpage.Text: **Résultats par page**

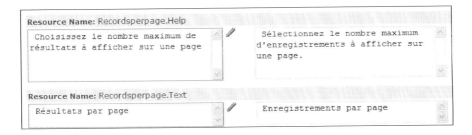

14. Click on **Save Resource File** (at the very bottom).

15. To see the effects, go to the ACME Employee page. Use the Language Selector control to switch between languages. See how the label and help text for both the English and French locales has been updated:

Creating your own module translations

Although the language packs you download and install handle the translation of the system labels and messages, custom modules that you develop will also have labels and other controls with values not found in the application-level resources.

To translate these unique module values you must create your own translations and save them in a local resource file. This recipe will extend the concepts shown in the previous recipe *Editing the language resource file* and show how to update the translation strings in your own modules.

Getting ready

In this recipe we will use the sample Employee project with labels created in *Chapter 6* and show how to localize the labels so that they will change when we switch between installed language packs. The sample Employee project already has English labels so in this recipe we will add labels in French (Canada).

To follow along with this recipe you must have completed the following recipe:

▶ *Displaying labels from the resource file*

▶ *Creating a bilingual site with a single portal*

▶ *Editing the language resource file*

How to do it...

1. Log in as SuperUser (`syshost` in our examples).

2. Look under the **Admin** menu and select **Languages.** The installed language packs for your portal are shown.

3. Click on the edit icon (the little pencil) next to Français (Canada) under Portal to enter the **Language Editor**.

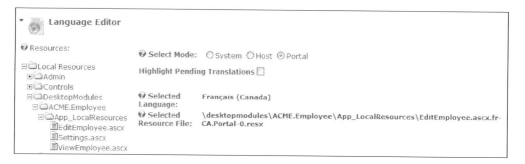

4. Click on **LocalResources** on the left. Expand the subfolder and drill down until you see `EditEmployee.ascx`.

5. Click on `EditEmployee.ascx` to display the available translation strings.

6. If this is the first time you are creating French language translations for this module, you will at first see English translations taken from the default language resource file we created back in the recipe *Displaying labels from the resource file*.

7. Substitute each English string for a French translation string as follows:

   ❑ `ControlTitle_edit.Text`: **Modifier Employé**

   ❑ `lblEmpFirstName.Help`: **Entrez le prénom de l'employé.**

   ❑ `lblEmpFirstName.Text`: **Prénom**

   ❑ `lblEmpLastName.Help`: **Entrez le nom de famille de l'employé.**

   ❑ `lblEmpLastName.Text`: **Nom de famille**

   ❑ `lblHireDate.Help`: **Entrez la date d'embauche de l'employé.**

   ❑ `lblHireDate.Text`: **Date d'embauche**

   ❑ `lblManagerNo.Help`: **Entrez le numéro d'identification du gérant salarié**

   ❑ `lblManagerNo.Text`: **Gestionnaire #**

   ❑ `lblSalary.Help`: **Entrez salaire annuel du salarié.**

   ❑ `lblSalary.Text`: **Salaire**

8. The page should start looking like this:

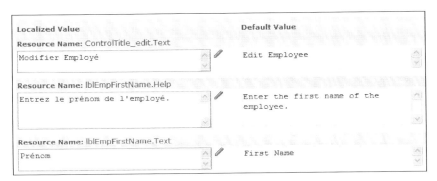

9. When you have typed in all the translations, click on the **Save Resource File** link at the bottom of the page.

10. To see the results, first select French as the language for your portal by clicking on the Language Selector control (see the recipe *Creating a bilingual site with a single portal* for an example).

11. Next, go to the Employee module and select an employee to edit.

12. When the **Edit Employee** control is displayed, the labels will now appear in French with the correct help messages:

Determining controls that need translations

There are times when your DNN form has many controls and you may have difficulty determining those that need a translation in the local resource file. DNN includes a technique to make each control on your form display the resource key it uses when there is no translation string in the resource file.

Getting ready

To follow along with this recipe you must have completed the following recipe from *Chapter 6*:

> ▶ *Displaying labels from the resource file*

How to do it...

1. Look on the DNN server and locate the root folder of the DNN installation.
2. Find the `web.config` file and open it in a text editor.
3. Scroll down through the file until you see the `ShowMissingKeys` key.
4. Set the value of this key to `true` with the following code:

```
<add key="AutoUpgrade" value="true" />
<add key="UseInstallWizard" value="true" />
<add key="InstallMemberRole" value="true" />
<!--Force controls to show missing translation keys -->
<add key="ShowMissingKeys" value="true" />
<add key="EnableWebFarmSupport" value="false" />
<add key="EnableCachePersistence" value="false" />
<add key="HostHeader" value="" />
```

5. Now log in the DNN site and navigate to the module you are developing.

6. The module will check for translation strings in the resource file. If no translation is found then the missing key is displayed. In this example, if we wanted to provide a translation for the collapsible panel we would need to add the key `Settings.Text` to the resource file.

7. To turn off this feature and restore the normal appearance of the module, set the `ShowMissingKeys` to `false`.

Localizing labels, titles, panels, and links

In this recipe we will continue the localization of the sample Employee project that we began in the recipe *Creating your own module translations*. In this example we will localize the labels, module title, collapsing panel, grid column titles, and links that appear on the `ViewEmployee` control. There are four things we must do:

1. Modify the Employee project to read a module title from the resource file.

2. Add the English text for the module title to the resource file.

3. Deploy the module to the test site.

4. Review all the English text strings for the module and create French translations for each one.

Getting ready

For this recipe we will use the `ViewEmployee` control from the sample Employee project. You also need to have created the English labels for the `ViewEmployee` control. This means to follow along you must have completed the previous recipes:

▶ _Populating a drop-down list from a stored procedure_

▶ _Creating your own module translations_

How to do it...

1. Start by launching the Development Tool and loading the **Employee** project.

2. First we will localize the title of the View Employee module. Open the `ViewEmployee.ascx.vb` file.

3. Scroll down to the `Event Handlers` region and look for the `Page_Init` procedure.

4. Add the following line of code at the top of the procedure:

```
Private Sub Page_Init(ByVal sender As System.Object,
                  ByVal e As System.EventArgs)
                              Handles MyBase.Init


    If Not Request.QueryString("CurrentPage") Is Nothing Then
        PageIndex = CType(Request.QueryString("CurrentPage"), Integer)
        End If


    ModuleConfiguration.ModuleTitle = Localization.GetString
                              ("ModuleTitle", LocalResourceFile)


        ' Format the columns of the grid control
```

5. This will read the title of the module from the resource file. (It's not perfect though. This can still be overridden by the title given when adding the module to a page).

6. Next, we need to add the English language text to the local resource file. Open the `ViewEmployee.ascx.resx` file.

7. Add the following entry:

   ❑ `ModuleTitle.Text`: **Current ACME Employees**

   ❑ `Settings.Text`: **Collapsible Panel**

8. Select **Save All** from the File menu.

9. Build and deploy the module to your DNN site.

10. Now we will create the matching French translations. Log in as SuperUser (`syshost` in our examples).

11. Look under the **Admin** menu and select **Languages.** The installed language packs for your portal are shown.

12. Click on the edit icon (the little pencil) next to **Français (Canada)** under Portal to enter the Language Editor.

13. Click on **LocalResources** on the left. Expand the subfolder and drill down until you see `ViewEmployee.ascx`.

14. Click on `ViewEmployee.ascx` to display the available translation strings.

15. If this is the first time you are creating French language translations for this module, you will at first see English translations taken from the default language resource file.

16. Substitute each English string for a French translation string as follows:

    ❑ `AddContent.Action`: **Ajouter des nouveaux employés**

    ❑ `lblManagerNo.Help`: **Choisissez un gestionnaire**

    ❑ `lblManagerNo.Text`: **Gestionnaire #**

    ❑ `lblSalaryRange.Help`: **Choisissez l'échelle salariale**

    ❑ `lblSalaryRange.Text`: **Échelle salariale**

    ❑ `ManagerPrompt.Text`: **Tous les gestionnaires**

    ❑ `ModuleTitle.Text`: **Les employés actuels de l'ACME**

    ❑ `SalaryPrompt.Text`: **Salaire Sélectionnez**

    ❑ `Settings.Text`: **Pliant Panneau**

17. The page should look like this:

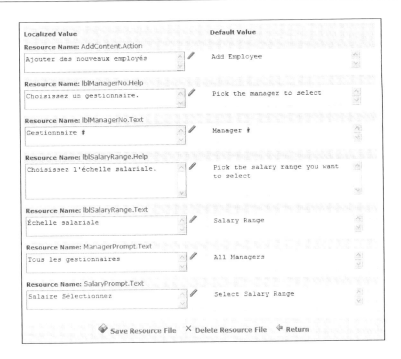

18. Click on **Save Resource File** (at the very bottom).

19. To see the results, go to the Employee module.

20. Use the Language Selector control to switch between languages. You will see the module title, the label on the collapsible panel, the drop-down labels, and the Add Employee link will now switch between English and French.

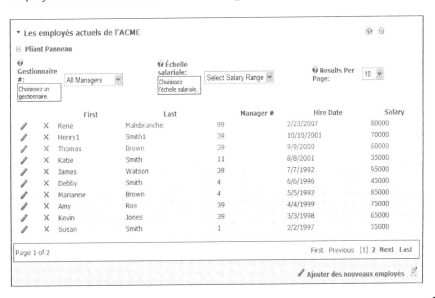

See also

In this recipe we localized some of the items on the sample `ViewEmployee` control. To see how to localize the remaining items, see the other recipes in this chapter.

Localizing a drop-down list with a stored procedure

As shown in *Chapter 6*, you can populate a drop-down list control from a stored procedure. In this recipe we will show how to localize a drop-down list by using the current locale to dynamically change the results returned from the stored procedure that populates the list.

Getting ready

To follow along you must have completed the following recipes:

- *Populating a drop-down list from a stored procedure*
- *Localizing labels, titles, panels, and links*

This recipe also requires a little data setup. To show how a drop-down list populates based on the selected locale, we need to create a special employee in the employee table. This employee will be the manager for employees working in Quebec.

How to do it...

1. Start by launching the Development Tool and loading the **Employee** project.

2. First we need to add a new field to the Employee table for each employee and manager. This new field is called `LocaleCode` and we will set the code so that we can tag some managers as English speaking and some as French speaking. The second task is to modify the `GetManagers` stored procedure from *Chapter 6* and add `CurrentLocale` as a parameter.

3. Double-click to open the `01.00.00.SqlDataProvider` file.

 If you have already installed this module once, you can create a new file called `01.00.01.SqlDataProvider` to hold the updated procedure. For details see the recipe *Deploying a new module version* in *Chapter 11*.

4. Change the table creation code to include the new field:

```
CREATE TABLE {databaseOwner}[{objectQualifier}ACME_Employee]
(
    [ModuleID] [int] NOT NULL,
    [ItemID] [int] NOT NULL IDENTITY(1, 1),
    [EmpFirstName] [nvarchar](30) NOT NULL,
    [EmpLastName] [nvarchar](30) NOT NULL,
    [ManagerNo] [int] NULL,
    [HireDate] [datetime] NOT NULL,
    [Salary] [float] NOT NULL,
    [LocaleCode] [nvarchar](10) NULL,
    [CreatedByUser] [int] NOT NULL,
    [CreatedDate] [datetime] NOT NULL
)
```

5. Next, scroll down and modify the `GetManagers` routine as indicated. Add the new parameter at the top and add it to the WHERE clause of the SELECT statement:

```
create procedure {databaseOwner}{objectQualifier}ACME_GetManagers

    @ModuleId int,
    @CurrentLocale  nvarchar(10)

as

select Emp.ModuleId,
       Emp.ItemId,
       EmpFirstName,
       EmpLastName,
       ManagerNo,
       HireDate,
       Salary,
       CreatedByUser,
       Emp.CreatedDate,
       'CreatedByUserName' = Usr.FirstName + ' ' + Usr.LastName
from {objectQualifier}ACME_Employee As Emp
inner join {objectQualifier}Users As Usr on Emp.CreatedByUser =
                                            Usr.UserId
where  ModuleId = @ModuleId And ManagerNo = 0
And LocaleCode = @CurrentLocale

GO
```

6. Next we need to update the routines that connect the employee controller to this stored procedure. Double-click to open the `DataProvider.vb` file.

7. Scroll down to the bottom of the file and look for the region of code called `Abstract methods`. Update the `GetManagers` function definition:

```
Public MustOverride Function GetManagers(ByVal ModuleId As
    Integer, ByVal LocaleCode As String) As IDataReader
```

8. Now, open the `SqlDataProvider.vb` and scroll to the bottom of the file to the `Public Methods` region. Add the new parameter:

```
Public Overrides Function GetManagers(ByVal ModuleId As Integer,
                ByVal LocaleCode As String) As IDataReader
          Return CType(SqlHelper.ExecuteReader(ConnectionString,
             GetFullyQualifiedName("GetManagers"), ModuleId,
             LocaleCode), IDataReader)
End Function
```

9. Next we need to change the `EmployeeController` file. Double-click on `EmployeeController.vb` and scroll down to the bottom of the `Public Methods` region. Add the following code:

```
Public Function GetManagers(ByVal ModuleId As Integer,
                ByVal LocaleCode As String) As List(Of EmployeeInfo)

     Return CBO.FillCollection(Of EmployeeInfo)
        (DataProvider.Instance().GetManagers(ModuleId,LocaleCode))

End Function
```

10. At this point we have the routines we need to populate the drop-down list. Double-click to open the `ViewEmployee.ascx.vb` file.

11. Scroll down to the bottom of the `Private Methods` region and find the procedure `BindManagerDropDown`.

12. We will modify the procedure to check the current language and pass it to the routine that populates the drop down. Add a new parameter to the call to `GetManagers` to pass the currently selected language:

```
Private Sub BindManagerDropDown()

    Dim objEmployeeController As New EmployeeController

    ' Get the current locale and pass it to the GetManagers
       routine
    ddlManagerNo.DataSource = objEmployeeController.GetManagers
       (ModuleId, CType
       (Page, DotNetNuke.Framework.CDefault).PageCulture.Name)
    ddlManagerNo.DataTextField = "ManagerName"
    ddlManagerNo.DataValueField = "ItemId"
```

13. Select **Save All** from the **File** menu.

14. To check the results, build and redeploy the module to your DNN site.

15. Next we need to prepare some sample employee data that will contain both English and French managers. We start by placing a special employee in the employee table who will be the manager of the employees in Quebec. Log into the DNN site as a SuperUser.

16. Go to the **ACME Employee** page.

17. Click on the **Add Employee** link.

18. Add a new employee as follows:

   ❑ **First Name**: René

   ❑ **Last Name**: Malebranche

   ❑ **Manager #**: 0

   ❑ **Hire Date**: 2/23/2007

   ❑ **Salary**: 80000

19. Next, we need to tag the employees with their active locale. Start by selecting **SQL** from the **Host** menu.

20. First we'll tag the English employees and managers (basically everybody who isn't Mr. Malebranche). Paste the following UPDATE statement into the text box:

```
UPDATE {databaseOwner}[{objectQualifier}ACME_Employee] SET
LocaleCode='en-US' WHERE EmpLastName<>'Malebranche';
```

21. Click on the **Execute** button.

22. Then we'll tag the new French speaking manager with the correct locale code. Paste the following UPDATE statement into the textbox:

```
UPDATE {databaseOwner}[{objectQualifier}ACME_Employee] SET
LocaleCode='fr-CA' WHERE EmpLastName='Malebranche';
```

23. Click on the **Execute** button.

24. To check the results, paste the following SQL query and click on Execute:

```
SELECT EmpFirstName,EmpLastName,ManagerNo,LocaleCode

FROM   {databaseOwner}[{objectQualifier}ACME_Employee];
```

25. Depending on the records in the table, you should see something like:

EmpFirstName	EmpLastName	ManagerNo	LocaleCode
John	Smith	0	en-US
Jane	Doe	0	en-US
Richard	Roe	0	en-US
Kevin	Jones	1	en-US
Amy	Roe	1	en-US
Marianne	Brown	8	en-US
Debbie	Smith	9	en-US
René	Malebranche	0	fr-CA

26. Now that we have some good sample data, we are ready to see the localization in action. Go to the **Employee** module.

27. Use the Language Selector control to switch between languages. The drop-down list should now change as the locale changes with both the prompt and the list of values changing from English to French:

See also

See the next recipe *Localizing a drop-down list with a DNN list* to localize a drop-down list that is built from a DNN list instead of an SQL query.

Localizing a drop-down list with a DNN list

As we saw in *Chapter 6*, you can populate a drop-down list control from a DNN list. Although the current version of DNN does not directly support localization with lists, we can create our own localization of a drop-down list control by dynamically switching the DNN list before binding it to the control.

In this recipe we will create a new DNN list in French then show how to use the current locale to pick the DNN list that populates the control.

Getting ready

To follow along you must have completed the following recipes:

- ▸ *Populating a drop-down list from a DNN list*
- ▸ *Creating your own module translations*

How to do it...

1. Log in as SuperUser (`syshost` in our examples).

2. Look under the **Host** menu and select **Lists**.

3. Make a new list by clicking on **Add List**.

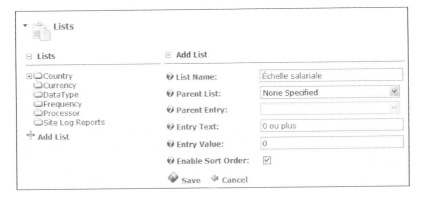

4. Type the details of our first entry:

   - **List Name**: `Échelle salariale`
   - **Parent List**: None Specified
   - **Parent Entry**: Blank
   - **Entry Text**: `0 ou plus`
   - **Entry Value**: `0`
   - **Enable Sort Order**: Checked

5. Click on **Save**.

 It is up to us to format the currency we're using in the list—DNN will not format it for us as real list localization is not supported.

6. Click on **Add Entry** and create the second list entry:

   - **Entry Text**: `30.000 ou plus`
   - **Entry Value**: `30000`

7. Click on **Save**.

8. Click on **Add Entry** and create the third list entry:

   - **Entry Text**: `60.000 ou plus`
   - **Entry Value**: `60000`

9. Click on **Add Entry** and create the fourth list entry:

   ❑ **Entry Text**: 100.000 ou plus

   ❑ **Entry Value**: 100000

10. Click on **Save**.

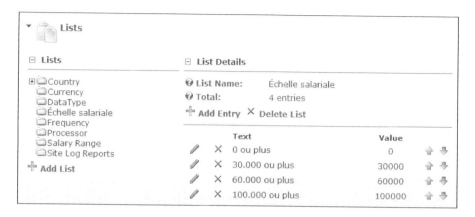

11. Now that we have a foreign language DNN list, we can use it inside our custom module. Launch the Development Tool and load the **Employee** project.

12. Next, open the ViewEmployee.ascx.vb file.

13. Scroll down until you find the BindSalaryDropDown procedure. If you don't see the procedure make sure you have completed the recipe *Populating a drop-down list from a DNN list* from *Chapter 6*.

14. Change the code of the procedure as follows:

```
Private Sub BindSalaryDropDown()

    Dim strListName As String
    Dim strPrompt As String
    strListName = Localization.GetString("SalaryListName",
                                LocalResourceFile)
    strPrompt = Localization.GetString("SalaryPrompt",
                                LocalResourceFile)

    Dim objList As New ListController()
    Dim lstSalary As ListEntryInfoCollection =
      objList.GetListEntryInfoCollection(strListName)

    ddlSalaryRange.DataSource = lstSalary
    ddlSalaryRange.DataTextField = "Text"
    ddlSalaryRange.DataValueField = "Value"
```

```
    Try
ddlSalaryRange.DataBind()

    ' add an extra value to always show a prompt in the drop down
    ddlSalaryRange.Items.Insert(0, New ListItem(strPrompt, "-1"))
    Catch ex As Exception
    End Try


End Sub
```

15. As we are now pulling our prompts from the resource files, we need to first add the English text by opening the `ViewEmployee.ascx.resx` file (under `/App_LocalResources`) and setting the text:

    ❑ `SalaryListName.Text`: **Salary Range**

    ❑ `SalaryPrompt.Text`: **Pick the salary range you want to select**

SalaryListName.Text	Salary Range
SalaryPrompt.Text	Select Salary Range

16. Select **Save All** from the **File** menu.

17. Build and deploy the module to your DNN site.

18. The last thing we need to do before we can test the results is create the French translations for our new salary prompts. Following the steps in the recipe *Localizing labels, titles, panels, and links* make sure the following French translations appear in the language editor:

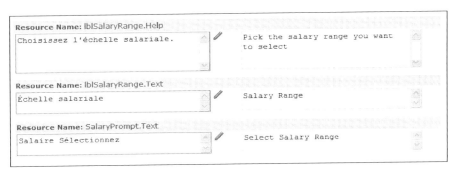

19. Click on **Save Resource File** (at the very bottom).

20. Go to the **Employee** module.

21. Use the Language Selector control to switch between languages. The drop-down list should now change as the locale changes with both the prompt and the list of values changing from English to French:

See also

See the recipe *Localizing a drop-down list with a stored procedure* to localize a drop-down list that is built from a stored procedure instead of a DNN list.

Localizing a stored procedure

In this chapter, we have seen several ways to localize the different kinds of module content. Although you can localize much in the module code, you may need to consider localizing in the backend stored procedures.

In this recipe we will see a simple example of passing the current locale to a stored procedure and using that information to change the results returned by the procedure.

Getting ready

To follow along with this recipe you must have completed the following recipes:

▸ *Creating stored procedures*

▸ *Localizing a DataGrid control*

In this example, we will demonstrate localization by applying a fixed exchange rate to the Salary values pulled from the database based on the locale. (Canadian dollars = Salary * 1.02642). This is not the most elegant way to perform currency conversion but it will suffice for this example.

How to do it...

1. Launch the Development Tool and load the **Employee** project.
2. Next, open the 01.00.00.SqlDataProvider file.
3. Scroll down until you find the ACME_GetEmployeesByFilter procedure.

4. We'll start by changing the procedure to add the desired locale as a parameter:

```
CREATE procedure {databaseOwner}{objectQualifier}ACME_
GetEmployeesByFilter
    @ModuleID int,
    @MgrFilter int,
    @SalaryFilter  int,
    @CurrentLocale  nvarchar(30),
    @PageIndex int,
    @PageSize int
AS
```

5. Next, we will change the SQL query to apply a fixed exchange rate to the employee salaries when the locale is French Canadian:

```
/** join the filtered Ids to the employee table to get our fields
**/

select {objectQualifier}ACME_Employee.ModuleId,
       {objectQualifier}ACME_Employee.ItemId,
       EmpFirstName,
       EmpLastName,
       ManagerNo,
       HireDate,
       CASE @CurrentLocale WHEN 'fr-CA' THEN Salary * 1.02642 ELSE
                                        Salary END As Salary,
       {objectQualifier}ACME_Employee.CreatedByUser,
       {objectQualifier}ACME_Employee.CreatedDate,
       'CreatedByUserName' = {objectQualifier}Users.FirstName + '
         ' + {objectQualifier}Users.LastName
FROM {objectQualifier}ACME_Employee
INNER JOIN {objectQualifier}Users on {objectQualifier}ACME_
Employee.CreatedByUser =
    objectQualifier}Users.UserId
    INNER JOIN #PageIndex PageIndex
      ON {objectQualifier}ACME_Employee.ItemId = PageIndex.ItemId
    WHERE ( (PageIndex.IndexID > @PageLowerBound) OR
      @PageLowerBound is null )
      AND ( (PageIndex.IndexID < @PageUpperBound) OR
        @PageUpperBound is null )
    ORDER BY
      PageIndex.IndexID

GO
```

6. Next, open the `DataProvider.vb` file and replace the `GetEmployeesByFilter` abstract method with this new version that has the `CurrentLocale` as a parameter:

```
Public MustOverride Function GetEmployeesByFilter(ByVal ModuleId
As Integer, ByVal MgrFilter As Integer, ByVal SalaryFilter
As Integer, ByVal CurrentLocale As String, ByVal PageIndex As
Integer, ByVal PageSize As Integer) As IDataReader
```

7. Repeat the process in the `SqlDataProvider.vb` file. Replace the entire `GetEmployeesByFilter` function with this new version:

```
Public Overrides Function GetEmployeesByFilter(ByVal ModuleId
As Integer, ByVal MgrFilter As Integer, ByVal SalaryFilter As
Integer, ByVal CurrentLocale As String, ByVal PageIndex As
Integer, ByVal PageSize As Integer) As IDataReader
    Return CType(SqlHelper.ExecuteReader(ConnectionString, GetF
ullyQualifiedName("GetEmployeesByFilter"), ModuleId, MgrFilter,
SalaryFilter, CurrentLocale, PageIndex, PageSize), IDataReader)
End Function
```

8. Next, open the `EmployeeController.vb` file and replace the first part of the `GetEmployeesByFilter` function with this new code:

```
Public Function GetEmployeesByFilter(ByVal ModuleId As Integer,
ByVal MgrFilter As Integer, ByVal SalaryFilter As Integer, ByVal
CurrentLocale As String, ByVal PageIndex As Integer, ByVal
PageSize As Integer, ByRef TotalRecords As Integer) As ArrayList
    Dim dr As IDataReader = DataProvider.Instance.
GetEmployeesByFilter(ModuleId, MgrFilter, SalaryFilter,
CurrentLocale, PageIndex, PageSize)
  Dim retValue As ArrayList = Nothing
  Try
  While dr.Read
     TotalRecords = Convert.ToInt32(dr("TotalRecords"))
  End While
  dr.NextResult()
  retValue = CBO.FillCollection(dr, GetType(EmployeeInfo))
   Finally
  If Not dr Is Nothing Then
     dr.Close()
  End If
   End Try
   Return retValue

End Function
```

9. Lastly, open the `ViewEmployee.ascx.vb` file.

10. Scroll down to the `BindData` procedure and change the call to `GetEmployeesByFilter` to include the current locale:

```
' use the filter procedure to retrieve the records
colEmployees =
        objEmployees.GetEmployeesByFilter(ModuleId,
        ddlManagerNo.SelectedItem.Value,
        ddlSalaryRange.SelectedItem.Value,
    Type(Page, DotNetNuke.Framework.CDefault).PageCulture.Name,
        CurrentPage, PageSize, TotalRecords)


If colEmployees.Count > 0 Then
```

11. Select **Save All** from the **File** menu.

12. To check the results, deploy the updated stored procedure code then build and deploy the module to your DNN site.

13. When the current locale is changed with the Language selector, the grid control will query the database and the salary values will change from US dollars (USD) to Canadian dollars (CAN) using the new exchange rate calculation:

First	Last	Manager #	Hire Date	Salary
Henry1	Smith1	0	10/10/2001	70000
Thomas	Brown	0	9/9/2000	60000
Katie	Smith	11	8/8/2001	35000
James	Watson	0	7/7/1992	95000
Debby	Smith	4	6/6/1996	45000

Prénom	Nom de famille	Gestionnaire #	Date d'embauche	Salaire
Henry1	Smith1	0	2001-10-10	71849,4
Thomas	Brown	0	2000-09-09	61585,2
Katie	Smith	11	2001-08-08	35924,7
James	Watson	0	1992-07-07	97509,9
Debby	Smith	4	1996-06-06	46188,9

How it works...

This is just a simple example of how a module can produce localized output. For simplicity we hardcoded the exchange rate, but a truly localized stored procedure would look up the correct daily exchange rate and use that in the formula.

Localizing a DataGrid control

The Datagrid control is a common way for a module to display content. DNN includes some support for localization of Datagrids and in this recipe we will see how it works and how to provide the translation strings the Datagrid needs.

Getting ready

To follow along you must have completed the following recipes:

- *Adding a paging control to a Datagrid*
- *Localizing labels, titles, panels, and link*

How to do it...

1. Launch the Development Tool and load the **Employee** project.

2. Open the `ViewEmployee.ascx.vb` file.

3. Scroll down to the `Page_Load` procedure.

4. In the procedure, find the calls to the binding routines and add the following code to trigger the localization of the Datagrid control:

```
If Not Page.IsPostBack Then


    If Not Request.QueryString("PageRecords") Is Nothing Then
    ddlRecordsPerPage.SelectedValue =
                            Request.QueryString("PageRecords")
    End If


    BindManagerDropDown()
    BindSalaryDropDown()


    ' have grid get column titles from resource file
    Localization.LocalizeDataGrid(grdResults, LocalResourceFile)


    BindData()


End If
```

5. Next, we need to add the English language text for our headings to the local resource file. Open the `ViewEmployee.ascx.resx` file.

6. Add the following entry:

   - ❏   `First.Header`: **First**
   - ❏   `Last.Header`: **Last**
   - ❏   `Hire Date.Header`: **Hire Date**
   - ❏   `Manager #.Header`: **Manager #**
   - ❏   `Salary.Header`: **Salary**

7. The file should now look like this:

First.Header	First
Last.Header	Last
Hire Date.Header	Hire Date
Manager #.Header	Manager #
Salary.Header	Salary

8. Build and deploy the module to your DNN site.

9. The last thing we need to do before we can test the results is create the French translations for our new grid headers. Following the steps in the recipe *Localizing labels, titles, panels, and links* make sure the following French translations appear in the language editor for `ViewEmploye.ascx`:

   ❑ `First.Header`: **Prénom**

   ❑ `Hire Date.Header`: **Date d'embauche**

   ❑ `Last.Header`: **Nom de famille**

   ❑ `Manager #.Header`: **Gestionnaire #**

   ❑ `Salary.Header`: **Salaire**

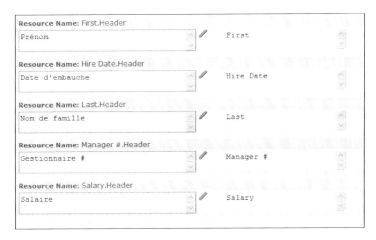

10. Click on **Save Resource File** (at the very bottom).

11. Go to the **Employee** module.

12. Use the Language Selector control to switch between languages. The column titles will be shown with the correctly translated values. Notice that the paging control has also been localized:

		Prénom	Nom de famille	Gestionnaire #	Date d'embauche	Salaire
🖊	✕	Henry1	Smith1	0	2001-10-10	70000
🖊	✕	Thomas	Brown	0	2000-09-09	60000
🖊	✕	Katie	Smith	11	2001-08-08	35000
🖊	✕	James	Watson	0	1992-07-07	95000
🖊	✕	Debby	Smith	4	1996-06-06	45000
🖊	✕	Marianne	Brown	4	1992-05-05	85000
🖊	✕	Amy	Roe	0	1999-04-04	75000
🖊	✕	Kevin	Jones	0	1998-03-03	65000
🖊	✕	Susan	Smith	1	1997-02-02	55000
🖊	✕	Richard	Roe	1	1995-01-01	35000

Page 1 de 2   Premier   Précédent   [1] 2   Suivant   Dernier

🖊 Ajouter des nouveaux employés 🖼

How it works...

Localizing the Datagrid headers requires using the LocalizeDataGrid API call found in the `DotNetNuke.Services.Localization` namespace. It requires that we provide the string translations in the local resource file.

See also

The LocalizeDataGrid routine will localize the Datagrid headers, but to have the query results change requires passing the current locale to the backend stored procedure that pulls the results from the database. To see how this is done, see the previous recipe *Localizing a stored procedure*.

10
Advanced Tricks with Existing Modules

- ▶ Using the HTML module with jQuery
- ▶ Using the HTML module with replacement tokens
- ▶ Using the HTML module with Flash
- ▶ Displaying an XML feed
- ▶ Controlling the friendly URL rewriting
- ▶ Tracking your site with Google Analytics
- ▶ Publishing calendar events as an RSS feed
- ▶ Designing your own forms
- ▶ Styling your own forms

Introduction

In previous chapters we saw recipes showing how to configure and use the core modules of DotNetNuke. As you become more familiar with administering a DNN portal and developing your own custom modules, you'll want to dig a little deeper and see what other features these modules offer.

In this chapter, we look at some new modules and explore what other features are available in DNN. We'll see how flexible the HTML module can be, how some of the underlying processing occurs, and how to extend the DNN database with your own custom forms.

Using the HTML module with jQuery

jQuery is a compact JavaScript library with a focus on the interaction between JavaScript and HTML. Since version 5, DNN has supported using jQuery code in your DNN pages.

In this recipe we will demonstrate a small jQuery program that extends the previous Image Bar example by adding thumbnails images that hover over the currently selected image.

Getting ready

To follow along with this recipe you must have completed the recipe from *Chapter 3*:

▸ *Using the HTML module*

How to do it...

1. Before coding in jQuery, it is important to check the version supported by your DNN installation. To see your version, start by logging in as SuperUser (`syshost` in our examples).

2. Select **Host Settings** from the **Host** menu.

3. Scroll down past the **Advanced Options** until you see **JQuery Settings**.

4. Under the **JQuery Settings** you will see the version your installation supports. In addition to the jQuery version you can see the available options. Here's a quick summary:

   ❑ Deslecting **Use jQuery debug version** will have DNN use the smaller, more compact library but will offer less debugging information.

   ❑ **Use Hosted jQuery Version** means DNN will use the library at the URL given. Unchecked, it will use the local copy of the library.

5. To see how to use jQuery in the HTML module, go to the page created in the recipe *Using the HTML module*.

6. Select **Edit Content** from the module menu (or click on the **Edit Content** icon).

7. When the HTML editor is displayed, click on the **HTML** button at the bottom. This will let us edit the HTML directly and avoid any automatic formatting.

8. To have a thumbnail image hover over the image bar, start by adding some new styles:

```
<style type="text/css">
.imagebar {
    height: 70px;
    width: 780px;
    border: 1px solid #ddd;
}
ul.image {
    float: left;
    list-style: none;
    margin: 0; padding: 0;
}
ul.image li {
    margin: 0; padding: 5px;
    float: left;
    position: relative;
    width: 120px;
    height: 60px;
}
ul.image li img {
    width: 120px; height: 60px;
    border: 1px solid #ddd;
    padding: 2px;
    background: #f0f0f0;
    position: absolute;
    left: 0; top: 0;
    -ms-interpolation-mode: bicubic;
}
#main_view {
    float: left;
    padding: 2px 0;
}
</style>
```

9. These styles format the images and position the hover image. We use `-ms-interpolation-mode: bicubic` to achieve a smooth image resizing.

10. Next, add the following jQuery code after the style elements and before the HTML:

```
<p><style type="text/css">
.imagebar {
    height: 70px;
    width: 780px;
```

```
      border: 1px solid #ddd;
   }
   ul.image {
      float: left;
      list-style: none;
      margin: 0; padding: 0;
   }
   ul.image li {
      margin: 0; padding: 5px;
      float: left;
      position: relative;
      width: 120px;
      height: 60px;
   }
   ul.image li img {
      width: 120px; height: 60px;
      border: 1px solid #ddd;
      padding: 2px;
      background: #f0f0f0;
      position: absolute;
      left: 0; top: 0;
      -ms-interpolation-mode: bicubic;
   }
   #main_view {
      float: left;
      padding: 2px 0;
   }
   </style></p>
   <script type="text/javascript">
   $(document).ready(function(){

   $("ul.image li").hover(function() {
      $(this).css({'z-index' : '10'});
      $(this).find('img').addClass("hover").stop()
         .animate({
            marginTop: '-100px',
            marginLeft: '-120px',
            top: '50%',
            left: '50%',
            width: '194px',
            height: '134px',
            padding: '20px'
         }, 400);

   } , function() {
      $(this).css({'z-index' : '0'});
      $(this).find('img').removeClass("hover").stop()
         .animate({
```

```
            marginTop: '0',
            marginLeft: '0',
            top: '0',
            left: '0',
            width: '120px',
            height: '60px',
            padding: '5px'
        }, 400);
    });

    });
    </script>
    <div class="imagebar">
    <ul class="image">
        <li><img alt="" src="/dotnetnuke/Portals/0/aspnet.gif" /></li>
        <li><img alt="" src="/dotnetnuke/Portals/0/
                                        redgate.gif" /></li>
        <li><img alt="" src="/dotnetnuke/Portals/0/WH4L.gif" /></li>
        <li><img alt="" src="/dotnetnuke/Portals/0/
                                        exacttarget.gif" /></li>
        <li><img alt="" src="/dotnetnuke/Portals/0/
                                        maximumasp.gif" /></li>
        <li><img alt="" src="/dotnetnuke/Portals/0/
                                        telerik.gif" /></li>
    </ul>
    </div>
```

11. Click on **Save** to see the results. The jQuery code defines a function that displays a larger thumbnail of the image when the mouse hovers over the image, then removes it when the mouse leaves.

How it works...

jQuery is a set of powerful JavaScript libraries with many features beyond the scope of this book. In addition to the simple example in this recipe, almost all jQuery functions can be added in the HTML module in the same way, including jQuery galleries, menu systems, and so on. To learn more about jQuery and how to write your own jQuery programs, visit the jQuery site at http://www.jQuery.com.

Using the HTML module with replacement tokens

The HTML module allows the substitution of dynamic content to replace special text tokens. With tokens you can include information from the DNN database in your HTML content.

Here are some of the tokens that we will use in this recipe:

Token	Description
[Portal:Email]	E-mail of the primary administrator.
[Portal:FooterText]	The site copyright text.
[Portal:HomeDirectory]	The home directory of the portal.
[Portal:PortalName]	The name of the portal.
[User:DisplayName]	The display name of the current user.
[User:Email]	The e-mail of the current user.
[Tab:Description]	Description of the current page.
[Tab:TabName]	Name of the current page.
[DateTime:Now]	Current date and time.

To see more examples of Token replacements, there's a good list on the Data Springs website: http://www.datasprings.com/Resources/ArticlesInformation/DNNTextHTMLTokenReplacementOptions.aspx.

Getting ready

To follow along with this recipe you should be familiar with the basic content management tasks from *Chapter 2, Managing Users and Site Setup* (such as *Adding a module to a page*).

How to do it...

1. Log in as Portal Administrator (sysadmin in our examples).
2. Add the HTML module to a new or existing page.
3. From the **HTML Module** menu, select **Settings** (or click on the Settings icon).
4. Scroll down to the **HTML Module Settings**:

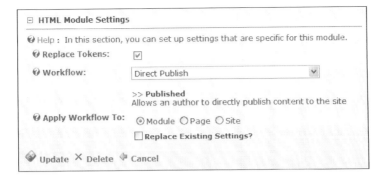

5. Make sure **Replace Tokens** is checked.

6. Click on **Update** to save your changes.

7. Select **Edit Content** from the module menu (or click on the **Edit Content** icon).

8. When the HTML editor is displayed, click on the **HTML** button at the bottom. This will let us edit the HTML directly and avoid any automatic formatting.

9. Type the following HTML into the editor:

```
<p>Site Status Report ([DateTime:Now])</p>
<hr />
<p><strong>Current User:</strong></p>
<p>Display Name: [User:DisplayName]</p>
<p>Email: [User:Email]</p>
<p><strong>Current Page:</strong></p>
<p>Name: [Tab:TabName]</p>
<p>Description: [Tab:Description]</p>
<p><strong>Portal Information:</strong></p>
<p>Name: [Portal:PortalName]</p>
<p>Contact: [Portal:Email]</p>
```

10. Click on **Save** to save your changes.

11. When the page is viewed, the tokens will be substituted with the current values from the portal settings:

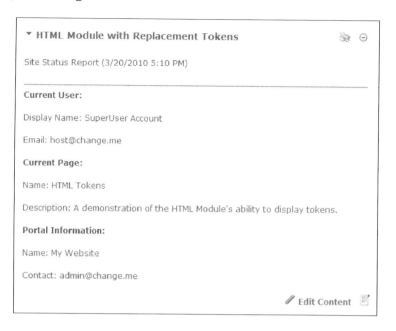

How it works...

Text token substitution gives you the ability to provide dynamic content from the normally static HTML module. Tokens are simple to use and give you direct access to values stored in the DNN database. That said, there are some limits on the use of tokens. Token replacement, which is done on-the-fly, conflicts with page caching which wants to preserve copies of the page for quick retrieval. This can kill performance if overused.

Using the HTML module with Flash

As the HTML module can display the same kind of code as a normal HTML file, we can embed Flash animation in the module just as we would in a normal web page. In this recipe we will see how to add a .swf file to the HTML module using the editor.

Getting ready

To follow along with this recipe you should be familiar with the basic content management tasks from *Chapter 2, Managing Users and Site Setup* (such as *Adding a module to a page*). You also need a sample Flash .swf file. For this example, we will use a sample flash from the Adobe site at http://www.adobe.com.

How to do it...

1. First we need a SWF file to use as an example. Open a browser to the following URL: `http://www.adobe.com/jp/events/cs3_web_edition_tour/swfs/perform.swf` and download the SWF file to a temporary folder.

2. Next, log in as Portal Administrator (`sysadmin` in our examples).

3. Add the HTML module to a new or existing page.

4. Select **Edit Content** from the module menu (or click on the **Edit Content** icon).

5. Place your cursor in the editor and click on the **Flash Manager** icon on the editor toolbar.

6. When the Flash Manager dialog is displayed, click on the **Select** button and navigate to the temporary folder where sample SWF file was saved.

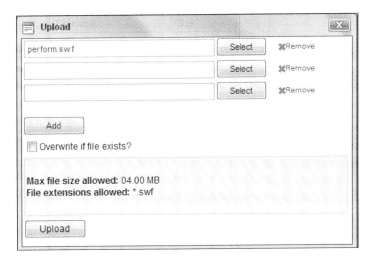

7. Click on **Upload** to load the SWF file.

8. Back on the Flash Manager dialog, set the width to 600 and the height to 400.

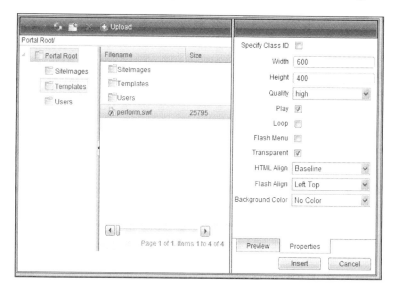

9. Leave the other options as default and click on **Insert**.

10. Click on **Save** to save your changes.

11. The Flash animation will now display on your page.

There's more...

In this recipe we saw how to display a SWF file in the HTML module. But there are other Flash formats that you can use. However, these depend on the user's browser having the proper plugins, so as administrator it is your decision whether to use other formats on your site.

Displaying an XML feed

The XML/XSL module is used to display a formatted XML data feed on a DNN page. There are many different kinds of publically available XML feeds and in this recipe will we see how to configure and format one.

Getting ready

To use the XML/XSL module you need a URL to a local or remote XML feed. In this recipe we will use the feed of a popular technology news site call Digg. We will also create a stylesheet to describe how the XML feed should be displayed. This is called the **XSL Transformation** (**XSLT**) file.

How to do it...

1. Before we can add an XML feed to our page, we must create a text file that describes how the information should be displayed.

2. Launch your normal Development Tool.

3. Select **New File...** from the **File** menu.

4. Select **General** as the **Category** and choose **XSLT File** as the template.

5. Click on **Open**.

6. A template XSL file will appear in the editor. Modify the file by adding the following code to describe how to display the XML elements:

```
<?xml version="1.0" encoding="utf-8"?>
<xsl:stylesheet version="1.0"
    xmlns:xsl="http://www.w3.org/1999/XSL/Transform"
```

```
                    xmlns:msxsl="urn:schemas-microsoft-com:xslt"
                                      exclude-result-prefixes="msxsl"
 >


   <xsl:param name="TITLE"/>

   <xsl:template match="rss">

     <xsl:for-each select="channel/item">
       <br>
         <strong>
             <xsl:value-of select="title"/>
         </strong>
         <br></br>

         <!-- only display markup for description if it's
                                              present -->
         <xsl:value-of select="description"
                           disable-output-escaping="yes"/>

       <a href="{link}" target="_main">
         [Click Here for More...]
       </a>

       </br>
       <br></br>
     </xsl:for-each>
   </xsl:template>

   <xsl:template match="description">
     <br>
       <xsl:value-of select="."/>
     </br>
   </xsl:template>

 </xsl:stylesheet>
```

7. Select **Save XSLTFile1.xslt As...** from the **File** menu.

8. Browse to a temporary folder and save the file as `news_feed.xsl`.

9. Now that we have a XSL file, log in as Portal Administrator (`sysadmin` in our examples).

10. Add the XML/XSL module to a new or existing page (if you don't see the XML/XSL module in the module drop-down list, see the recipe *Installing standard DNN modules* in *Chapter 1, Installation and Setup*).

11. From the Module menu, select **Edit XML/XSL Options** (or click on the **Edit XML/XSL Options** link).

12. Provide the following link information:

    ❑ **Link Type**: **URL (A Link To An External Resource)**

    ❑ **Location:** http://feeds.digg.com/digg/container/
       technology/popular.rss

13. Under the **XSL Transformation Settings**:

    ❑ **Link Type**: **File (A File On Your Site)**

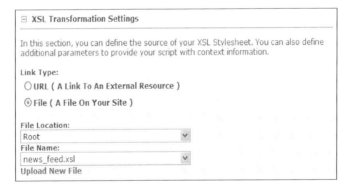

14. Click on **Upload New File** then click on the **Browse** button.

15. Browse to the news_feed.xsl you created in the temporary folder.

16. Click on **Upload Selected File**.

17. Click on **Update** to save your changes.

18. The XML feed will now display with the formatting described in the XSLT file.

Controlling the friendly URL rewriting

Since version 3, DNN has provided a mechanism to automatically convert the real URLs used for DNN pages to "friendly" URLs more compatible with people and search engines. For example, as search engines tend to ignore pages that use parameters, the URL `http://www.dotnetnuke.com/default.aspx?Tabid=527` could be converted to the more friendly URL `http://www.dotnetnuke.com/tabid/527/default.aspx`.

This URL Rewriting is done automatically by following a set of rules saved in a special file called `SiteURls.config` found in the root folder of the DNN installation. But there are situations where you may want to change how the automatic rewriting is done.

In this recipe, we will show how to override the URL rewriting to create our own friendly URL mapping to a specific DNN page.

Getting ready

For this recipe imagine we have a DNN page we created with the URL `http://localhost/dotnetnuke/default.aspx?tabid=123`. As this is an awkward URL, we will create a friendly "alias" called `http://localhost/dotnetnuke/SamplePage.aspx` that goes to the same place.

 The rules for URL rewriting are written using Regular Expressions. You can learn more about the syntax of regular expressions at `http://www.regular-expressions.info`.

How to do it...

1. Look on the DNN server and locate the root folder of the DNN installation.

2. Find the `SiteURls.config` file and open it in a text editor.

```xml
<?xml version="1.0" encoding="utf-8" ?>
<RewriterConfig>
    <Rules>
        <RewriterRule>
            <LookFor>.*DesktopDefault.aspx(.*)</LookFor>
            <SendTo>~/Default.aspx$1</SendTo>
        </RewriterRule>
        <RewriterRule>
            <LookFor>.*EditModule.aspx(.*)</LookFor>
            <SendTo>~/Default.aspx$1</SendTo>
        </RewriterRule>
        <RewriterRule>
            <LookFor>.*/TabId/(\d+)(.*)/Logoff.aspx</LookFor>
            <SendTo>~/Admin/Security/Logoff.aspx?tabid=$1</SendTo>
        </RewriterRule>
        <RewriterRule>
            <LookFor>.*/TabId/(\d+)(.*)/rss.aspx</LookFor>
            <SendTo>~/rss.aspx?TabId=$1</SendTo>
        </RewriterRule>
        <RewriterRule>
            <LookFor>.*Telerik.RadUploadProgressHandler.ashx(.*)
            </LookFor>
            <SendTo>~/Telerik.RadUploadProgressHandler.ashx$1
            </SendTo>
        </RewriterRule>
        <RewriterRule>
            <LookFor>[^?]*/TabId/(\d+)(.*)</LookFor>
            <SendTo>~/Default.aspx?TabId=$1</SendTo>
        </RewriterRule>
        <RewriterRule>
            <LookFor>.*BannerClickThrough.aspx(.*)</LookFor>
            <SendTo>~/DesktopModules/Admin/Banners/
                                    BannerClickThrough.aspx$1
            </SendTo>
        </RewriterRule>
    </Rules>
</RewriterConfig>
```

3. To create our own URL rewrite, add the following rule:

```
<?xml version="1.0" encoding="utf-8" ?>
<RewriterConfig>
    <Rules>
        <RewriterRule>
            <LookFor>.*/SamplePage.aspx</LookFor>
            <SendTo>~/default.aspx?tabid=123</SendTo>
        </RewriterRule>
        <RewriterRule>
            <LookFor>.*DesktopDefault.aspx(.*)</LookFor>
            <SendTo>~/Default.aspx$1</SendTo>
        </RewriterRule>
```

4. Save the file.

5. With this rule in place anyone navigating to `http://www.yoursite.com/SamplePage.aspx` will automatically redirect to `http://www.yoursite.com/default.aspx?tabid=123`.

See also

One word of warning when creating your own redirecting URL: you can get unexpected results if you redirect to a similarly named file that exists in another location called by the site. So always test your changes on a development site before making them on a production site.

Tracking your site with Google Analytics

Google Analytics is a tool from Google for tracking the activity on your website. It works by placing a tracking ID on your pages that Google can log and report on as people visit your site.

To use Analytics in DNN, you need to configure the Google Analytics module and you need a publically accessible DNN portal so that you can track your visitors. You also need to sign up for an Analytics account though you can use your Google Gmail account if you have one.

Getting ready

In this recipe we will use a sample Gmail account to log into Google Analytics and get a tracking number we can use in our DNN site.

To follow along with this recipe you must have the following:

- An Analytics or Gmail account (you can get a free one by going to `http://mail.google.com` and clicking on the **Create an Account** button).
- The username and password to your account.

How to do it...

1. The first step is to get an Analytics tracking ID from Google. If you already have a Tracking ID, skip to step 13, otherwise start by opening your favorite web browser and going to the Google Analytics home page (`http://www.google.com/analytics`).

2. If you have already signed up Analytics click on the **Access Analytics** button. Otherwise click on the **Sign Up Now** link.

3. You can sign in with your Gmail address and password.

4. If you are new to Analytics, you will see the Google Analytics **Sign Up** button.

5. Click on the **Sign Up** button.

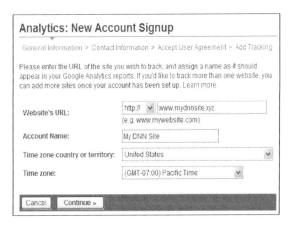

6. When prompted for account information, give the URL of your public DNN site and pick the name you want to see on the reports:

   ❏ **Website's URL** : `www.mydnnsite.xyz`

   ❏ **Account Name**: `My DNN Site`

   ❏ **Time zone country or territory**: Pick your country

   ❏ **Time zone**: Pick your time zone

7. Click on the **Continue** button.

8. For the contact information, provide your first and last name and your country or territory.

9. Click on the **Continue** button.

10. Read through the Terms of Service and check **Yes, I agree to the above terms and conditions**.

11. Click on the **Create New Account** button.

12. When your account is created you will see the Tracking Instructions page. Scroll down and click on the **Save and Finish** button at the bottom of the page.

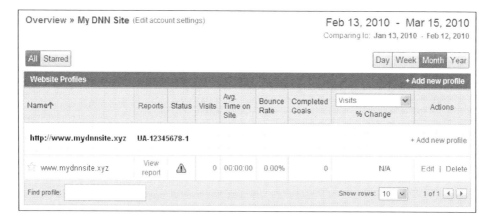

13. You will now see the Analytics overview page showing your website and the current analytics. Look at the number shown next to your URL—this is the tracking ID.

14. To put this tracking number in your DNN site, start by logging in as Portal Administrator (`sysadmin` in our examples).

15. From the **Admin** menu, select **Google Analytics**.

16. Type in the tracking ID from the Analytics overview page.

17. Click on **Update** to save your changes. You should see a message that your configuration was successfully updated.

18. To confirm that Google is correctly tracking your site, return to the Google Analytics overview page.

19. Look for the **Check Status** link near the top of your site profile. Click on the link and Google will check your site for the presence of the tracking ID and confirm that tracking is installed.

How it works...

Google Analytics works by inserting a small piece of JavaScript containing a unique tracking ID into each page you want to track. As visitors view your DNN pages, Google records the ID and offers the results on your Analytics Overview page. In addition, if you use a Google Webmaster account it will give you access to other Google options.

Publishing calendar events as an RSS feed

As we saw in *Chapter 3, Easy Tricks with Existing Modules*, the Events module displays a list of upcoming events in a calendar format. Beyond the basic calendar functionality, the Events module offers additional features for managing and publishing events.

In this recipe, we will see how to publish your calendar events as an RSS feed your users can subscribe to and view outside of your DNN site.

Getting ready

To follow along with this recipe you must have completed the following recipe from *Chapter 3 Easy Tricks with Existing Modules*:

▸ *Creating a calendar of events*

How to do it...

1. Start by logging in as Portal Administrator (`sysadmin` in our examples).
2. Go to the page holding your calendar.
3. Using the Add Event icon, create three sample events as follows (see the recipe *Creating a calendar of events* in *Chapter 3, Easy Tricks with Existing Modules*, for instructions):
    - ❑ **Title** : Groundhog Day Celebration
    - ❑ **Date**: February 2, 2010
    - ❑ **Description**: Join the whole office in celebrating Groundhog Day and a quick end to winter!
    - ❑ **Title** : Earth Day Observation
    - ❑ **Date**: April 22, 2010
    - ❑ **Description**: Join us for this year's Earth Day Observation in the central conference room.
    - ❑ **Title** : Office Summer Picnic
    - ❑ **Date**: June 25, 2010
    - ❑ **Description**: Everyone is invited to this year's summer picnic. See the signup sheet for details.
4. Select **Settings** from the Module menu (or click on the Settings icon).
5. Scroll down to the **Event Module Settings**.
6. Expand the **RSS Settings**.

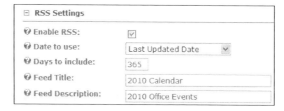

    - ❑ **Enable RSS**: Checked
    - ❑ **Days to use**: **Last Updated Date**

- ❑ **Days to include**: 365
- ❑ **Feed Title**: 2010 Calendar
- ❑ **Feed Description**: 2010 Office Events

7. Click on **Update** to save your changes.

8. When you return to the Events page you will see a small RSS icon has appeared at the top of the calendar:

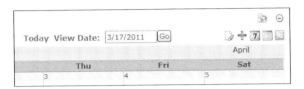

9. Clicking on the icon will allow users to subscribe to the RSS and see the events in a browser. For example, in a browser like Firefox the feed would appear as:

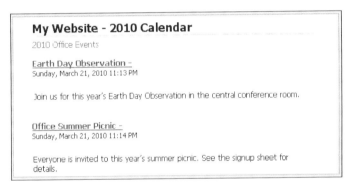

There's more...

One of the things you can do with a feed of calendar events is create an "Upcoming Events" page by consuming the feed within your own portal.

Designing your own forms

Forms and Lists (the successor of User Defined Table) is a powerful DNN module for creating your own forms and displaying them on your pages. As Portal Administrator you can define the data you want to collect and grant access to your users to add, update, and delete the records.

In this recipe we will see how to define a new form with the data types provided by DNN and how to collect the data and display it in a searchable list.

To make it easier to define the forms, DNN provides special data types to describe the data. This table shows some of the available types that we will use in this recipe.

Data Type	Description
Text	Used to hold text information from edit boxes, radio buttons, or drop-down lists.
Currency	Holds a value rounded to 2 digits and formatted using the currency symbol of the current culture setting.
Date	Holds a date value. When used in a form DNN will provide a pop-up calendar.
Download	Holds a file attached to the record.
Email	Creates a mailto link.
Image	Holds an image with optional dimensions.
Integer	Holds an integer number.
User Profile Link	Displays a hyperlink to a user profile.
Separator	Used to group columns on the form.
True/False	Displays a checkbox.
URL	Holds a formatted URL.

Getting ready

In this recipe we will define a Department form to record the departments in a company. We will store the unique department number, the department name, and other relevant information.

How to do it...

1. Start by logging in as Portal Administrator (sysadmin in our examples).

2. Add the **Form and List** module to a new or existing page (if you don't see the Form and List module in the module drop-down list, see the recipe *Installing standard DNN modules* in *Chapter 1, Installation and Setup*).

> ▼ **New Department**
> *No templates available.*
> Create a new Form or List based on a template from the list above, or design your own in **Form and List Configuration**.

3. To define a new form, click the **Form and List Configuration** link or icon.

4. A form template will display showing the basic audit columns. To add your own columns, click on the **Add New Column** link.

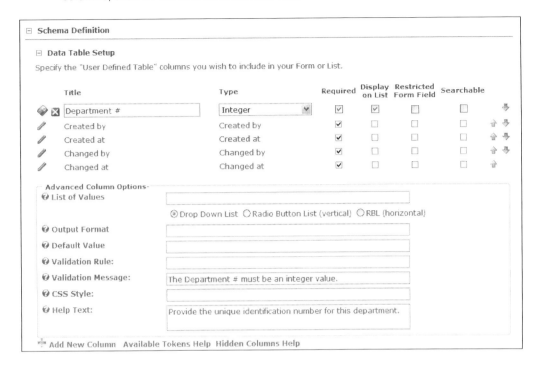

5. Define the first column:

   - **Title**: Department #
   - **Type**: **Integer**
   - **Required**: Checked
   - **Display on List**: Checked
   - **Restricted Form Field**: Unchecked
   - **Searchable**: Unchecked

6. You can add a help message by scrolling down to the **Advanced Column Options** and adding the following text:

   - Help Text: **Provide the unique identification number for this department**.

7. Click on **Add Column** to save your changes and add the next column.

8. Repeat these steps to add the remaining columns as shown below:

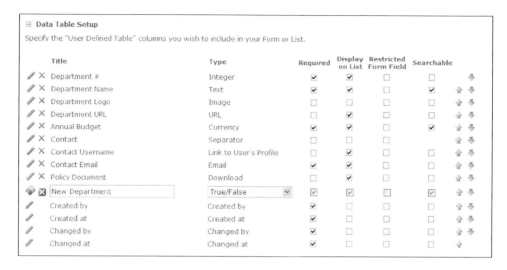

9. When all the columns have been added, click the **Save Configuration and Return** link at the bottom of the page.

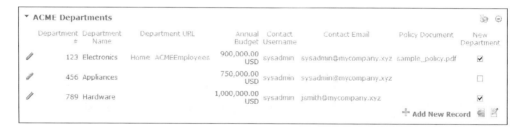

10. The form is now ready to use. Click on the **Add New Record** link to add department records.

11. Based on the columns you defined, the edit form will display. Note how the help messages you provided for the columns appear as **?** icons on the form:

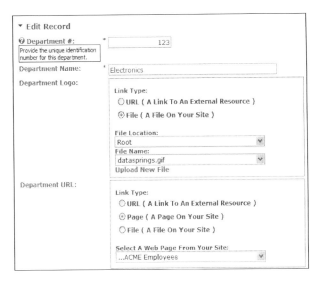

12. In addition, the edit form offers ways to attach documents, specify URLs, or upload images based on the column data types you selected.

13. The form will also perform basic validation based on the column data type. For example, we defined `Department #` to be an integer, so if we try to use text for a department number we will see a validation message:

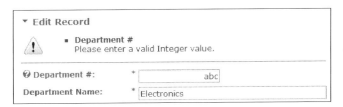

14. Another feature of the Form and List module is the ability to provide searching on the records. To see how searching works, start by clicking on the **Form and List Configuration** link in the lower-right corner.

15. Scroll down to **List Settings** and expand it.

16. Make sure the following are checked:

    ❑ **Show Search Box**: Checked

    ❑ **Simple Search**: Checked

    ❑ **Show no records until Search**: Checked

17. Click on the **Save Configuration and Return** link at the bottom of the page.

18. Now the list of departments is hidden and replaced with a simple search box. To perform a search, type in the search box and click on the **Search** link.

How it works...

The Form and List module saves your form definitions in a table called UserDefinedFields in the DNN database. As new records are created, the values for each of the columns are saved in a table called UserDefinedData. If you would like to export your custom records from the DNN database see the recipe *Exporting from a user defined form* in *Chapter 11, Challenging Custom Modules*.

There's more...

Simple search will look for the text contained within any searchable column. If you are looking for a field starting with a given text use "|elec" or look for trailing parts using "onics|" and exact matches by "|electronics|". Advanced Search offers these options in a drop-down list and allows you to specify the column to search in.

See also

To learn more about the Form and List module and see how to control the format of the lists, see the next recipe *Styling your own forms*.

Styling your own forms

As we saw in the recipe *Designing your own forms*, the Form and List module will collect custom data and display it as a list of records. But the module also gives you the ability to control how the records are displayed.

In this recipe we will take the Department form created in the previous recipe and format the list of departments using an XSL stylesheet.

Getting ready

To follow along with this recipe you must have completed the previous recipe:

▶ *Designing your own forms*

How to do it...

1. Start by logging in as Portal Administrator (sysadmin in our examples).

2. Go to the page holding the department form from the previous recipe.

3. Click on the **Form and List Configuration** icon in the lower right corner.

4. Scroll down to **List Settings** and expand it.

5. For the **Rendering Method**, select **XSLT using built-in stylesheets**.

6. Use the drop-down list and select **cardview.xsl**.

7. Click on the **Save Configuration and Return** link at the bottom of the page.

8. Now the departments are displayed with all fields shown in a formatted list:

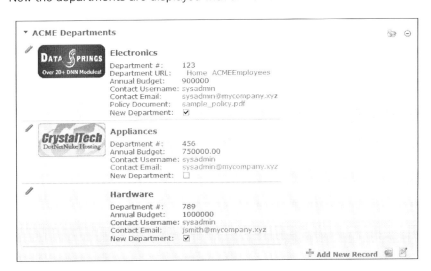

9. You can experiment with the other available stylesheets to see what looks best on your page.

How it works...

The XSL stylesheet describes how the columns of the form should display. You can create your own stylesheets by selecting the XSLT using self-made or generated stylesheets options and uploading a custom stylesheet.

For more information on XSL stylesheets, visit `http://www.w3.org/Style/XSL`.

11
Challenging Custom Modules

- ▶ Making modules searchable
- ▶ Exporting module data
- ▶ Importing module data
- ▶ Exporting and importing user defined tables
- ▶ Creating custom module actions
- ▶ Using HTML in the manifest
- ▶ Deploying a new module version
- ▶ Using multiple database connections

Introduction

So far in this book we have looked at the different modules that are available in DNN along with how to develop your own custom modules. In this chapter, we will look at some advanced module development techniques. We will learn more about the DNN interfaces for searching, importing, exporting, and updating modules. We will also explore some lesser known techniques such as using HTML in the manifest and using multiple database connections.

DNN offers several module interfaces for developers. Unlike the one-way APIs used in previous DNN versions, these interfaces represent a two-way interaction between the developer and the portal framework. All modules can access these interfaces because they inherit from the `PortalModuleBase` class, but custom modules need custom code to link to the interface. The recipes in this chapter demonstrate four of the interfaces:

- ► `iSearchable`
- ► `iPortable`
- ► `iActionable`
- ► `iUpdatable`

Making modules searchable

Most websites offer the ability for a visitor to search the site content. DNN provides a built-in search engine plus an interface for indexing the content coming from your modules.

In this recipe we will add code to the sample Employee module that will take the content from the `GetEmployees` stored procedure and index it in the DNN default data store. When the data has been indexed it becomes searchable using the DNN search tool (depending on your site's skin this appears as a little magnifying glass in the upper-right corner of the portal).

Getting ready

To follow along with this recipe you must have completed the following recipe from *Chapter 5, Building, Debugging, and Deploying Modules*:

- ► *Deploying a module as a standalone package*

As the developer you must also decide which columns will be searchable for your module. You do not need to make all your fields searchable. Instead, choose the most important fields that help identify a unique record. For example, it is better to index the description and summary of a document, rather than the entire document itself. In this example we will use Employee full name, hire date, and salary as the searchable fields. As text fields make the best fields for searching we will format the date and salary fields into a searchable text string.

To help identify how the values from a module should be indexed, DNN offers different properties we can assign to our module data:

Property	Description
Title	Text that is displayed in the search results (first and last name in this example).
Description	Text that summarizes the content of the search results (name, hire date, and e-mail address in this example).
Content	The fields users can search on (salary, hire date, e-mail address, new hire flag, and imageURL in this example).

Property	Description
SearchKey	The content's unique ID (ItemID in this example) within the module.
Author	The ID of the user that created the content (CreatedBy in this example).
PubDate	The date the content was made available to the search engine (CreatedDate in this example).
GUID	A unique identifier used when syndicating the module contents (ItemID in this example). It can also be used for displaying the appropriate record (as it appears as part of the query string).

How to do it...

1. Start by launching the Development Tool and loading the Employee project.

2. Double-click to open the `EmployeeController.vb` file.

3. Scroll down to the **Optional Interfaces** region and look for the `GetSearchItems` function.

4. When the sample module was generated by the Starter Kit, it created a basic searchable interface. We need to replace some of the generated code with the specific fields of our module:

```
Public Function GetSearchItems(ByVal ModInfo As
    Entities.Modules.ModuleInfo) As
        DotNetNuke.Services.Search.SearchItemInfoCollection Implements
        DotNetNuke.Entities.Modules.ISearchable.GetSearchItems


' define our own strings to hold the values for the SearchItem
    Dim strTitle As String
    Dim strDescription As String
    Dim intAuthor As Integer
    Dim dtePubDate As Date
    Dim strSearchKey As String
    Dim strContent As String


    Dim SearchItemCollection As New SearchItemInfoCollection


    ' use the template GetEmployees() routine to get all employee
        records from the database table (without filtering)
    Dim colEmployees As List(Of EmployeeInfo) =
                                GetEmployees(ModInfo.ModuleID)
    Dim objEmployee As EmployeeInfo
    For Each objEmployee In colEmployees
```

```
' build the strings with the fields we want to index
strTitle = ModInfo.ModuleTitle + " - " +
                                    objEmployee.ContactInfo()
strDescription = objEmployee.EmpFirstName & " " &
                 objEmployee.EmpLastName & " - Hired " &
                 objEmployee.FormattedHireDate &
                 " New Hire: " & objEmployee.NewHire &
                 " Email:" & objEmployee.EmailAddress
intAuthor = objEmployee.CreatedByUser
dtePubDate = objEmployee.CreatedDate
strSearchKey = objEmployee.ItemId.ToString
strContent = System.Web.HttpUtility.HtmlDecode
            (objEmployee.EmpFirstName & " " &
             objEmployee.EmpLastName &
             " " & objEmployee.Salary.ToString & " " &
             objEmployee.HireDate.ToString &
             " " & objEmployee.EmailAddress)


' Create a search item and pass the strings as arguments
Dim SearchItem As SearchItemInfo = New SearchItemInfo(strTitle,
        strDescription, intAuthor, dtePubDate,
        ModInfo.ModuleID, strSearchKey, strContent, "ItemId=" &
        objEmployee.ItemId.ToString)
SearchItemCollection.Add(SearchItem)


    Next


    Return SearchItemCollection


End Function
```

5. Now that we have defined what is searchable in the module, rebuild and redeploy the module.

6. The next step is to index the module data to make it searchable. Log in as SuperUser.

7. Select **Search Admin** from the **Host** menu.

8. Click on the **Re-Index Content** link to index the module data. You will see the message **Content Re-indexed** when it finishes. (Note: On a large site this may take a while.)

9. To search the module data look for the search box (just above the **Login/Logout** link on the default skin).

10. Type **25000** (or other sample employee salary) and click on the search icon.

11. The search results will display:

12. As we defined in the code, the Title in the search results is the module name, employee name, and hire date. The description is the name, hire information, and e-mail that appear just below the title. The link is generated from the ItemId and leads to the ACME employee page.

How it works...

As we did in previous recipes, we used the `EmployeeInfo` class to get the information for indexing. The important thing is to select the best `SearchItem` property for each piece of data so DNN has an idea of what kind of data we are indexing.

By coding this `iSearchable` interface, DNN will extract all the employee information from the module (by calling the `GetEmployees` stored procedure) and save this information in the data store. When the data is in the store it becomes available for searching.

There's more...

We are using the `System.Web.HttpUtility.HtmlDecode` function in this code to clean our content and make it safe for the Web in case this content will be syndicated (plus it's also good programming practice). However, it's best to avoid embedding HTML in your search results because even with `HtmlDecode` it might cause unexpected formatting of the results.

Exporting module data

One of the features available to a DNN module is the ability to export data from the database into an XML file. This makes it possible to save or transfer data collected through one portal to another portal or other application. This feature appears in the module action menu but also for the page export and portal template creation. Exporting and importing are done with the `iPortable` interface and require defining what fields from the module should be in the export.

In this recipe we'll use the sample Employee module from *Chapter 5, Building, Debugging, and Deploying Modules* and see the code we must add to implement the interface and perform an export.

Getting ready

To follow along with this recipe you must have completed the following recipe from *Chapter 5*:

▸ *Deploying a module as a standalone package*

How to do it...

1. Start by launching the Development Tool and loading the Employee project.
2. Double-click to open the `EmployeeController.vb` file.
3. Scroll down to the **Optional Interfaces** region and look for the `ExportModule` function.
4. We need to define the fields of the module that are available for export. The original Starter Kit created one temporary field called Content. We need to replace Content with the actual module fields as follows:

```
Public Function ExportModule(ByVal ModuleID As Integer) As String
    Implements DotNetNuke.Entities.Modules.IPortable.ExportModule

    Dim strXML As String = ""

    Dim colEmployees As List(Of EmployeeInfo) =
                                   GetEmployees(ModuleID)
    If colEmployees.Count <> 0 Then
    strXML += "<Employees>"
    Dim objEmployee As EmployeeInfo
    For Each objEmployee In colEmployees
        strXML += "<Employee>"

                strXML += "<EmpFirstName>" &
```

```
                    XMLEncode(objEmployee.EmpFirstName) & "</EmpFirstName>"
                        strXML += "<EmpLastName>" &
                    XMLEncode(objEmployee.EmpLastName) & "</EmpLastName>"
                        strXML += "<ManagerNo>" &
                    XMLEncode(objEmployee.ManagerNo) & "</ManagerNo>"
                        strXML += "<HireDate>" &
                    XMLEncode(objEmployee.HireDate) & "</HireDate>"
                        strXML += "<Salary>" &
                        XMLEncode(objEmployee.Salary) & "</Salary>"


            strXML += "</Employee>"
    Next
    strXML += "</Employees>"
      End If


      Return strXML


    End Function
```

5. That's all the code that is needed. To test the results, start by rebuilding and redeploying the module.

6. Go to the page with the Employee module and select **Export Content** from the module action menu.

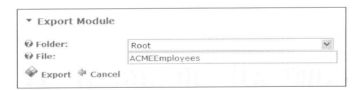

7. Select a temporary folder (Root for example) and click on the **Export** link.

8. To view the XML file it created look in the root folder of your portal (for example, dotnetnuke\Portals\0). Look for the file content.ACMEEmployee. ACMEEmployees.xml.

9. Depending on how many records were in the employee table, the file will look something like this:

```
<?xml version="1.0" encoding="utf-8" ?>
- <content type="ACMEEmployee" version="01.00.00">
  - <Employees>
    - <Employee>
      - <EmpFirstName>
        - <![CDATA[ John
      ]]>
```

```
        </EmpFirstName>
      -  <EmpLastName>
        -  <![CDATA[ Smith
  ]]>
        </EmpLastName>
      -  <ManagerNo>
        -  <![CDATA[ 0
  ]]>
        </ManagerNo>
      -  <HireDate>
        -  <![CDATA[ 3/23/2010
  ]]>
        </HireDate>
      -  <Salary>
        -  <![CDATA[ 25000
  ]]>
        </Salary>
      </Employee>
    </Employees>
  </content>
```

How it works...

Adding the code to the `ExportModule` function provided the XML tags needed to save our custom data in the XML file. The `iPortable` interface did the rest.

There's more...

You may be tempted to export all the fields in your module but there are a few simple rules when picking the export fields:

▶ Do not include ModuleId or ItemId as these are regenerated by the system on import

▶ Similarly, there is no need to export create and update dates

▶ You do not need to include calculated fields unless the export is for another module or application

▶ In general, export only the fields needed for the insert routine used by your import code (the `AddEmployee` routine for example)

See also

To see how to load your module table with the records from this export, see the next recipe *Importing module data*.

Importing module data

As we saw in the _Exporting module data_ recipe, DNN provides tools for importing and exporting data in and out of the database using the `iPortable` interface. To use the interface we must define the fields in the export file and define how to save these fields when the file is imported.

In this recipe we'll use the export file from the previous recipe to import into the sample Employee module.

Getting ready

To follow along with this recipe you must have completed the following previous recipes:

▸ _Deploying a module as a standalone package_

▸ _Exporting module data_

How to do it...

1. Start by launching the Development Tool and loading the Employee project.

2. Double-click to open the `EmployeeController.vb` file.

3. Scroll down to the **Optional Interfaces** region and look for the `ImportModule` subroutine.

4. We need to define the fields in the XML file we can import. The original starter kit created one temporary field called Content. We need to replace Content with the actual fields as follows:

```
Public Sub ImportModule(ByVal ModuleID As Integer,
  ByVal EmpFirstName As String, ByVal Version As String,
  ByVal UserId As Integer) Implements
    DotNetNuke.Entities.Modules.IPortable.ImportModule

    Dim xmlEmployee As XmlNode
    Dim xmlEmployees As XmlNode = GetContent(EmpFirstName,
                                             "Employees")
    For Each xmlEmployee In xmlEmployees.SelectNodes("Employee")
    Dim objEmployee As New EmployeeInfo
    objEmployee.ModuleId = ModuleID

    objEmployee.EmpFirstName =
            xmlEmployee.SelectSingleNode("EmpFirstName").InnerText
    objEmployee.EmpLastName =
            xmlEmployee.SelectSingleNode("EmpLastName").InnerText
    objEmployee.ManagerNo =
```

```
                    xmlEmployee.SelectSingleNode("ManagerNo").InnerText
           objEmployee.HireDate =
                    xmlEmployee.SelectSingleNode("HireDate").InnerText
           objEmployee.Salary =
                    xmlEmployee.SelectSingleNode("Salary").InnerText


           objEmployee.CreatedByUser = UserId
           AddEmployee(objEmployee)
            Next


        End Sub
```

5. That's all the code that is needed on the import side. To test the results, start by rebuilding and redeploying the module.

6. Go to the page with the Employee module and select **Import Content** from the module action menu.

7. Select `Root` for the Folder and select the file from your previous export.

8. Click on the `Import` link.

9. The records from the XML export file will now load into the Employee table. If you are importing back into the table that created the export, you will likely see duplicate records. This occurs because we don't include ItemID in our export. When the new records are imported, new ItemIDs are generated.

How it works...

Adding the code to the `ImportModule` function defined how the fields from the XML file fit into the `EmployeeInfo` object which saves the data in the database.

Exporting and importing user defined tables

In the previous two recipes we saw how to import and export data in and out of a module using an XML file. This is built-in functionality that is available to all DNN modules. With the Form and List module you have an extra option to import and export data from your custom table using a Comma Separated Values (CSV) file instead of XML.

Getting ready

To follow along with this recipe you must have completed the following recipe from
Chapter 10, Advanced Tricks with Existing Modules:

▶   _Designing your own forms_

How to do it...

1.   Start by logging in as Portal Administrator.

2.   Go to the page holding the Department form from the recipe _Designing Your_
     Own Forms.

3.   From the module action menu, select **Export to CSV file.**

4.   Select a temporary folder (like `Templates/`) and name the file `ACMEDepartments`.

5.   Select comma (**,**) for the delimiter.

6.   Click on the **Export** link.

7.   This will create a CSV file called `ACMEDepartments.csv` in the `Templates` folder
     of your portal (for example, `\dotnetnuke\Portals\0\Templates`). If you have
     a spreadsheet application such as Microsoft Excel or OpenOffice Calc, you can open
     the file and see your user defined records: In addition, you can edit these records and
     resave as a CSV file for import into the Forms and Lists module.

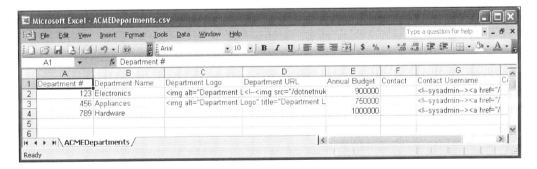

8. To import the CSV file back into your Form and List module, the process is very similar. Start by selecting **Import from CSV File** from the module action menu.

9. Select the folder where you saved the CSV file and choose comma (**,**) for the delimiter.
10. Click on **Import** to load the file.

 Because the export file in this example includes the unique identifier, it will not import records that already exist in your custom table. To see the import work you may need to delete some records from the table before trying the import.

Creating custom module actions

In many recipes we have used the module action menu that appears next to the module title and is used to select additional module features. Modules that inherit from the `PortalModuleBase` class receive several default actions in the menu (things like Import/ Export Content). In this recipe we will show how to add your own actions in the module menu using the `iActionable` interface.

There are three basic tasks to define our own module actions:

- Define the custom action menu item
- Create a subroutine to handle the `Click` event
- Connect the `Click` event handler to the menu item

Getting ready

To follow along with this recipe you must have completed the following recipe from *Chapter 5 , Building, Debugging, and Deploying Modules:*

- *Deploying a module as a standalone package*

For this recipe we will demonstrate the action menu processing by creating a simple HTML table of statistics on the View Employee form that is hidden until we click on the **Show Statistics** action menu item.

How to do it...

1. Start by launching the Development Tool and loading the Employee project.

2. Double-click to open the `ViewEmployee.ascx` file. Scroll down to the bottom of the file and add this new hidden HTML table:

```
<table id="tblStats" cellspacing="2" cellpadding="2" border="0"
    runat="server" style="width: 100%" visible="false">
    <tr>
        <td width="25%" class="SubHead">
            Total Company Sales:
        </td>
        <td width="75%">
            $1,234,567.00
        </td>
    </tr>
    <tr>
        <td width="25%" class="SubHead">
            Total Company Expenses:
        </td>
        <td width="75%">
            $234,567.00
        </td>
    </tr>
</table>
```

3. Next, double-click to open the `ViewEmployee.ascx.vb` file.

4. At the top of the file add the necessary import directive:

```
Imports DotNetNuke.Entities.Modules.Actions
```

5. Scroll down to the **Optional Interfaces** region and look for the `ModuleActions` property.

```
Public ReadOnly Property ModuleActions() As Entities.Modules.
Actions.ModuleActionCollection Implements Entities.Modules.
IActionable.ModuleActions
    Get
    Dim Actions As New Entities.Modules.Actions.
ModuleActionCollection
    Actions.Add(GetNextActionID, Localization.GetString(Entities.
Modules.Actions.ModuleActionType.A
    ddContent, LocalResourceFile),
    Entities.Modules.Actions.ModuleActionType.AddContent, "", "",
    EditUrl(), False, Security.SecurityAccessLevel.Edit, True,
                                                                False)
```

```
        Return Actions
      End Get
  End Property
```

6. If you look at the code that was originally created by the Starter Kit, there is already one action defined. This is the `Add Content` action we use to add a new Employee record.

7. Now that we see what an action looks like, let's create a second action that will make visible the new HTML table:

```
Public ReadOnly Property ModuleActions() As
  Entities.Modules.Actions.ModuleActionCollection Implements
  Entities.Modules.IActionable.ModuleActions
    Get
  Dim Actions As New
    Entities.Modules.Actions.ModuleActionCollection
  Actions.Add(GetNextActionID,
    Localization.GetString(Entities.Modules.Actions.
    ModuleActionType.AddContent, LocalResourceFile),
    Entities.Modules.Actions.ModuleActionType.AddContent, "", "",
    EditUrl(), False, Security.SecurityAccessLevel.Edit, True,
                                                            False)


  Actions.Add(GetNextActionID, "Show Statistics",
    Entities.Modules.Actions.ModuleActionType.AddContent,
    "ShowStats", "view.gif", "", False,
    Security.SecurityAccessLevel.View, True, False)


        Return Actions
      End Get
  End Property
```

8. This creates a new item in the module action menu called `Show Statistics`. The next step is to create a subroutine to perform the action when the menu item is selected. Scroll down to the bottom of the **Optional Interfaces** region.

9. Add the following subroutine:

```
Private Sub ModuleAction_Click(ByVal sender As Object,
                               ByVal e As ActionEventArgs)
    Select Case e.Action.CommandArgument
    Case "ShowStats"
        tblStats.Visible = True
    End Select
End Sub
```

10. This routine will make the HTML visible when the action is selected. The last step is to connect the action menu item to this click handler. Scroll to the `Page_Load` routine and add the following code just before the check for post back:

```
Private Sub Page_Load(ByVal sender As System.Object,
                      ByVal e As System.EventArgs) Handles MyBase.Load
    Try

        'Add an Action Event Handler to the Skin
        AddActionHandler(AddressOf ModuleAction_Click)

        If Not Page.IsPostBack Then
```

11. Select **Save All** from the **File** menu to save your changes.

12. Rebuild and redeploy the module.

13. Go to the page with the Employee module. When you first see the page, the statistics table should be invisible.

14. Look under the module action menu. You should see the new menu option **Show Statistics.**

15. Select **Show Statistics** from the menu and the statistics table should display at the bottom of the page.

How it works...

When calling `Actions.Add()` to define the new action, nine key arguments are passed. In this table you can see the arguments and how they were used in this example:

Argument	Original template action	New action
Title	Pulled from resource file	Hardcoded `"Show Statistics"`
Command name/Action	`AddContent`	`AddContent`
Optional Parameter	None	`"ShowStats"`
Icon to display	None	`"view.gif"`
Optional URL	`EditUrl()`	None
Action event T/F	`False`	`False`
Required security level	`Edit`	`View`
Visible T/F	`True`	`True`
New window T/F	`False`	`False`

There's more...

In this example we hardcoded our menu item text `"Show Statistics"` and the numbers for our statistics. This was done to make the example easier to read. In real modules you should avoid hard coding text by using the resource file (something like `Localization.GetString("StatisticsPrompt", LocalResourceFile)`).

Using HTML in your manifest

Although the manifest file is primarily for telling DNN where to install the various pieces of your module, the manifest does contain text for things like the release notes and the user license. Rather than using plain text for these documents it is possible to use HTML to format the information.

In this recipe we will enhance the manifest file by using HTML formatting.

Getting ready

To follow along with this recipe you must have completed the following recipe from *Chapter 5, Building, Debugging, and Deploying Modules*:

▸ *Editing the Manifest File*

How to do it...

1. Start by launching the Development Tool and loading the Employee project.

2. Double-click to open the `Employee.dnn` file.

3. Scroll down until you see the section labeled `<license>`.

   ```
   <license src="license.txt" />.
   ```

4. Replace the reference to `license.txt` with a character data tag (CDATA) and the HTML representing your formatted license text:

   ```
   <license>
   <![CDATA[
       <h1>SAMPLE END USER LICENSE AGREEMENT (EULA)</h1>

       This End-User License Agreement ("EULA") is a legal agreement
         made and entered into by you ("LICENSEE"), the person,
         business or other entity which will be bound by and subject
         to the terms and conditions set forth in this EULA, and ACME
         Incorporated ("ACME"), the author of SOFTWARE (as defined
         below). By installing and using the SOFTWARE, LICENSEE agrees
         to be bound by all of the terms and conditions of this EULA.
         If LICENSEE does not agree to the terms of this EULA,
         LICENSEE may not install or use the SOFTWARE.

       <p>

       <h3>INTRODUCTION</h3>

       <h3>DEFINITIONS</h3>

       <h3>MORE STUFF LIKE THIS...</h3>
   ]]>
   </license>
   ```

5. The same trick also works in the release notes section. Try the following code for the release notes:

   ```
   <releaseNotes>
   <![CDATA[
   <h1>RELEASE NOTES</h1>
   These are some sample release notes demonstrating HTML formatting.
   <h3>Version 01.00.00</h3>
   <table border="1">
   <tr>
   <th>Change ID</th>
   <th>Date</th>
   <th>Description</th>
   </tr>
   <tr>
   <td>12345</td>
   ```

```
<td>10/01/2010</td>
<td>Fixed bug in manifest file.</td>
</tr>
</table>
]]>
</releaseNotes>
```

6. Finally, you can use this same technique to provide a better company URL and e-mail link in the **Owner** section. Normally when the owner is displayed in the package information the URL and e-mail are displayed as fixed text:

❷ Owner:	John Smith
❷ Organization:	ACME Corporation
❷ Url:	http://www.mycompany.xyz
❷ Email Address:	support@mycompany.xyz

7. You can turn the company URL into a real hyperlink and the e-mail address into a `mailto:` link with the following code:

```
<owner>
    <name>John Smith</name>
    <organization>ACME Corporation</organization>
    <url><![CDATA[<a href="http://www.mycompany.xyz/">
        http://www.mycompany.xyz/</a>]]></url>
    <email><![CDATA[<a href="mailto:support@mycompany.xyz">
        support@mycompany.xyz</a>]]></email>
</owner>
```

8. To check the results, log in as SuperUser and use the **Install Extension Wizard** to deploy the module.

9. When the wizard displays the **Package Information** page the new links will appear:

▾ **Install Extension**

Package Information

The following information was found in the package manifest.

❷ Name:	ACME.Employee
❷ Type:	Module
❷ Friendly Name:	ACME Employees
❷ Description:	A list of current ACME employees.
❷ Version:	1.0.0
❷ Owner:	John Smith
❷ Organization:	ACME Corporation
❷ Url:	http://www.mycompany.xyz/
❷ Email Address:	support@mycompany.xyz

10. When the **Release Notes** display they will appear in formatted HTML:

11. Similarly, the license agreement will appear in formatted HTML:

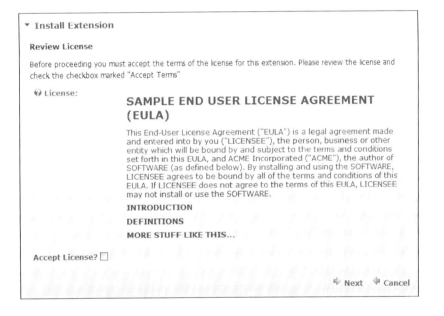

Deploying a new module version

In previous recipes we have seen how to create and deploy a DNN module. But what happens when you have a new version that you want to deploy? How do you redeploy a module so it upgrades the previous version rather than replacing it?

In this recipe we will see how to assign version numbers to a module and update the manifest file to create a seamless module upgrade.

There are three things to consider when planning a module upgrade:

▶ What changes do you need to make to the database?

▶ Has the assemble (the DLL file) changed?

▶ Have you added any new files (images, forms, and so on)?

Getting ready

To follow along with this recipe you must have completed the following recipe from *Chapter 5, Building, Debugging, and Deploying Modules*:

▶ *Deploying a module as a standalone package*

In this recipe we will enhance the sample Employee project by adding three new fields to the employee table: `DepartmentID`, `EmployeeURL`, and `SecurityLevel`. This means adding new table columns, updating a stored procedure, and rewriting the manifest file.

How to do it...

1. We'll start by creating a new `SqlDataProvider` script that will create the new fields in the database. Launch the Development Tool and load the Employee project.

2. In the Solution Explorer, right-click on the Employee project.

3. Select **New Item...** from the **Add** pop-up menu.

4. Pick **Text File** as the template and called it `01.01.00.SqlDataProvider`.

5. Click on **Add** to create the file.

6. To create the three new fields in the Employee table, add the following code to the top of the file:

```
/** Alter Table **/

if not exists (select * FROM syscolumns WHERE (name =
  'DepartmentID') AND (id = OBJECT_ID(N'{databaseOwner}
    [{objectQualifier}ACME_Employee]')))
```

```
BEGIN

    ALTER TABLE {databaseOwner}[{objectQualifier}ACME_Employee]
    ADD DepartmentID VARCHAR (30) ;

    ALTER TABLE {databaseOwner}[{objectQualifier}ACME_Employee]
    ADD EmployeeURL VARCHAR (120);

    ALTER TABLE {databaseOwner}[{objectQualifier}ACME_Employee]
    ADD SecurityLevel VARCHAR (30);

END

GO
```

7. Next, we'll add the code to drop the existing `GetEmployeesByFilter` procedure from version one and replaced it with an improved version:

```
/** Drop Existing Stored Procedures   **/

if exists (select * from dbo.sysobjects where id =
  object_id(N'{databaseOwner}[{objectQualifier}
    ACME_GetEmployeesByFilter]') and OBJECTPROPERTY(id,
      N'IsProcedure') = 1)
   drop procedure {databaseOwner}{objectQualifier}ACME_
GetEmployeesByFilter
GO

/** Recreate stored procedure with new columns   **/

CREATE procedure {databaseOwner}{objectQualifier}ACME_
GetEmployeesByFilter
    @ModuleID int,
    @MgrFilter int,
    @SalaryFilter  int,
    @PageIndex int,
    @PageSize int
AS

/** If we pass -1 for a numeric filter it means ignore the filter
**/

    DECLARE @PageLowerBound int
```

```
        DECLARE @PageUpperBound int

/** Calculate the upper and lower bonds based on the PageIndex and
PageSize  **/

    SET @PageLowerBound = @PageSize * @PageIndex
    SET @PageUpperBound = @PageLowerBound + @PageSize + 1

/** create a temp table to hold the Ids of our results  **/

    CREATE TABLE #PageIndex
    (
        IndexID      int IDENTITY (1, 1) NOT NULL,
        ItemId   int
    )

/** populate the temp temp with the filtered results **/

    INSERT INTO #PageIndex (ItemId)
    SELECT ItemId
    FROM {objectQualifier}ACME_Employee
    WHERE (ModuleId = @ModuleId) AND  (ManagerNo = @MgrFilter OR
                  @MgrFilter = -1) AND (Salary >= @SalaryFilter)
    ORDER BY ItemId DESC

/** remember the count of the results  **/

    SELECT COUNT(*) as TotalRecords
    FROM #PageIndex

/** join the filtered Ids to the employee table to get our fields
**/

select {objectQualifier}ACME_Employee.ModuleId,
       {objectQualifier}ACME_Employee.ItemId,
       EmpFirstName,
       EmpLastName,
       ManagerNo,
       HireDate,
       Salary,
       DepartmentID,
```

```
        EmployeeURL,
        SecurityLevel,
        {objectQualifier}ACME_Employee.CreatedByUser,
        {objectQualifier}ACME_Employee.CreatedDate,
        'CreatedByUserName' = {objectQualifier}Users.FirstName + '
                        ' + {objectQualifier}Users.LastName
FROM {objectQualifier}ACME_Employee
INNER JOIN {objectQualifier}Users on
                {objectQualifier}ACME_Employee.CreatedByUser =
                                {objectQualifier}Users.UserId
    INNER JOIN #PageIndex PageIndex
        ON {objectQualifier}ACME_Employee.ItemId = PageIndex.ItemId
    WHERE ( (PageIndex.IndexID > @PageLowerBound) OR
                                @PageLowerBound is null )
        AND ( (PageIndex.IndexID < @PageUpperBound) OR
                                @PageUpperBound is null )
    ORDER BY
        PageIndex.IndexID


    GO
```

8. Next we need to update the manifest file to include the new `01.01.00.SqlDataProvider file`. Double-click to open the `Employee.dnn` file.

9. At the top of the file, update the version number to `01.01.00`:

```
<packages>
  <package name="ACME.Employee" type="Module"
          version="01.01.00">
    <friendlyName>ACME Employees</friendlyName>
```

10. Scroll down until you see the `<scripts>` section and add the following code:

```
<scripts>
  <basePath>DesktopModules\ACME.Employee</basePath>
  <script type="Install">
    <name>01.00.00.SqlDataProvider</name>
    <version>01.00.00</version>
  </script>
  <script type="Install">
    <name>01.01.00.SqlDataProvider</name>
    <version>01.01.00</version>
  </script>
  <script type="UnInstall">
    <name>Uninstall.SqlDataProvider</name>
    <version>01.00.00</version>
  </script>
</scripts>
```

11. The last change for the manifest is to update the version number on the assembly:

```
<assemblies>
    <assembly>
        <path>bin</path>
        <name>Employee.dll</name>
        <version>01.01.00</version>
    </assembly>
</assemblies>
```

12. Select **Save All** from the **File** menu to save your changes.

13. Rebuild the project and create an installation ZIP file according to the instructions in the recipe *Deploying a module as a standalone package* from *Chapter 5, Building, Debugging, and Deploying Modules*. Include both the `01.00.00` and `01.01.00` `SqlDataProvider` files.

14. Name the new ZIP file `Employee_01.01.00_Install.zip`.

15. The `Employee_01.01.00_Install.zip` file should now contain the following:

Name	Type ▲	Packe...	Has ...	Size
App_LocalResources	File Folder	0 KB		0 KB
Bin	File Folder	0 KB		0 KB
EditEmployee.ascx	ASP.NET User Control	1 KB	No	4 KB
Settings.ascx	ASP.NET User Control	1 KB	No	1 KB
ViewEmployee.ascx	ASP.NET User Control	2 KB	No	5 KB
Employee.dnn	DNN File	2 KB	No	6 KB
01.00.00.SqlDataProvider	SQLDATAPROVIDER File	2 KB	No	8 KB
01.01.00.SqlDataProvider	SQLDATAPROVIDER File	1 KB	No	3 KB
Employee.SqlDataProvider	SQLDATAPROVIDER File	1 KB	No	3 KB
Uninstall.SqlDataProvider	SQLDATAPROVIDER File	1 KB	No	2 KB

16. To check the results, log in as SuperUser and use the **Install Extension Wizard** to deploy the new ZIP file. The module should install over the existing module without error.

17. You can use the **Database Explorer** in the Development tool to confirm the upgrade added the new columns:

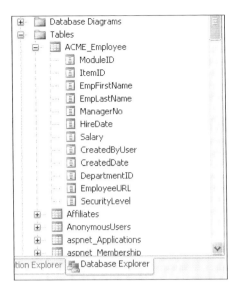

18. The **Database Explorer** will also show the updated stored procedure.

How it works...

It is important that you think carefully about the changes you need to make in your module upgrade. Keep in mind you must perform the upgrade without affecting the previous module versions. For example, to add columns to the Employee table we used the ALTER TABLE command rather than the DROP TABLE command. This preserves any records that might already be in the table.

Incremental updates like this are tricky and should be well tested before releasing your update. They also require a solid understanding of SQL.

There's more...

In this example we did not create any new objects so the original uninstall file still applies. If we create a new table for example, then we have to update the uninstall file with a new version number. As we never do incremental uninstalls, we only need to have one uninstall file.

Using multiple database connections

There are some situations when you need to access a database that is not the one running the DNN installation. Perhaps you need to run a query against a legacy database or extract information from a different company database.

In this recipe we will see how to create a second database connection and use it to populate the **Manager** drop-down list from the recipe *Populating a drop-down list from a stored procedure*.

For this recipe we will use the sample Northwind database that comes with MS Access.

Getting ready

To follow along with this recipe you must have completed the following recipe from *Chapter 6, Data Entry Tricks*:

▶ *Populating a drop-down list from a stored procedure*

How to do it...

1. Download the sample Northwind database from the Microsoft site by going to `http://www.microsoft.com/downloads` and searching for **Northwind Traders Sample Database**.

2. Select **Access 2000 Tutorial: Northwind Traders Sample Database** and click on the **Download** button to begin the download.

3. When prompted, select **Run** and agree to the install and license agreement.

4. Place the file on the C drive (`c:\Nwind.mdb`) of the DNN server.

5. Look on the DNN server and locate the root folder of the DNN installation.

6. Find the `web.config` file and open it in a text editor.

7. Scroll down through the file until you see `<connectionStrings>` and add the following key:

```
<add name="LegacyAccess"
   connectionString="Provider=Microsoft.Jet.OLEDB.4.0;Data
   Source=C:\Nwind.mdb; User Id=admin;Password=;" />
```

8. Next, double-click to open the `ViewEmployee.ascx.vb` file.

9. As we are accessing an old MS Access database in this recipe, we need to use the OLE DB provider. So start by adding the necessary import directive at the top of the file:

```
Imports System.Data.OleDb
```

10. Next we'll create a new routine to connect to the MS Access database file using the connection string we saved in the `web.config` file. Scroll down to the bottom of the `Public Methods` region and add the following code:

```
Public Function GetLegacyManagers() As OleDbDataReader

        Dim sqlConn As OleDbConnection
        Dim sqlCmd As OleDbCommand
        Dim strConnection As String
```

```
Dim sdrResults As OleDbDataReader

 Try
 'Use connection string from Web.Config
 strConnection = ConfigurationManager.ConnectionStrings
                              ("LegacyAccess").ConnectionString

  ' open the connection and run the SQL
  sqlConn = New OleDbConnection(strConnection)
  sqlCmd = New OleDbCommand("Select EmployeeId As ManagerNo,
               LastName + ', ' + FirstName As ManagerName
               FROM Employees", sqlConn)

  sqlConn.Open()
  sdrResults = sqlCmd.ExecuteReader
                              (CommandBehavior.CloseConnection)
   Catch ex As Exception
  sqlConn.Close()
   End Try


   Return sdrResults

 End Function
```

11. To test the new routine, start by opening the file `ViewEmployee.ascx.vb`.

12. Scroll down to the `Private Methods` region and change the `BindManagerDropDown` routine as follows:

```
Private Sub BindManagerDropDown()

    Dim objEmployeeController As New EmployeeController
    ddlManagerNo.DataSource =
                     objEmployeeController.GetLegacyManagers()
    ddlManagerNo.DataBind()


End Sub
```

13. This will populate the Manager drop-down list from the legacy database using the new connection. To test the results, start by rebuilding and redeploying the module.

14. Go to the page with the Employee module. The names in the Manager drop-down list are now coming from a second database connection to an MS Access database.

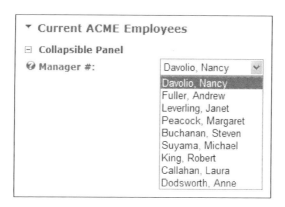

How it works...

In this example we used an OLE connection to a MS Access 2000 database, but this technique works with other database types. Here are some other example connection strings for different types of databases:

Database type	Sample connection string

Oracle Database using a `TNSNames.ora` file	`<add name="LegacyOracle" connectionString=`
	`"Data Source=LEGACY;User Id=legacyuser;`
	`    Password=legacypassword;" />`

MS Access	`<add name="LegacyAccess" connectionString="`
	`Provider=Microsoft.Jet.OLEDB.4.0;Data Source=C:\`
	`northwind.mdb;User Id=legacyuser;Password=legacypa`
	`ssword;" />`

SQL Server Express	`<add name="LegacyExpress" connectionString="Data`
	`Source=.\SQLExpress;Initial`
	`Catalog=LegacyDatabase;User ID=legacyuser;Password`
	`=legacypassword" />`

MySQL	`<add name="LegacyMySQL" connectionString="Server=l`
	`ocalhost;Port=3306;`
	`Database=LegacyMySQL;Uid=legacyuser;Pwd=legacypass`
	`word;" />`

12
Advanced Modules and Security

- ▶ Creating a secondary View control
- ▶ Controlling navigation with NavigateURL
- ▶ Module messages and event Logging
- ▶ Creating your own CBO Hydrator
- ▶ Using Active Directory with DNN
- ▶ Synchronizing security roles with DNN
- ▶ Correcting Active Directory issues

Introduction

In this chapter, we will touch on some advanced module development topics and look at extending DNN security. We'll start by seeing how to create a secondary View control and navigation links to it. Then we'll see how to create custom display messages and use the event log for debugging messages. Lastly we'll see how to add Active Directory Authentication and synchronize it with DNN.

Creating a secondary View control

In this recipe we will see how to move beyond the basic View, Edit, and Settings controls to create a second View control. We'll start with the Datagrid project from *Chapter 6, Data Entry Tricks* and add a new control to it. Then in the next recipe we'll see how to navigate to the new control from the Datagrid.

There are six steps to create a secondary View control:

1. Design the layout of the control.
2. Create the new web control in your project.
3. Add the code that will populate the control the page loads.
4. Add a return link that takes the user back to the primary view control.
5. Add the local resources for the labels.
6. Update the manifest with the new files.

The View control we will create is organized in a simple HTML table and displays an image along with the employee information. The layout looks like this:

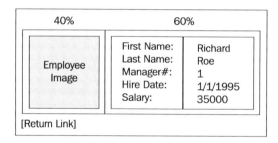

Getting ready

To follow along with this recipe you must have completed the following recipe from *Chapter 6, Data Entry Tricks*:

▸ *Displaying a Datagrid with filter controls*

How to do it...

1. Launch the Development Tool and load the Employee project.
2. We'll start by creating a new `DisplayEmployee` control that will show the employee details using labels. Similar to the `EditEmployee` control, but it will be display only.
3. In the Solution Explorer, right-click on the **Employee** project.

4. Select **New Item...** from the **Add** pop-up menu.

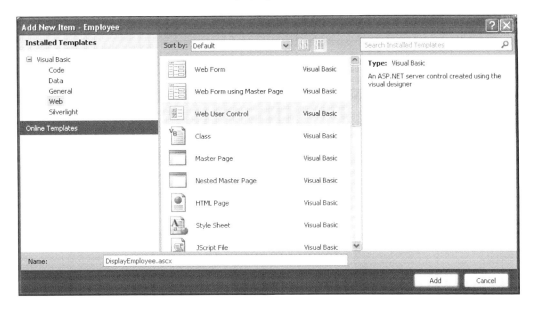

5. Pick **Web User Control** as the template and call it `DisplayEmployee.ascx`.

6. Click on **Add** to create the file.

7. Double-click to open the new `DisplayEmployee.ascx` file.

8. To display the employee information, we'll create some label controls and organize them in an HTML table. Add the following code to the top of the file:

```
<%@ Control Language="vb" AutoEventWireup="false"
    CodeBehind="DisplayEmployee.ascx.vb"
    Inherits="ACME.Modules.Employee.DisplayEmployee" %>
<%@ Register TagPrefix="dnn" TagName="Label"
    Src="~/controls/LabelControl.ascx" %>
```

9. Below that place an HTML table holding the controls:

```
<table width="650" cellspacing="0" cellpadding="0" border="0"
     summary="Display Table">
    <tr>
        <td width="40%" valign="top" align="center">
            <asp:Image ID="imgEmployee" runat="server"
                 ImageUrl="~/images/thumbnail.jpg" />
        </td>
        <td width="60%">
            <table width="100%" >
                <tr valign="top">
                    <td class="SubHead" width="125">
```

```
                    <dnn:label id="lblEmpFirstName"
                            runat="server"
                            controlname="lblEmpFirstNameValue"
                            suffix=":">
                     </dnn:label>
                </td>
                <td>
                    <dnn:label id="lblEmpFirstNameValue"
                            runat="server" >
                    </dnn:label>
                </td>
            </tr>
            <tr valign="top">
                <td class="SubHead" width="125">
                    <dnn:label id="lblEmpLastName"
                            runat="server"
                            controlname="lblEmpLastNameValue"
                            suffix=":">
                    </dnn:label>
                </td>
                <td>
                    <dnn:label id="lblEmpLastNameValue"
                            runat="server" >
                    </dnn:label>
                </td>
            </tr>
            <tr valign="top">
                <td class="SubHead" width="125">
                    <dnn:label id="lblManagerNo"
                            runat="server"
                            controlname="lblManagerNoValue"
                            suffix=":">
                    </dnn:label>
                </td>
                <td>
                    <dnn:label id="lblManagerNoValue"
                            runat="server" >
                    </dnn:label>
                </td>
            </tr>
            <tr valign="top">
                <td class="SubHead" width="125">
                    <dnn:label id="lblHireDate" runat="server"
                        controlname="lblHireDateValue"
```

```
                                         suffix=":">
                             </dnn:label>
                         </td>
                         <td>
                             <dnn:label id="lblHireDateValue"
                                         runat="server" >
                             </dnn:label>
                         </td>
                     </tr>
                     <tr valign="top">
                         <td class="SubHead" width="125">
                             <dnn:label id="lblSalary" runat="server"
                                         controlname="lblSalaryValue"
                                         suffix=":">
                             </dnn:label>
                         </td>
                         <td>
                             <dnn:label id="lblSalaryValue"
                                         runat="server" >
                             </dnn:label>
                         </td>
                     </tr>
                 </table>
             </td>
         </tr>
     </table>
```

10. Next, we'll add a Return link at the bottom of the control to navigate back to the View control:

```
<p>
     <asp:linkbutton cssclass="CommandButton" id="cmdReturn"
                     resourcekey="cmdReturn" runat="server"
                     borderstyle="none" text="Return"
                     causesvalidation="False">
     </asp:linkbutton>
</p>
```

11. Next, double-click to open the new `DisplayEmployee.ascx.vb` file.

12. In this file we'll need to add code to the `Page_Load` routine to populate our labels with the values of the selected employee. Replace the empty `Page_Load` routine with the following code:

```
Private Sub Page_Load(ByVal sender As Object, ByVal e As
                                System.EventArgs) Handles MyBase.Load

    Try
```

```
' Determine ItemId of Employee to Update
If Not (Request.QueryString("ItemId") Is Nothing) Then
    ItemId = Int32.Parse(Request.QueryString("ItemId"))
End If


If Page.IsPostBack = False Then

    If Not Common.Utilities.Null.IsNull(ItemId) Then
    ' get content
    Dim objEmployees As New EmployeeController
    Dim objEmployee As EmployeeInfo =
                    objEmployees.GetEmployee(ModuleId, ItemId)
    If Not objEmployee Is Nothing Then
        lblEmpFirstNameValue.Text = objEmployee.EmpFirstName
        lblEmpLastNameValue.Text = objEmployee.EmpLastName
        lblManagerNoValue.Text = objEmployee.ManagerNo
        lblHireDateValue.Text = objEmployee.HireDate
        lblSalaryValue.Text = objEmployee.Salary


    Else ' security violation attempt to access item not related
                                                to this Module
        Response.Redirect(NavigateURL(), True)
    End If


    End If
End If


Catch exc As Exception     'Module failed to load
ProcessModuleLoadException(Me, exc)
    End Try
End Sub
```

13. The last piece of code for this file is to add a handler for the Return link at the very bottom:

```
#Region "Optional Interfaces"


Private Sub cmdReturn_Click(ByVal sender As Object, ByVal e As
EventArgs) Handles cmdReturn.Click
    Try
    Response.Redirect(NavigateURL(), True)
    Catch exc As Exception     'Module failed to load
```

```
        ProcessModuleLoadException(Me, exc)
          End Try
      End Sub


      #End Region


      End Class
```

14. The last step is to create a new resource file for the View control where we will save our label text. In the Solution Explorer, right-click on the `App_LocalResources` folder.

15. Select **New Item...** from the **Add** pop-up menu.

16. Select **Resources File** as the template and call it `DisplayEmployee.ascx.resx`.

17. Click on **Add** to create the file and then add the following entries:

   ❑ `ControlTitle_display.Text`: **Display Employee**

   ❑ `lblEmpFirstName.Text`: **First Name**

   ❑ `lblEmpLastName.Text`: **Last Name**

   ❑ `lblManagerNo.Text`: **Manager #**

   ❑ `lblHireDate.Text`: **Hire Date**

   ❑ `lblSalary.Text`: **Salary**

18. The file should now look like this:

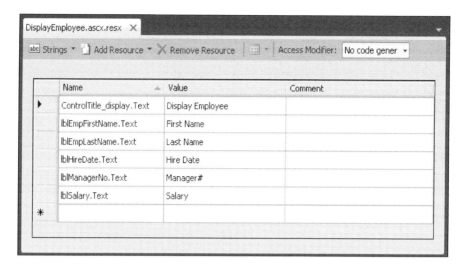

19. With the new user control in place and the resource file created, all that is left is to add the new files to the manifest. Double-click to open the `Employee.dnn` file.

20. Scroll down and add the following text:

```
<control>
    <src>DesktopModules/ACME.Employee/ViewEmployee.ascx</src>
    <type>View</type>
    <helpurl></helpurl>
</control>
<control>
    <key>AcmeEmployeeDisplay/key>
    <title>Display Employee</title>
    <src>DesktopModules/ACME.Employee/DisplayEmployee.ascx</src>
    <type>View</type>
    <helpurl></helpurl>
</control>
```

21. Scroll down a little and add:

```
<file>
  <name>ViewEmployee.ascx</name>
</file>
<file>
  <name>DisplayEmployee.ascx</name>
</file>
<file>
  <name>EditEmployee.ascx</name>
</file>
```

22. Scroll down a little more and add:

```
<file>
  <path>App_LocalResources</path>
  <name>ViewEmployee.ascx.resx</name>
</file>
<file>
  <path>App_LocalResources</path>
  <name>DisplayEmployee.ascx.resx</name>
</file>
<file>
  <path>App_LocalResources</path>
  <name>EditEmployee.ascx.resx</name>
</file>
```

23. Select **Save All** from the **File** menu to save all the changes.

24. Build and deploy the module to your DNN site (for instructions see the recipe *Deploying a module as a standalone package* in *Chapter 5, Building, Debugging, and Deploying Modules*). Include both the new files: `DisplayEmployee.ascx` and `DisplayEmployee.ascx.resx`.

25. Although we cannot yet navigate to the new control (as it still needs to be hooked up to the Datagrid), when deployed it looks like this:

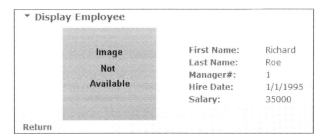

26. The next recipe will show how to call this new View control from the Datagrid of employees.

How it works...

In this recipe we used an HTML table to layout our new control, but that was just to keep the example simple. As we saw in the previous chapters it is better to use CSS styling to control the layout as it is much more flexible for skinning,

There's more...

A very important part of this recipe is found when we are adding the form to the manifest. For a secondary view control to work it must have a unique key that we'll use to identify the form when we navigate to it. In this example, we gave the new form the key `AcmeEmployeeDisplay` when we defined it in the manifest with the `<key>AcmeEmployeeDisplay</key>` element.

Controlling navigation with NavigateURL

In this recipe we'll see how to control navigation within a module using NavigateURL. In this example, we will hook up the Datagrid of employees so that when the link for an employee is clicked, navigation will pass to the secondary View control created in the previous recipe and display the employee details.

 Note: this technique is for navigation within a module, not outside to other modules or pages.

Getting ready

To follow along with this recipe you must have completed the following recipe:

▸ *Creating a secondary View control*

How to do it...

1. Start by launching the Development Tool and loading the Employee project.

2. The first step is to add a link to the Datagrid of employees that will go to the secondary View control. Double-click to open the `ViewEmployee.ascx` file.

3. We add a new column in the Datagrid with the following code:

    ```
    <dnn:imagecommandcolumn CommandName="Display" ImageUrl="~/images/
    view.gif" EditMode="URL" KeyField="ItemID" />
    <dnn:imagecommandcolumn CommandName="Edit" ImageUrl="~/images/
    edit.gif" EditMode="URL" KeyField="ItemID" />
    <dnn:imagecommandcolumn CommandName="Delete" ImageUrl="~/images/
    delete.gif" KeyField="ItemID" />
    ```

4. The next step is to modify the `Page_Init` routine so that the correct navigate URL is put in the Datagrid when it is populated. Double-click to open the `ViewEmployee.ascx.vb` file.

5. Scroll down to the `Page_Init` routine and add the following code, just before the code for the `Edit` link. The important part here is we are passing the key value `AcmeEmployeeDisplay` that we defined in the manifest representing the secondary view control.

```
If imageColumn.CommandName = "Delete" Then
    imageColumn.OnClickJS = Localization.GetString("DeleteItem")
    End If


    'Set the link the the secondary view control using NavigateURL
    If imageColumn.CommandName = "Display" Then
    Dim formatString As String = NavigateURL(TabId,
"AcmeEmployeeDisplay", "mid=" & CStr(ModuleId), "ItemId=KEYFIELD")
    formatString = formatString.Replace("KEYFIELD", "{0}")
    imageColumn.NavigateURLFormatString = formatString
    End If


    'Manage Edit Column NavigateURLFormatString
    If imageColumn.CommandName = "Edit" Then
```

6. Rebuild and redeploy the module.

7. Go to the page with the Employee module. When the employees are shown in the Datagrid, you will see a new view icon (looking like a magnifying glass):

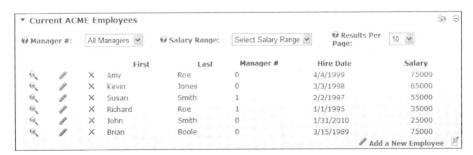

8. When you click on the view icon next to an employee, you will navigate to the secondary View control and see the employee information displayed. In this example, we included a sample image from the standard DNN images to demonstrate how an employee detail control might look:

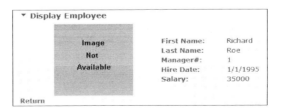

How it works...

DNN does a lot of work behind the scenes to handle navigation through the site (things like friendly URL rewriting). Most navigation is handled automatically but if you need to control specific navigation in your module you can use NavigateURL with the appropriate parameters.

Displaying module messages and event logging

When developing DNN modules, they are many times when it is useful to display a message on the page or log a message to the event log for later analysis. In this recipe we will see how to use the `AddModuleMessage` and `AddLog` methods.

`AddModuleMessage` is a method in the `DotNetNuke.UI.Skins.Skin` namespace useful for simple messages you want to display on the page. There are four message types you can use to highlight your message:

- `BlueInfo`: This is a good type to use when you want to inform the user something has happened, but it's not a success or failure type of action.

- `GreenSuccess`: This is a good type to use when the user has performed some action and you want to draw their attention to its success. If you use a message upon success, it's a good idea to also use a message upon failure.

- `YellowWarning`: A useful type when an action did not fully succeed but it's not certain the action was a failure.

- `RedError`: Most effective if used in moderation. This is good for serious errors or cases when the user cannot proceed until the error is fixed.

`AddLog` is found in the `DotNetNuke.Services.Log.EventLog` namespace and writes a message to the site event log. It is useful when you want to record that an event has taken place but you do not want to display a message to the user. This is very useful for debugging a live site. Note that logging can be turned off by the Portal Administrator so you'll need to make sure logging is turned on to follow this recipe.

Getting ready

To follow along with this recipe you must have completed the following recipe from *Chapter 6, Data Entry Tricks*:

- *Displaying a Datagrid with filter controls*

How to do it...

1. Start by launching the Development Tool and loading the Employee project.

2. Double-click to open the `EditEmployee.ascx.vb` file.

3. Scroll down to the `Page_Load` routine. We will add some log messages just after the code that loads the selected employee record:

```
If Not objEmployee Is Nothing Then
    txtEmpFirstName.Text = objEmployee.EmpFirstName
    txtEmpLastName.Text = objEmployee.EmpLastName
    txtManagerNo.Text = objEmployee.ManagerNo
    txtHireDate.Text = objEmployee.HireDate
    txtSalary.Text = objEmployee.Salary


    ' log the employee information
    Dim objEventLog As New Services.Log.EventLog.
EventLogController
    objEventLog.AddLog(objEmployee, PortalSettings, UserId,
UserInfo.Username, _
    Services.Log.EventLog.EventLogController.EventLogType.ADMIN_
ALERT)


    ' print a success message on the page
    UI.Skins.Skin.AddModuleMessage(Me, "Employee record
successfully loaded.", UI.Skins.Controls.ModuleMessage.
ModuleMessageType.GreenSuccess)
```

4. Rebuild and redeploy the module.

5. Go to the page with the Employee module and select an employee to edit. When the employee record is displayed, you will see a new success message at the top of the page. The large green icon is displayed because we chose `GreenSuccess` as the message type:

6. To see the other log message we created, select **Event Viewer** from the **Admin** menu:

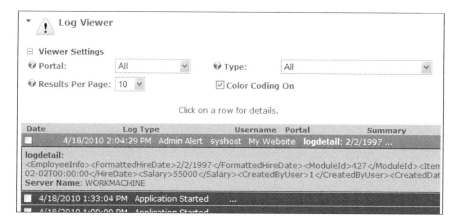

How it works...

The AddLog routine is overloaded to accept different parameters. In this case we passed the employee object as part of the log message. This is very useful for debugging when we want to see the status of an entire object. AddLog will automatically convert the values in the given object to an XML string and display it in the event log.

There's more...

When using the EventLogController there are many types of events you can log. These are color coded in the Log Viewer and you can filter the messages by type. In this recipe, we logged our message using ADMIN_ALERT as the event type but there are many more event types you can use. Here are a few examples:

- ► ADMIN_ALERT
- ► HOST_ALERT
- ► APPLICATION_START
- ► APPLICATION_END
- ► USER_CREATED
- ► PORTAL_CREATED
- ► MODULE_CREATED
- ► TAB_CREATED
- ► LOGIN_SUCCESS
- ► LOGIN_FAILURE

Creating your own CBO Hydrator

DNN includes a useful core service called CBO Hydrator. The CBO Hydrator is a collection of methods for populating one or more Custom Business Objects (CBOs) from the database. We've seen in previous recipes how the CBO EmployeeInfo pulls records from the database and uses the CBO Hydrator to populate a Datagrid.

As a DNN developer you have the ability to write your own Hydrator by implementing the IHydrator interface. Implementing IHydrator is more efficient and it also gives you the option of customizing it to any special situations in your module, including "massaging" the data before it is passed to the presentation layer or perhaps filtering the results based on the user's security.

In this recipe, we will use the sample Employee project to demonstrate the two pieces required to implement the IHydrator interface: a property called KeyID and a method called Fill.

Getting ready

To follow along with this recipe you must have completed the following recipe from *Chapter 6, Data Entry Tricks* :

▸ *Displaying a Datagrid with filter controls*

How to do it...

1. Start by launching the Development Tool and loading the Employee project.
2. Double-click to open the EmployeeInfo.vb file.
3. Look at the top of the file and add the following Implements statement:

```
Public Class EmployeeInfo
    Implements Entities.Modules.IHydratable

    ' local property declarations
```

4. Next, scroll down to the bottom of the file, just after the last property and add the following new Optional Interfaces region and Fill routine:

```
#Region "Optional Interfaces"

        Public Sub Fill(ByVal dr As IDataReader) Implements
                    DotNetNuke.Entities.Modules.IHydratable.Fill

        ItemId = Convert.ToInt32
                    (Null.SetNull(dr.Item("ItemID"), ItemId))
```

```
                    ModuleId = Convert.ToInt32
                         (Null.SetNull(dr.Item("ModuleID"), ModuleId))
                    EmpFirstName = Convert.ToString
                              (Null.SetNull(dr.Item("EmpFirstName"),
                              EmpFirstName)) + " (first)"
                    EmpLastName = Convert.ToString
                              (Null.SetNull(dr.Item("EmpLastName"),
                              EmpLastName)) + " (last)"
                    ManagerNo = Convert.ToInt32
                         (Null.SetNull(dr.Item("ManagerNo"), ManagerNo))
                    HireDate = Convert.ToDateTime
                         (Null.SetNull(dr.Item("HireDate"), HireDate))
                    Salary = Convert.ToInt32
                         (Null.SetNull(dr.Item("Salary"), Salary))


            End Sub


    #End Region
```

5. Note how we are customizing the data a little by adding a short text suffix (first) and (last) to the first and last name fields.

6. Finally, we need to supply a `KeyID` property after the `Fill` routine:

```
Public Property KeyID() As Integer Implements
                         DotNetNuke.Entities.Modules.IHydratable.KeyID
    Get
    Return ItemId
     End Get
     Set(ByVal value As Integer)
    ItemId = value
     End Set
End Property


    #End Region
```

7. That's all we need to do. No other code changes are needed and the switch to the new `Fill` routine is automatic.

8. To prove that it is working, rebuild and redeploy the module.

9. Go to the page with the Employee module and see how the (first) and (last) suffixes are now showing in the grid. That's how we know that DNN has automatically switched to our custom `IHydrator` code:

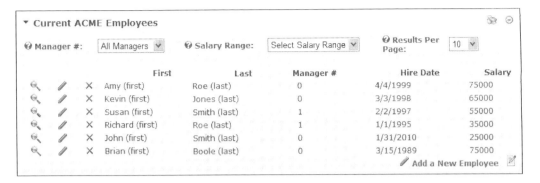

Using Active Directory with DNN

As we saw in _Chapter 2, Managing Users and Site Setup,_ DNN comes with built-in user security with roles and grants. This is fine in many cases, but sometimes your DNN site is located on a network that already has Active Directory (AD) security. How can you configure a DNN portal to use the existing security and not have to recreate all the AD users?

The answer is to add the Active Directory Authentication provider to work along with the DNN security provider. In this way you can log in with user names defined in DNN or in Active Directory.

In this recipe we will see how to configure a DNN portal to use Active Directory authentication along with the default DNN authentication.

Getting ready

To follow along with this recipe you'll need access to a network that uses Active Directory with a valid username and password. Note that on some networks access to Active Directory may be restricted. Check with the network administrator if you have trouble using this recipe.

How to do it...

1. Start by logging in as **SuperUser**.

2. Select **Extensions** from the **Host** menu.

3. Scroll down to **Authentication System** section.

Authentication System			
🖉	Default Authentication	The Default UserName/Password Authentication System for DotNetNuke.	1.0.0
🖉 ✕	DNN_ActiveDirectoryAuthentication	The DotNetNuke Active Directory Authentication Project is an Authentication provider for DotNetNuke that uses the Windows Active Directory authentication protocol to authenticate users.	5.0.2
🖉 ✕	DNN_LiveIDAuthentication	The DotNetNuke LiveID Authentication Project is an Authentication provider for DotNetNuke that uses the LiveID authentication protocol to authenticate users.	1.0.1
🖉 ✕	DNN_OpenIDAuthentication	The DotNetNuke OpenID Authentication Project is an Authentication provider for DotNetNuke that uses the OpenID authentication protocol to authenticate users.	2.0.0

4. You should see Active Directory listed. If not, select **Install Available Extensions** from the action menu and install it.

5. Once you have confirmed Active Directory Authentication is installed, select **Extensions** from the **Admin** menu.

6. Scroll down to the list of authentication systems and click on the edit icon next to **DNN_ActiveDirectoryAuthentication.** This will display the **Authentication Settings** page.

7.   Provide the following information:

    ❑ **Enabled?**: Checked (means the portal will use AD)

    ❑ **Hide Login Controls?**: Unchecked (don't hide the Windows Login button)

    ❑ **Synchronize Role?**: Unchecked (don't synch the DNN roles with the AD roles)

    ❑ **Do Not Automatically Create Users?**: Unchecked (allow existing AD users to use the portal)

    ❑ **Provider**: Leave the default **ADSIAuthenticationProvider**

    ❑ **Authentication Type**: Leave the default **Delegation**

    ❑ **Root Domain**: If you know the root domain of your network then use that, otherwise leave blank

    ❑ **User Name**: Provide a valid user name for your Windows network that can access Active Directory

    ❑ **Password**: Provide the valid password for the user

- ❑ **Email Domain**: Leave blank (specifies the **Email Domain** if AD is not available)

- ❑ **Default Domain**: Provide the default domain of your users (if left blank the user will need to specify with their login for example MYDOMAIN\jsmith)

- ❑ **Auto-Login IP Address**: Leave blank (optional: enables automatic login based on IP address)

8. Click on **Update Authentication Settings** to save your changes. After a pause you should see a success message.

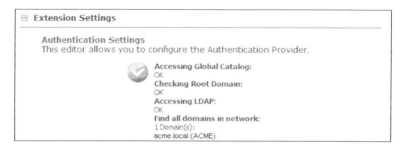

9. If you do not see a success message, confirm you have supplied a valid domain, a valid user name and password, and also that Active Directory is available on your network.

10. Click on **Cancel** to close the configuration page.

11. To test the results, log out as SuperUser.

12. Windows will now try to log you back into the portal. If all goes well, you will be prompted for your Active Directory username and password and then the DNN home page will display.

How it works...

Once logged in, your users can come and go without logging in again until the security cookie times out (or they use the logoff link) and then they'll need to give their username and password again through the login page.

There's more...

If DNN is installed on an older version of Windows (before Vista/Windows 7) you might get an error "Error while processing Windows Authentication. Check your IIS settings. DesktopModules/AuthenticationServices/ActiveDirectory/WindowsSignin.aspx should NOT allow anonymous access." In this case see the next recipe for instructions for fixing this issue or rolling back and disabling Active Directory security.

See also

In this recipe we enabled Active Directory Authentication to allow AD users to access your DNN portal without existing in DNN. In the next recipe we will see how to synchronize the security roles between Active Directory and DNN so you can grant access to your pages and modules to the Active Directory roles.

Synchronizing Security Roles with DNN

Once you're using Active Directory for your DNN security, the next step is to synchronize your AD security roles (or groups) with DNN so you can control access to pages and modules based on role, not just the username.

This does not automatically create the security roles (you have to manually do that); instead it syncs what roles the user has. So if you revoke a role in AD, the user automatically loses that role in DNN as well.

In this recipe we will assume there is a security role called Users in your Active Directory. It is important that when you recreate the roles in DNN that you spell them exactly the same as they appear in Active Directory.

Getting ready

To follow along with this recipe you must have completed the following recipes:

- *Creating and Assigning Security Roles.*
- *Granting Access to Modules*
- *Using Active Directory with DNN*

How to do it...

1. Start by logging in as portal Administrator.

2. Look under the Admin menu and select **Security Roles.**

3. This page will display all the security roles you currently have. Use the **Add New Role** link to create a new role called **Users**.

4. Now that we have a role defined both in Active Directory and DNN, we need to turn on role synchronizing. Select **Extensions** from the **Admin** menu.

5. Scroll down to the list of authentication systems and click the edit icon next to **DNN_ActiveDirectoryAuthentication.** This will display the configuration page.

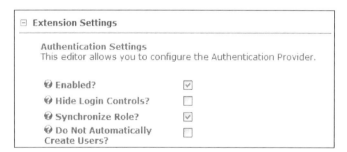

6. Find the checkbox called **Synchronize Role** and make sure it is **checked**.

7. Click **Update Authentication Settings** to save your changes. After a pause you should see a success message.

8. Lastly, pick a module in your portal that anonymous users (those not logged in) cannot see. Use the instructions from the recipe *Granting access to modules* to grant read access to this module to the Users role you created above. Since you did not grant the Users role to anyone, the only way a user will see this module is if the synchronizing works.

9. After granting access to the role, use the Logoff link and log off as Administrator.

10. Refresh the browser and you will now log in using your Active Directory credentials. You should successfully log into the DNN portal and see the module granted to the Users role.

How it works...

By configuring the Active Directory Authentication to keep roles synchronized, grants and revokes made in Active Directory will automatically apply to the matching DNN role.

Correcting Active Directory issues

Changing security providers in DNN is a little risky because if something goes wrong, you might get locked out of your site. In this recipe we'll see how to fix a common access issue and also how to roll back the Active Directory provider should you need to start all over.

Getting ready

To follow along with this recipe you must have completed the following recipe:

▸ *Using Active Directory with DNN*

How to do it...

1. If you encounter the error `WindowsSignin.aspx` should NOT allow anonymous access. while setting up Active Directory security in DNN, you will need to manually tweak the security on the `WindowsSignin.aspx` file as follows:

2. On the web server, open the IIS Manager and expand the folder `DesktopModules/ AuthenticationServices/ActiveDirectory` until you can see `WindowsSignin.aspx` listed.

3. Right click on `WindowsSignin.aspx` and select **Properties**.

4. On the **File Security** tab should be a section called **Anonymous access and authentication control**.

5. Click on the **Edit** button and uncheck Anonymous Access.

6. Click **OK** to close the dialog then **OK** again to close the properties.

7. Relaunch your browser and the error should go away.

8. If you cannot get the Active Directory security working with your DNN portal and find you cannot log back into your portal as SuperUser, you can disable Active Directory security and restore the DNN security with the following steps:

9. Use the Development tool to connect to the database.

10. Find the table called **PortalSettings**. Open the table and look for the record for `AD_WindowsAuthentication` for `PortalId` of 0.

11. Change the value to `False`.

0	AD_SynchronizePassword	False	1	4/16/2010 8:57:...	2	4/17/201
0	AD_SynchronizeRole	False	1	4/16/2010 8:57:...	2	4/17/201
0	AD_UserName		1	4/16/2010 8:57:...	2	4/17/201
0	AD_WindowsAuthentication	False	1	4/16/2010 8:57:...	2	4/17/201
0	DefaultAdminSkin	[G]skins/minimal...	1	2/20/2010 10:1...	1	2/24/201
0	DefaultPortalSkin	[G]skins/minimal	1	2/20/2010 10:1	1	2/24/201

12. Close the table then close and reopen the browser. The portal will default back to normal DNN security and you can log in as Administrator.

13
Advanced Skinning

- ▶ Using the Rotator widget
- ▶ Using the Visibility widget
- ▶ Using the Stylesheet widget
- ▶ Creating and deploying a custom widget
- ▶ Using a custom widget in a skin
- ▶ Using the rounded corner Super Stylesheet
- ▶ Showing portal settings in a skin
- ▶ Adding animation to a menu

Introduction

In this chapter, we will take a deeper look at the topic of skinning that we explored back in *Chapter 8, Basic Skinning*. We will see several examples of skin widgets, how to add animation to a menu, super stylesheets, and using variables in skins.

Most of the recipes we have seen so far are driven by code placed on the DNN server (modules and so forth). Skin widgets are a way of creating client-side code residing directly in the skin to give local functionality without having to run back and forth to the server.

Widgets contain pieces of JavaScript that can be placed in a skin and run on the client side. They are very similar to the Skin Objects we demonstrated in *Chapter 8, Basic Skinning*, but have a lot more functionality and can be customized to include our own JavaScript. To use a widget, you reference them in the skin using the HTML `object` element with `PARAMS` for the configuration options.

DNN includes several useful widgets found in the `\Resources\Widgets` folder on the DNN server and in this chapter we will explore a few of them and see how to make our own.

Using the Rotator widget

In this recipe we'll see how to use the Rotator skin widget that automatically rotates between different graphic images one after another. This is useful for things such as animated banner ads or photo slide shows.

The Rotator widget comes with different options controlling how the images are swapped and how long they are displayed. To use the Rotator widget we need a set of images to rotate. For this example we will use some of the standard vendor images that come with a normal DNN installation.

The Rotator uses an index variable to track the rotation, so the images must include a number in the filename such as `image1.gif`, `image2.gif`, `image3.gif`.

Getting ready

To follow along with this recipe you must have completed the following recipe from *Chapter 8, Basic Skinning*:

▸ *Creating a simple ASCX skin*

The available parameters to the Rotator widget are:

Parameters	Description	Examples
Direction	The direction the images move during transition.	Left, Right, Up, Down, or Blend
Height	The height of the image.	120
Width	The width of the image.	60
ImageCount	The number of images in the rotation.	6
ImageTemplate	Specifies the names of all the image files to use.	vendor{INDEX}.gif
ImageURL	The location of the images folder.	<%=SkinPath %>images/
Interval	How many milliseconds to display each image before the next image is displayed. There are 1000 milliseconds per second so 2500 means display each image for two and half seconds before changing to the next image.	2500
Transition	The style of the transition. Like a photo slideshow, you can have each image gently slide in or suddenly snap in.	Slide or Snap

How to do it...

1. Find the folder called `SampleASCXSkin` that was created in the recipe *Creating a simple ASCX skin*.

2. Create a new folder within called `/images`.

3. From the DNN installation, take any six of the sample vendor images from the `\dotnetnuke\Portals\0` folder and copy them into the `/images` folder.

4. Rename the image files `vendor1.gif`, `vendor2.gif` all the way to `vendor6.gif`. At this point the `/images` folder should contain the following images:

vendor1.gif	vendor2.gif	vendor3.gif
vendor4.gif	vendor5.gif	vendor6.gif

5. Now launch the Development Tool.

6. Select **Open File...** from the **File** menu.

7. Browse to the `SampleASCXSkin` folder and open the `SampleASCXSkin.ascx` file.

8. Scroll down to the HTML table holding the different panes and add the following code to the `Left Pane`:

```
<div class="content">
    <table width="100%" border="0" cellspacing="0" cellpadding="0">
      <tr>
      <td valign="top" id="LeftPane" class="LeftPane"
          runat="server" visible="false">

        <object id="ContentRotator" codetype="dotnetnuke/client"
            codebase="RotatorWidget" declare="declare">
          <param name="imageCount" value="6" />
          <param name="imageURL" value="<%=SkinPath %>images/" />
          <param name="imageTemplate" value="vendor{INDEX}.gif" />
```

```
            <param name="width" value="120" />
            <param name="height" value="60" />
            <param name="transition" value="slide" />
            <param name="direction" value="left" />
            <param name="interval" value="3000" />
        </object>

        </td>
        <td valign="top" id="ContentPane" class="ContentPane"
            runat="server" visible="false">
        </td>
        <td valign="top" id="RightPane" class="RightPane"
            runat="server" visible="false">
        </td>
         </tr>
      </table>
   </div>
```

9. As we want to include the vendor images in the skin package, we need to update the manifest so that when we redeploy the skin, the images will upload to the server.

 The Rotator widget works equally well with images that reside in a specific folder on your portal and are not part of the skin. If you are using images that are not part of your skin you don't need to add them to the manifest and can skip this last part of the recipe.

10. Open the `SampleASCXSkin.dnn` file.

11. Scroll down to the `skinFiles` element and add the following:

```
<skinFile>
   <name>skin.css</name>
</skinFile>
<skinFile>
   <path>images</path>
   <name>vendor1.gif</name>
</skinFile>
<skinFile>
   <path>images</path>
   <name>vendor2.gif</name>
</skinFile>
<skinFile>
   <path>images</path>
```

```
        <name>vendor3.gif</name>
    </skinFile>
    <skinFile>
       <path>images</path>
       <name>vendor4.gif</name>
    </skinFile>
    <skinFile>
       <path>images</path>
       <name>vendor5.gif</name>
    </skinFile>
    <skinFile>
       <path>images</path>
       <name>vendor6.gif</name>
    </skinFile>
  </skinFiles>
```

12. Select **Save All** from the **File** menu to save your changes.

13. To see how the new skin will look on our site, log in as the SuperUser.

14. Deploy the skin from the skin folder to the DNN portal as described in the recipe *Deploying your skins and containers*. Be sure to include the new /images folder in the ZIP file.

15. Once the skin is deployed, look under the **Admin** menu and select **Skins**.

16. Select the **SampleASCXSkin** from the **Skins:** drop-down list and click on the **Preview** link.

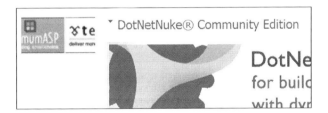

17. As we placed the Rotator widget in the left pane, on the left side of the page you will see the first image. After a moment, the image will change as the rotation begins. We picked an interval value of 3000 so the image should change every 3 seconds. We chose slide as the transition and left as the direction, so the next image should slide in from the right side to the left.

There's more...

You can experiment with different parameter values and see the results. For example, changing the transition to `Snap` will have the images immediately replace each other without the slide animation and using a longer interval is helpful when the images are larger.

See also

If you look closely you will see the ImageURL contains a reference to the `<%=SkinPath %>` `variable`. To learn more about other portal variables usable in skins, see the recipe *Showing portal settings in a skin* at the end of this chapter.

Using the Visibility widget

In this recipe we will take a look at the Visibility skin widget. The Visibility widget creates a button on your skin that dynamically toggles the visibility of an HTML element without calling the server.

 As we are using JavaScript behind the scenes, the target element must be accessible in the Document Object Module (DOM). The DOM is an easy way to reference elements in an HTML form (like the DIV element). You can learn more at `http://www.w3.org/DOM/`.

To demonstrate the widget we'll modify the sample ASCX skin from the recipe *Creating a simple ASCX skin*, adding `BREADCRUMB` and `TEXT` controls inside a `DIV` element, then redeploying the skin to see the change.

Getting ready

To follow along with this recipe you must have completed the following recipe from *Chapter 8 , Basic Skinning:*

▶ *Creating a simple ASCX skin*

How to do it...

1. Find the folder called `SampleASCXSkin` that was created in the recipe *Creating a simple ASCX skin*.
2. Launch the Development Tool.
3. Select **Open File...** from the **File** menu.
4. Browse to the `SampleASCXSkin` folder and open the `SampleASCXSkin.ascx` file.

5. We're going to add the BREADCRUMB and TEXT controls to our skin so begin by adding the following registers at the top of the file:

```
<%@ Register TagPrefix="dnn" TagName="USER"
            Src="~/Admin/Skins/User.ascx" %>
<%@ Register TagPrefix="dnn" TagName="LOGIN"
            Src="~/Admin/Skins/Login.ascx" %>
<%@ Register TagPrefix="dnn" TagName="TEXT"
            Src="~/Admin/Skins/Text.ascx" %>
<%@ Register TagPrefix="dnn" TagName="BREADCRUMB"
            Src="~/Admin/Skins/BreadCrumb.ascx" %>
```

6. Next, scroll down to the HTML table holding the different panes and add the following code to the ContentPane:

```
<div class="content">
   <table width="100%" border="0" cellspacing="0" cellpadding="0">
      <tr>
      <td valign="top" id="LeftPane" class="LeftPane"
          runat="server" visible="false">
      </td>
      <td valign="top" id="ContentPane" class="ContentPane"
          runat="server" visible="false">

    <object id="VisibiltyButton" codetype="dotnetnuke/client"
            codebase="VisibilityWidget" declare="declare">
       <param name="title" value="Hide/Show Breadcrumbs" />
       <param name="collapseClassName" value="collapse_icon" />
       <param name="expandClassName" value="expand_icon" />
       <param name="targetElementID" value="testElement" />
    </object>

    <div id="testElement">
       <dnn:TEXT runat="server" id="dnnTEXT"
               CssClass="breadcrumb_text" Text="You are here >"
               ResourceKey="Breadcrumb" /> <span>
       <dnn:BREADCRUMB runat="server" id="dnnBREADCRUMB"
                   CssClass="Breadcrumb" RootLevel="0"
                   Separator=" > " />
    </div>

      </td>
      <td valign="top" id="RightPane" class="RightPane"
runat="server" visible="false">
      </td>
      </tr>
   </table>
</div>
```

7. This gives us a text prompt, a breadcrumb, and the Visibility widget. What we need now is a little button to click on. To display a hide/show image on the button we must define the images in the `skin.css` file. Open the `skin.css` file.

8. Scroll down and add the follow style elements just after **Control Styles**:

```
/* Control Styles */
#login_style                           {float: right; padding: 10px 17px
0px 10px;}


/* Visibility widget */

.collapse_icon,
.expand_icon
{
    width: 14px;
    height: 14px;
    float: right;
    margin-top: 5px;
    background-repeat: no-repeat;
    cursor: pointer;
    border: 0;
    background-color: Transparent;
}


.collapse_icon
{
    background-image: url("/dotnetnuke/images/minus2.gif");
}


.expand_icon
{
    background-image: url("/dotnetnuke/images/plus2.gif");
}
```

9. This creates a small icon button that will show a plus or minus sign that changes as the visibility toggles. For simplicity we'll use some icons that come with DNN.

10. Finally, select **Save All** from the **File** menu to save your changes.

11. To see how the new skin will look on the site, log in as the SuperUser.

12. Deploy the skin from the skin folder to the DNN portal as described in the recipe *Deploying your skins and containers*.

13. Once the skin is deployed, look under the **Admin** menu and select **Skins**.

14. Select the **SampleASCXSkin** from the **Skins:** drop-down list and click on the Preview link.

15. A small minus sign icon will appear next to the breadcrumb we added. If you click on the minus sign, the breadcrumb will disappear and a plus sign icon will remain:

16. Clicking on the plus sign icon will restore the breadcrumb.

How it works...

This is a handy trick to save "real estate" on your pages by hiding large elements that do not always need to be visible. As the widget operates on the client side it is a very quick and efficient way to show and hide DOM elements.

There's more...

In this example we used some common DNN plus and minus icon images, but you are free to create your own images and add them to the skin. Just change the path in the CSS file to point to your images and add the images to the skin manifest.

Using the Stylesheet widget

Just as the Rotator widget can dynamically cycle through a set of images on the client side, the Stylesheet skin widget lets you dynamically switch between different stylesheets for your skin. This can be a very powerful tool for changing the entire appearance of your DNN pages on the client side with very little coding.

In this recipe we will create three simple stylesheets specifying font sizes (small, medium, and large) then add the Stylesheet widget to switch between them.

Getting ready

To follow along with this recipe you must have completed the following recipe from *Chapter 8, Basic Skinning*:

▶   *Creating a simple ASCX skin*

How to do it...

1. Find the folder called `SampleASCXSkin` that was created in the recipe *Creating a simple ASCX skin*.

2. Create a new folder within called `/css`.

3. To show switching between different stylesheets, we need to create three new CSS files and put them in this folder. Start by launching the Development Tool.

4. Then select **New File...** from the **File** menu.

5. At the **New File** dialog, select **Text File** and click **Open**.

6. Put the following code in the file:

    ```
    *
    {
        font-size:  8pt;
    }
    ```

7. Save the file as `small_font.css` in the `/css` folder.

8. Create another text file and add the following code:

    ```
    *
    {
        font-size:  14pt;
    }
    ```

9. Save the file as `med_font.css` in the `/css` folder.

10. Create one more text file and add the following code:

    ```
    *
    {
        font-size:  28pt;
    }
    ```

11. Save the file as `large_font.css` in the `/css` folder.

12. The `/css` folder should now look like this:

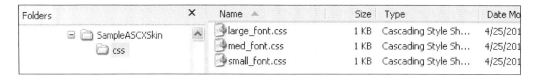

13. Next, select **Open File...** from the **File** menu and open the `SampleASCXSkin.ascx` file.

14. Scroll down to the HTML table holding the different panes and add the following code to the left pane:

```
<div class="content">
    <table width="100%" border="0" cellspacing="0" cellpadding="0">
      <tr>
        <td valign="top" id="LeftPane" class="LeftPane"
            runat="server" visible="false">

          <object id="TextSizeSelector" codetype="dotnetnuke/client"
                codebase="StyleSheetWidget" declare="declare">
            <param name="baseUrl" value="<%= SkinPath %>css/" />
            <param name="template" value="&lt;input type='button'
                title='{TEXT}' value='{TEXT}' {ID} {CLASS} /&gt; " />
            <param name="default" value="small_font" />

            <param name="Small Font" value="small_font" />
            <param name="Med Font" value="med_font" />
            <param name="Large Font" value="large_font" />
          </object>

        </td>
        <td valign="top" id="ContentPane" class="ContentPane"
            runat="server" visible="false">
        </td>
        <td valign="top" id="RightPane" class="RightPane"
            runat="server" visible="false">
        </td>
      </tr>
    </table>
</div>
```

15. As we want to include the new stylesheets as part of the skin package, we need to update the manifest so that when we redeploy the skin, the CSS files will upload to the server.

16. Open the `SampleASCXSkin.dnn` file.

17. Scroll down to the `skinFiles` element and add the following:

```
    <skinFile>
      <name>skin.css</name>
    </skinFile>
    <skinFile>
      <path>css</path>
      <name>small_font.css</name>
    </skinFile>
```

```
<skinFile>
  <path>css</path>
  <name>med_font.css</name>
</skinFile>
<skinFile>
  <path>css</path>
  <name>large_font.css</name>
</skinFile>
</skinFiles>
```

18. Select **Save All** from the **File** menu to save your changes.

19. To see how the new skin will look on the site, log in as the SuperUser.

20. Deploy the skin from the skin folder to the DNN portal as described in the recipe *Deploying your skins and containers*. Be sure to include the new /css folder in the ZIP file.

21. Once the skin is deployed, look under the **Admin** menu and select **Skins**.

22. Select the **SampleASCXSkin** from the **Skins:** drop-down list and click on the Preview link.

23. As we placed the Stylesheet widget in the left pane, you will see three buttons have appeared. Clicking on the buttons will switch between the small, medium, and large font stylesheets we created. This causes the fonts on the page to dynamically change size.

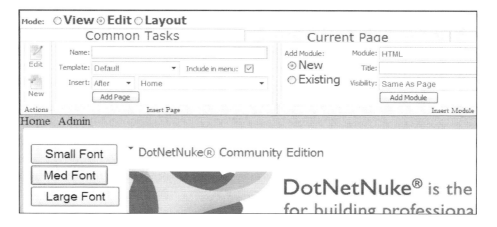

There's more...

In this example we used extremely simple stylesheets, doing nothing more than changing font sizes. But the power of this widget is limited only by your creativity in your stylesheet code. You can experiment with other CSS elements and more CSS files to really see all the possibilities of this widget.

Once again we used the `<%=SkinPath %>` variable in the skin. To learn more about other portal variables usable in skins, see the recipe *Showing portal settings in a skin* at the end of this chapter.

Creating and deploying a custom widget

In the previous recipes we saw how the different skin widgets that come with DNN can be used in our skins to provide interesting and creative client-side functionality. In this recipe we will see how to make our own skin widgets using the sample template that comes with DNN and adding our own JavaScript.

There's a lot you can do with custom widgets. In this recipe we will demonstrate a simple "fading" widget that fades out and disappears when you click on it. It works by adjusting the opacity of the element.

To make it work we need to do three things:

1. Make a copy of the DNN widget template that we can edit.
2. Edit the template JavaScript file and add our own click handler.
3. Update the manifest and deploy the skin.

To help us get our feet wet with custom skin widgets, DNN thoughtfully provides a complete sample widget with a JavaScript template. All we need to do is modify the button click handler to trigger the functionally. We start by copying the sample widget template from the DNN installation to a temporary folder. Then we will rename the files and edit them to create the custom widget.

To follow along with this recipe you must have completed the following recipe from *Chapter 8, Basic Skinning*:

▶   *Creating a simple ASCX skin*

How to do it...

1. Start by creating a new folder and naming it `ACME.SampleWidget`.

2. Look on the DNN server and locate the folder `\Resources\Widgets\User\YourCompany`.

3. Copy the files in this folder to the new `ACME.SampleWidget` folder.

4. Rename the JavaScript file `YourCompany.Widgets.SampleWidget.js` to `ACME.Widgets.SampleWidget.js`.

5. Delete the subfolder called `/EmbedWidgetResources` as we will not use it in this recipe.

6. This folder should now contain the following files:

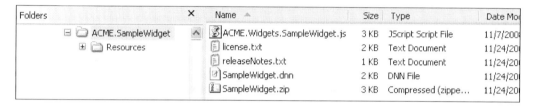

7. Launch the Development Tool.

8. Select **Open File...** from the **File** menu.

9. Browse to the `ACME.SampleWidget` folder and open the `ACME.Widgets.SampleWidget.js` file.

10. The first thing we need to do is change the text "YourCompany" in the script. Instead of YourCompany, you can place your actual company name or initials. We do this with a simple search and replace: Under the **Edit** menu, look under **Find and Replace** and select **Quick Replace** (or just press *Ctrl+H*).

11. When prompted:
    - **Find What**: `YourCompany`
    - **Replace with**: `ACME`
    - **Look in**: **Current Document**

12. Click on **Replace All**.

13. To add our own little custom JavaScript, scroll down to the bottom of the template script and find the `ClickHandler` function. We need to add some code to fade the text when a link is clicked:

```
ACME.Widgets.SampleWidget.clickHandler = function(sender)
{
    var clickedObject = sender.target;
```

```
    // perform a simple loop to increase the Opacity

    var i=0;
    for (i=0;i<=100;i++)
    {
        divFade.style.filter = "Alpha(Opacity=" + i + ",style=3)";
    }

}
```

14. It's not much, but it is enough to show the JavaScript triggering from the mouse click in the widget.

15. Lastly, as we will deploy the skin as an extension, we also need to update the manifest for the widget. Open the file `SampleWidget.dnn`.

16. As we did before, we must change the text "YourCompany" to our sample company "ACME". Change the following highlighted lines:

```
<dotnetnuke type="Package" version="5.0">
  <packages>
    <package name="ACME.SampleWidget" type="Widget"
            version="1.0.0">
      <friendlyName>Sample Widget</friendlyName>
      <description>The Sample Widget is a demonstration widget for
                                                    DotNetNuke.
      </description>
      <owner>
        <name>DotNetNuke</name>
        <organization>DotNetNuke Corporation</organization>
        <url>www.dotnetnuke.com</url>
        <email>support@dotnetnuke.com</email>
      </owner>
      <license src="license.txt" />
      <releaseNotes src="releasenotes.txt" />
      <components>
        <component type="Widget">
          <widgetFiles>
            <basePath>ACME</basePath>
            <widgetFile>
              <name>ACME.Widgets.SampleWidget.js</name>
            </widgetFile>
            <widgetFile>
              <name>license.txt</name>
            </widgetFile>
```

```
            <widgetFile>
              <name>releasenotes.txt</name>
            </widgetFile>
          </widgetFiles>
        </component>
      </components>
    </package>
  </packages>
</dotnetnuke>
```

17. Select **Save All** from the **File** menu to save your changes.

18. To deploy the widget create a compressed ZIP file containing the following files:

    ❏ `ACME.Widgets.SampleWidget.js`

    ❏ `license.txt`

    ❏ `releaseNotes.txt`

    ❏ `SampleWidget.dnn`

19. Save the ZIP file as `SampleWidget.zip`.

20. To deploy the widget, log in as SuperUser.

21. From the **Host** menu, select **Extensions** and pick **Install Extension Wizard** from the action menu.

22. When prompted, browse to the `ACME.SampleWidget` folder and select the new ZIP file `SampleWidget.zip`.

23. Complete the wizard to install the extension. It should now appear in the list of Widgets installed on your site.

24. To see the new widget in action we must include it in a skin. The next recipe will describe the steps to use the widget in a skin.

How it works...

The widget functionality is coded in the JavaScript file. In this example we kept it very simple but you are free to add as much functionality as your JavaScript skills can create.

> To see more examples of skin widgets and how they work, download and examine the Extropy skin available from www.codeplex.com (just search for "Extropy").

There's more...

In this recipe we created a simple custom widget and deployed it to the DNN site so that the widget is available to skins. In the next recipe we will see how to use the custom widget in a skin.

Using a custom widget in a skin

Once a custom skin widget has been created and installed on the server it becomes available just like the widgets that come with DNN. In this recipe we will see how to use the custom skin widget created in the previous recipe by combining it with the SampleASCXSkin from *Chapter 8, Basic Skinning*.

There are three things we need to do:

1. Make sure you have completed the previous recipe and updated the template JavaScript.
2. Add the custom Widget control to the ASCX file.
3. Deploy the skin and test it.

Getting ready

To follow along with this recipe you must have completed the following recipes:

- ► *Creating a simple ASCX skin*
- ► *Creating and deploying a custom widget*

How to do it...

1. To use the `ACME.SampleWidget` widget in a skin, we'll need to edit the sample ASCX skin files from the recipe *Creating a simple ASCX skin*. Start by finding the folder called `SampleASCXSkin`.
2. Launch the Development Tool.
3. Select **Open File...** from the **File** menu.
4. Browse to the `SampleASCXSkin` folder and open the `SampleASCXSkin.ascx` file.

5. We're going to place the new widget in the `LeftPane` so add the following code:

```
<div class="content">
    <table width="100%" border="0" cellspacing="0" cellpadding="0">
        <tr>
        <td valign="top" id="LeftPane" class="LeftPane"
            runat="server" visible="false">

            <div id="divFade" style="background-color:
                    Silver;width:200px; height:45px;text-align:center;">
                Sample Fading Text

                <object id="CustomWidget" codetype="dotnetnuke/client"
                            codebase="ACME.Widgets.SampleWidget"
                            declare="declare">
                    <param name="widgetFolder" value="ACME.SampleWidget"
            />
                    <param name="text" value="[Click to Fade]" />
                </object>

            </div>

        </td>
        <td valign="top" id="ContentPane" class="ContentPane"
            runat="server" visible="false">
        </td>
        <td valign="top" id="RightPane" class="RightPane"
            runat="server" visible="false">
        </td>
        </tr>
    </table>
</div>
```

6. Select **Save All** from the **File** menu to save your changes.

7. To see how the new skin will look on our site, log in as the SuperUser.

8. Deploy the skin from the skin folder to the DNN portal as described in the recipe *Deploying your skins and containers*.

9. Once the skin is deployed, look under the **Admin** menu and select **Skins**.

10. Select the **SampleASCXSkin** from the **Skins:** drop-down list and click on the **Preview** link.

11. On the left side you will see a small block with text. Clicking on the widget text will cause the text in the DIV to fade out:

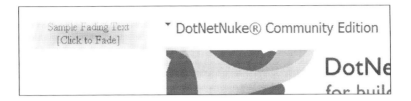

How it works...

This custom ACME.SampleWidget fades elements by using a simple JavaScript click handler that dynamically modifies the Opacity of the DIV element containing the sample text when you click on it. That is enough to demonstrate how the custom widgets work, but a more complicated example would require a good bit more JavaScript and a more in-depth discussion of JavaScript programming.

 Creating custom DNN widgets is really an art all to itself. You can learn more about crafting your own widgets from this excellent blog by Nik Kalyani: http://www.kalyani.com/2009/12/dotnetnuke-widgets-guide-part-1-of-4.

Using the rounded corner Super Stylesheet

Super Stylesheets is a new feature in DNN version 5 that offers ways to reuse HTML layouts by maximizing the use of CSS. At the time of this writing there are three super stylesheets available: the Yahoo YUI Library, the DNN layouts stylesheet, and the rounded corners stylesheet.

In this recipe we will demonstrate how to import and use the rounded corners stylesheet to create a graphic box around skin content.

To achieve the box effect, we start with a set of custom images for the box border, then create a set of nested DIVs in the skin and then use the dnn-roundedcorners.css file provided by DNN to link the graphic images to the DIV elements. This is very similar to the recipe *Styling a container with images* from *Chapter 8, Basic Skinning* but this time the rounded Corners stylesheet will position the images using CSS instead of an HTML table.

Getting ready

To follow along with this recipe you must have completed the following recipe from *Chapter 8, Basic Skinning*:

▶ *Creating a simple ASCX skin*

When all the pieces are in place the graphic box will look like this:

> You can place any size content in your skin and the RoundedCorners stylesheet will automatically resize the graphic box around it.

How to do it...

1. Find the folder called `SampleASCXSkin` that was created in the recipe *Creating a simple ASCX skin*.

2. Create a new folder inside to hold the images called `\images`.

3. We'll use some images to make the border of the box. In this example we'll use the following images:

   ❑ `box_e.png`: The right side of the graphic box

   ❑ `box_n.png`: The first top side of the graphic box

   ❑ `box_ne.png`: The upper-right corner of the graphic box

   ❑ `box_nw.png`: The upper-left corner of the graphic box

   ❑ `box_s.png`: The bottom of the graphic box

   ❑ `box_se.png`: The lower-right corner of the graphic box

   ❑ `box_sw.png`: The lower-left corner of the graphic box

   ❑ `box_w.png`: The left side of the graphic box

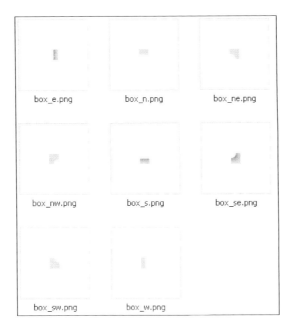

4. With the images in the correct folder, launch the Development Tool.

5. Select **Open File...** from the **File** menu and open the `skin.css` file.

6. Add an import statement at the top of the file to bring in the DNN `roundedcorners.` `css` file. If DNN is running on the localhost then the code would be:

```
@import url("http://localhost/dotnetnuke/resources/shared/
stylesheets/dnn-roundedcorners.css");
```

7. Below that, add the following code to link the images to the style elements from DNN:

```
.RoundedCorners .N{background-image: url("images/box_n.png"); }
.RoundedCorners .NE{background-image: url("images/box_ne.png"); }
.RoundedCorners .E{background-image: url("images/box_e.png"); }
.RoundedCorners .SE{background-image: url("images/box_se.png"); }
.RoundedCorners .S{background-image: url("images/box_s.png"); }
.RoundedCorners .SW{background-image: url("images/box_sw.png"); }
.RoundedCorners .W{background-image: url("images/box_w.png"); }
.RoundedCorners .NW{background-image: url("images/box_nw.png"); }

/* General Styles */
```

8. Now that the stylesheet is set, the next step is to modify the control. Select **Open File...** from the **File** menu and open the `SampleASCXSkin.ascx` file.

9. Scroll down to the HTML table holding the different panes and add the following code to the left pane:

```
<div class="content">
    <table width="100%" border="0" cellspacing="0" cellpadding="0">
      <tr>
      <td valign="top" id="LeftPane" class="LeftPane"
          runat="server" visible="false">
      </td>
      <td valign="top" id="ContentPane" class="ContentPane"
          runat="server" visible="false">

      <div class="RoundedCorners">
          <div class="W">
        <div class="E">
            <div class="N">
            <div class="NW">
              <div class="NE" align="center"
                  style="padding: 10px; vertical-align: middle">
              You can place any amount of content in your skin
                                        and the RoundedCorners
              stylesheet will automatically resize the graphic
                              box around it. Even if your
              content needs to wrap, the graphic box will resize
                                        accordingly.
              </div>
            </div>
            </div>
        <div class="S">
            <div class="SW">
            <div class="SE" align="center">
              [ You can put your footer content here ]
            </div>
            </div>
        </div>
         </div>
        </div>
      </div>

      </td>
      <td valign="top" id="RightPane" class="RightPane"
          runat="server" visible="false">
      </td>
       </tr>
    </table>
</div>
```

10. The last step is to modify the manifest file to include our images before we deploy the skin. Open the SampleASCXSkin.dnn file.

11. Scroll down to the `SkinFiles` element and add the following:

```
<skinFile>
  <name>skin.css</name>
</skinFile>
<skinFile>
  <path>images</path>
  <name>box_n.png</name>
</skinFile>
<skinFile>
  <path>images</path>
  <name>box_ne.png</name>
</skinFile>
<skinFile>
  <path>images</path>
  <name>box_e.png</name>
</skinFile>
<skinFile>
  <path>images</path>
  <name>box_se.png</name>
</skinFile>
<skinFile>
  <path>images</path>
  <name>box_s.png</name>
</skinFile>
<skinFile>
  <path>images</path>
  <name>box_sw.png</name>
</skinFile>
<skinFile>
  <path>images</path>
  <name>box_w.png</name>
</skinFile>
<skinFile>
  <path>images</path>
  <name>box_nw.png</name>
</skinFile>
</skinFiles>
```

12. Select **Save All** from the **File** menu to save your changes.

13. To see how the new skin will look on our site, log in as the SuperUser.

14. Deploy the skin from the skin folder to the DNN portal as described in the recipe *Deploying your skins and containers*. Be sure to include the new /`images` folder in the ZIP file.

15. Once the skin is deployed, look under the **Admin** menu and select **Skins**.

16. Select the **SampleASCXSkin** from the **Skins:** drop-down list and click on the Preview link.

17. As we placed the `DIV` elements in the Content Pane the graphic box with the content will display at the top of the page:

> You can place any amount of content in your skin and the RoundedCorners stylesheet will automatically resize the graphic box around it. Even if your content needs to wrap, the graphic box will resize accordingly.
>
> [You can put your footer content here]

How it works...

To use the rounded corners super stylesheet we had to do three things: first import the DNN rounded corners stylesheet into the skin CSS file. Then add some additional rules to define our custom border images, and then add a set of nested DIV elements to wrap our images around our content.

Showing portal settings in a skin

As we saw in some of the previous recipes, it is possible to reference some DNN variables in our skins. We saw an example of this where we used the variable SkinPath (`<%= SkinPath %>`) to retrieve the path to the current skin. But there are other values we can access in the skin and in this recipe we will see how to access portal settings variables in skins.

The following chart shows some of the portal setting variables we can use:

Variable	Description
`<%=PortalSettings.ActiveTab.TabName %>`	Name of the current page.
`<%=PortalSettings.ActiveTab.TabID %>`	ID of the current page.
`<%= iif(Request.IsAuthenticated,"Logged In","Logged Out") %>`	Displays login status.
`<%=PortalSettings.ActiveTab.Title %>`	Title of the current page.
`<%= PortalSettings.PortalName %>`	Name of the current portal.
`<%= PortalSettings.PortalId %>`	The current portal ID (0, 1, 2, and so on).
`<%= PortalSettings.AdministratorRoleName %>`	The name of the administrators role.

Variable	Description
`<%= PortalSettings.Email %>`	The e-mail address of the portal administrator.
`<%= PortalSettings.FooterText %>`	The text that appears in the footer.
`<%= PortalSettings.HomeDirectory %>`	Home directory of the current portal.
`<%= PortalSettings.Version %>`	The DNN version of your site.
`<%= PortalSettings.UserInfo.DisplayName %>`	The display name of the current user.
`<%= PortalSettings.UserInfo.IsSuperUser %>`	Is the current user a SuperUser (true/false).

To demonstrate the portal settings variables we will add a status box to the sample skin to display some of the current portal settings.

Note: many of these settings variables are more easily (and safely) accessed using Tokens (like `[User:DisplayName]`) inside a Text skin object. See the recipe *Creating a simple HTML skin* in *Chapter 8, Basic Skinning* for examples.

Getting ready

To follow along with this recipe you must have completed the following recipe from *Chapter 8, Basic Skinning*:

▶ *Creating a simple ASCX skin*

How to do it...

1. Find the folder called `SampleASCXSkin` that was created in the recipe *Creating a simple ASCX skin*.

2. Launch the Development Tool.

3. Select **Open File...** from the **File** menu and open the `SampleASCXSkin.ascx` file.

4. We're going to add a small HTML table to act as a status panel. Place it in the `LeftPane` with the following code:

```
<div class="content">
    <table width="100%" border="0" cellspacing="0" cellpadding="0">
        <tr>
        <td valign="top" id="LeftPane" class="LeftPane"
            runat="server" visible="false">
```

```
<table width="200" border="0"  style="font-family: Impact;
    font-size: small">
  <tr>
      <td colspan="2" align="center">
      <u>Portal Status</u>
      </td>
      <td >

      </td>
  </tr>
  <tr>
      <td>
          Name:
      </td>
      <td>
          <%= PortalSettings.PortalName %> ( ID= <%=
                              PortalSettings.PortalId %> )
      </td>
  </tr>
  <tr>
      <td>
          Home:
      </td>
      <td>
          <%= PortalSettings.HomeDirectory %>
      </td>
  </tr>
  <tr>
      <td>
          Version:
      </td>
      <td>
          <%= PortalSettings.Version %>
      </td>
  </tr>
  <tr>
      <td>
          Status:
      </td>
      <td>
```

```
                <%= iif(Request.IsAuthenticated,"Logged
                                    In","Logged Out") %>
        </td>
    </tr>
    <tr>
        <td>
            Current Page:
        </td>
        <td>
            <%=PortalSettings.ActiveTab.TabName %>
        </td>
    </tr>
    <tr>
        <td>
            User:
        </td>
        <td>
            <%= PortalSettings.UserInfo.DisplayName %>
        </td>
    </tr>
    <tr>
        <td>
            User Email:
        </td>
        <td>
            <%= PortalSettings.UserInfo.Email %>
        </td>
    </tr>
    <tr>
        <td>
            SuperUser?:
        </td>
        <td>
            <%= PortalSettings.UserInfo.IsSuperUser %>
        </td>
    </tr>
    <tr>
        <td>
            Footer:
        </td>
        <td>
```

```
                    <%= PortalSettings.FooterText %>
            </td>
        </tr>
    </table>

    </td>
    <td valign="top" id="ContentPane" class="ContentPane"
        runat="server" visible="false">
    </td>
    <td valign="top" id="RightPane" class="RightPane"
        runat="server" visible="false">
    </td>
    </tr>
    </table>
</div>
```

5. Select **Save All** from the **File** menu to save your changes.

6. To see how the new skin will look on our site, log in as the SuperUser.

7. Deploy the skin from the skin folder to the DNN portal as described in the recipe *Deploying your skins and containers*.

8. Once the skin is deployed, look under the **Admin** menu and select **Skins**.

9. Select the **SampleASCXSkin** from the **Skins:** drop-down list and click on the Preview link.

10. As we placed the HTML table in the LeftPane the status panel will appear on the left side of the page:

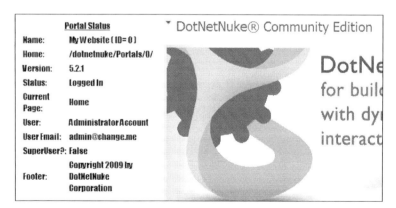

How it works...

This technique will only get the information of the current portal. Also, PortalSettings is a shared class that is only directly accessible from skins and not from containers.

Adding animation to a menu

Back in *Chapter 8 , Basic Skinning* the recipe *Styling a menu with images* showed how to enhance the basic DNN NAV menu with custom graphic images. In this recipe we will revisit the graphic menu and show how you can easily add animation to visually enhance how the menus open and close.

As part of the NAV control DNN provides CustomAttributes that we can define to control the menu animation. In this chart we can see some of the attributes that are available:

Attribute	Description	Examples
`AnimationType`	Is a type of menu animation. `Slide` makes the menu rollout straight down. `Expand` is similar but a little more gentle. `Diagonal` opens the menu from the upper left to lower right and `ReverseDiagonal` is the same but from the lower right to upper left.	`Slide`, `Expand`, `Diagonal`, `ReverseDiagonal`
`EasingType`	The mathematical equation to control the animation. A math function can provide a more interesting animation than a simple linear motion.	`Bounce`, `Circ`, `Cubic`, `Expo`, `Quad`, `Quint`, `Quart`, `Sine`
`EasingDirection`	Direction of animation as you switch from one menu to another.	`easeIn`, `easeOut`, `easeInOut`
`AnimationLength`	Number of seconds to run the animation as the menu opens. A longer time makes for better animation but too long and the user will become impatient waiting for the menu to open. One second is a good compromise.	`1`
`AnimationInterval`	How often to update the animation (in milliseconds). This controls the "smoothness" of the animation. Longer intervals are more efficient but can cause "jerky" animation.	`10`

Getting ready

To follow along with this recipe you must have completed the following recipe from *Chapter 8, Basic Skinning*:

▶ *Styling a menu with images*

How to do it...

1. Find the folder called `ASCXMenuSkin` that was created in the recipe *Styling a menu with images*.

2. Launch the Development Tool.

3. Select **Open File...** from the **File** menu.

4. Browse to the `ASCXMenuSkin` folder and open the `ASCXMenuSkin.ascx` file.

5. Start by adding a register directive at the top of the file:

```
<%@ Register TagPrefix="dnn" Namespace="DotNetNuke.UI.Skins"
             Assembly="DotNetNuke" %>
```

6. Then, scroll down a little until you see the NAV control. To add the new custom attributes, change the NAV control from this:

```
<div class="menu_style">
    <dnn:NAV runat="server" id="dnnNAV"
            ProviderName="DNNMenuNavigationProvider"
            IndicateChildren="false"
            ControlOrientation="Horizontal"
            CSSControl="mainMenu" />
</div>
```

To this:

```
<div class="menu_style">
    <dnn:NAV runat="server" id="dnnNAV"
            ProviderName="DNNMenuNavigationProvider"
            IndicateChildren="false"
            ControlOrientation="Horizontal"
            CSSControl="mainMenu" mouseouthidedelay="100">
        <customattributes>
            <dnn:customattribute value="Expand" name="AnimationType" />
            <dnn:customattribute value="Sine" name="EasingType" />
            <dnn:customattribute value="In" name="EasingDirection" />
            <dnn:customattribute value="1" name="AnimationLength" />
            <dnn:customattribute value="10" name="AnimationInterval" />
        </customattributes>
    </dnn:NAV>
</div>
```

7. That's all we need to do. By adding the custom attributes we need for menu animation the skin is ready to go.

8. To preview the skin, start by logging in as the SuperUser.

9. Deploy the skin from the skin folder to the DNN portal as described in the recipe *Deploying your skins and containers*.

10. Once the skin is deployed, look under the **Admin** menu and select **Skins**.

11. Select the **ASCXMenuSkin** from the **Skins:** drop-down list and click on the **Preview** link.

12. The menus appear the same as before but now they employ animation to gently slide open and close. You can adjust the speed by changing the value of `AnimationLength` in the above code sample. A value of `1` moves at the normal rate while a value of `10` would create a very slow menu opening.

There's more...

You can experiment with the available options and see how the menu animation changes. For example, the `EasingType` is probably the most fun option to play with. `Sine` creates a nice smooth menu opening, `Bounce` creates a kind of hesitant expansion. `Circ` offers a cleaner "snappy" opening while Quad makes a more "mellow" animation.

Index

Symbols

Thank you for buying
DotNetNuke 5.4 Cookbook

About Packt Publishing

Packt, pronounced 'packed', published its first book "*Mastering phpMyAdmin for Effective MySQL Management*" in April 2004 and subsequently continued to specialize in publishing highly focused books on specific technologies and solutions.

Our books and publications share the experiences of your fellow IT professionals in adapting and customizing today's systems, applications, and frameworks. Our solution based books give you the knowledge and power to customize the software and technologies you're using to get the job done. Packt books are more specific and less general than the IT books you have seen in the past. Our unique business model allows us to bring you more focused information, giving you more of what you need to know, and less of what you don't.

Packt is a modern, yet unique publishing company, which focuses on producing quality, cutting-edge books for communities of developers, administrators, and newbies alike. For more information, please visit our website: www.packtpub.com.

About Packt Open Source

In 2010, Packt launched two new brands, Packt Open Source and Packt Enterprise, in order to continue its focus on specialization. This book is part of the Packt Open Source brand, home to books published on software built around Open Source licences, and offering information to anybody from advanced developers to budding web designers. The Open Source brand also runs Packt's Open Source Royalty Scheme, by which Packt gives a royalty to each Open Source project about whose software a book is sold.

Writing for Packt

We welcome all inquiries from people who are interested in authoring. Book proposals should be sent to author@packtpub.com. If your book idea is still at an early stage and you would like to discuss it first before writing a formal book proposal, contact us; one of our commissioning editors will get in touch with you.

We're not just looking for published authors; if you have strong technical skills but no writing experience, our experienced editors can help you develop a writing career, or simply get some additional reward for your expertise.

open source
community experience distilled

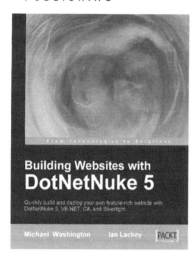

Building Websites with DotNetNuke 5

ISBN: 978-1-847199-92-8   Paperback: 336 pages

Quickly build and deploy your own feature-rich website with DotNetNuke 5, VB.NET, and C#

1. Create and manage your own website with DotNetNuke 5

2. Customize and enhance your site with custom modules

3. Code provided in VB.NET and C# using Visual Studio 2010

4. Covers module development using Silverlight and Linq to SQL

DotNetNuke Skinning Tutorial

ISBN: 978-1-847192-78-3   Paperback: 156 pages

A simple, clear, step-by-tutorial to creating DotNetNuke skins to put you in control of the look and feel of your DotNetNuke website

1. Take control of the look and feel of your DotNetNuke website

2. Simple, clear, tutorial to creating DotNetNuke skins

3. Practical step-by-step guidance

4. No knowledge of DotNetNuke skinning required

Please check **www.PacktPub.com** for information on our titles

Building Websites with VB.NET and DotNetNuke 4

ISBN: 978-1-904811-99-2   Paperback: 336 pages

A practical guide to creating and maintaining your own DotNetNuke website, and developing new modules and skins

1. Specially revised and updated version of this acclaimed DotNetNuke book

2. Create and manage your own website with DotNetNuke

3. Customize and enhance your site with skins and custom modules

4. Extensive coverage of the DAL and DAL+ for custom module development

Ext JS 3.0 Cookbook

ISBN: 978-1-847198-70-9   Paperback: 376 pages

Clear step-by-step recipes for building impressive rich internet applications using the Ext JS JavaScript library

1. Master the Ext JS widgets and learn to create custom components to suit your needs

2. Build striking native and custom layouts, forms, grids, listviews, treeviews, charts, tab panels, menus, toolbars and much more for your real-world user interfaces

3. Packed with easy-to-follow examples to exercise all of the features of the Ext JS library

Please check **www.PacktPub.com** for information on our titles

Made in the USA
Lexington, KY
08 November 2011